ESTATE PUBL

CW00734834

WILTSHIRE

Street maps with index
Administrative Districts
Population Gazetteer
Road Map with index
Postcodes

COUNTY RED BOOKS

This atlas is intended for those requiring street maps of the historical and commercial centres of towns within the county. Each locality is normally presented on one or two pages and although, with many small towns, this space is sufficient to portray the whole urban area, the maps of large towns and cities are for centres only and are not intended to be comprehensive. Such coverage in Super and Local Red Books (see page 2).

Every effort has been made to verify the accuracy of information in this book but the publishers cannot accept responsibility for expense or loss caused by any error or omission. Information that will be of assistance to the user of these maps will be welcomed.

The representation of a road, track or footpath on the maps in this atlas is no evidence of the existence of a right of way.

Street plans prepared and published by ESTATE PUBLICATIONS, Bridewell House, TENTERDEN, KENT.
The Publishers acknowledge the co-operation of the local authorities of towns represented in this atlas.

Ordnance Survey® This product includes mapping data licensed from Ordnance Survey® with the permission of the Controller of Her Majesty's Stationery Office.

COUNTY RED BOOK

WILTSHIRE

contains street maps for each town centre

SUPER & LOCAL RED BOOKS

are street atlases with comprehensive local coverage

CHIPPENHAM & CALNE

including: Box, Corsham, Draycot Cerne, Hullavington, Kington Langley, Kington St. Michael, Rudloe, Stanton St. Quintin, Malmesbury etc.

SALISBURY & WILTON

including: Alderbury, Amesbury, Bulford, Bulford Camp, Downton, Durrington, Larkhill, Mere, Porton, Quidhampton, Redlynch, Shrewton, Tisbury, Winterbourne Gunner etc.

SWINDON

including: Broad Blunsdon, Calne, Chippenham, Chiseldon, Cricklade, Highworth, Lydiard Millicent, Marlborough, Purton, Wootton Bassett, Wroughton etc.

CONTENTS

COUNTY ADMINISTRATIVE DISTRICTS: pages 4-5

GAZETTEER INDEX TO ROAD MAP: pages 6-7
(with populations)

COUNTY ROAD MAP: pages 8-11

TOWN CENTRE STREET MAPS:

Aldbourne	page 12	Marlborough	30-31
Amesbury	13	Melksham	32
Avebury	12	Mere	28
Bradford-on-Avon	14-15	North Tidworth	33
Bulford	16	Pewsey	34
Calne	17	Potterne	34
Chippenham	18-19	Redlynch	25
Corsham	20	Salisbury	35-39
Cricklade	21	Swindon	40-47
Devizes	22-23	Tisbury	51
Downton	24	Trowbridge	48-50
Durrington	16	Warminster	52-53
Highworth	26	Westbury	54
Holt	21	Wilton	55
Ludgershall	27	Wootton Bassett	56
Lyneham	28	Wroughton	51
Malmesbury	29		

INDEX TO STREETS: page 57

LEGEND TO STREET MAPS

One-Way Street	→	Post Office	●
Pedestrianized	▨	Public Convenience	⊙
Car Park	P	Place of Worship	+

Scale of street plans: 4 Inches to 1 mile (unless otherwise stated on the map).

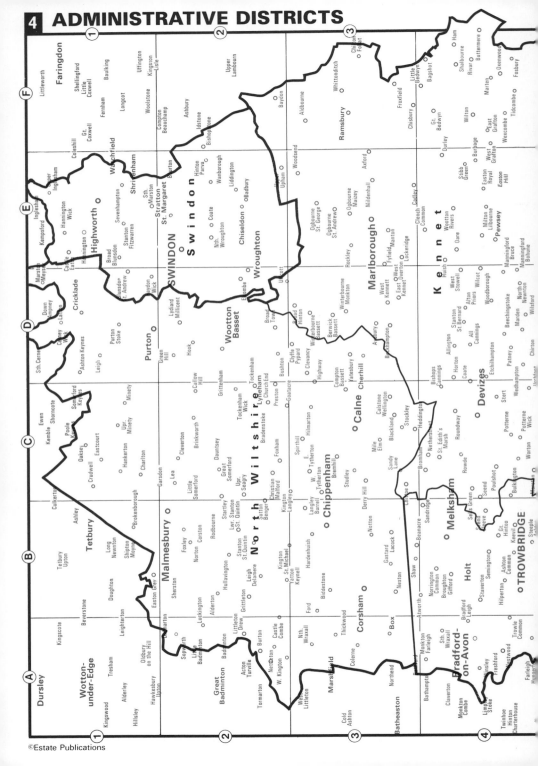

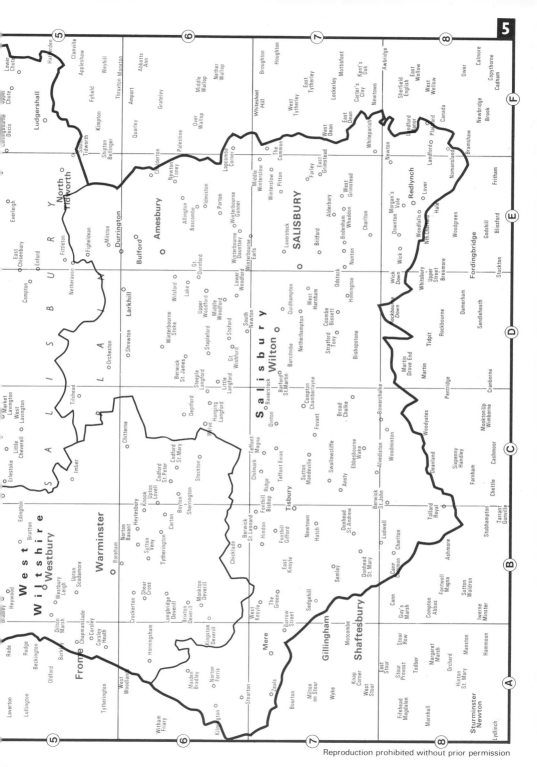

GAZETTEER INDEX TO ROAD MAP

with Populations   County of **Wiltshire** population **564,471**

Wiltshire Districts:

Kennett	68,526
North Wiltshire	111,974
Salisbury	105,318
Thamesdown	170,850
West Wiltshire	107,803

Aldbourne **1,682**	9 G3
Alderbury **1,859**	11 F9
Alderton	8 B2
All Cannings **555**	9 E5
Allington **469**	8 D5
Allington	11 F8
Alton Priors **230**	9 E5
Alvediston **85**	10 C10
Amesbury **6,656**	11 F7
Ansty **100**	10 C9
Ashton Common	8 B5
Ashton Keynes **1,399**	8 D1
Atworth **943**	8 B4
Avebury **562**	9 E4
Axford	9 F4
Badbury	9 F3
Bagshot	9 G4
Barford St Martin **568**	10 D9
Barrow Street	10 B9
Baverstock	10 D8
Baydon **512**	9 G3
Beanacre	8 C4
Beckhampton	9 E4
Beechingstoke **147**	9 E5
Berwick Bassett **51**	9 E4
Berwick St James **153**	10 D8
Berwick St John **260**	10 C10
Berwick St Leonard **34**	10 C8
Biddestone **466**	8 B3
Bishops Cannings **1032**	8 D5
Bishopstone (Salisbury) **566**	10 D9
Bishopstone (Swindon) **620**	9 G2
Bishopstrow **112**	*
Blackland	8 D4
Blunsdon St Andrew **2,195**	9 E1
Bodenham	11 F9
Boreham	10 C7
Boscombe	11 F8
Bowerchalke **335**	10 D10
Box **3,789**	8 B4
Boyton **162**	10 C8
Bradenstoke	8 D3
Bradford Leigh	8 B5
Bradford-on-Avon **8,815**	8 B5
Bratton **1,193**	10 C6
Braydon **49**	*
Bremhill **984**	8 C4
Brinkworth **1,167**	8 D2
Britford **440**	11 F9
Brixton Deverill **63**	10 B8
Broad Blunsdon	9 E1
Broad Chalke **584**	10 D9
Broad Hinton **629**	9 E3
Broad Town **567**	9 E3
Brokenborough **199**	8 C2
Bromham **1,860**	8 C4
Broughton Gifford **901**	8 B5
Bulford **5,255**	11 F7
Bulkington **268**	8 C5
Burbage **1,434**	9 F5
Burcombe **151**	10 D9
Burton	8 B3
Bushton	8 D3
Buttermere **43**	9 H5
Cadley	9 F4
Callow Hill	8 D2
Calne **13,530**	8 D4

Calstone Wellington	8 D4
Castle Combe **347**	8 B3
Castle Eaton **225**	9 E1
Chapmanslade **588**	10 B7
Charlton (Malmesbury) **428**	8 C2
Charlton (Salisbury)	11 F9
Charlton (Shaftesbury)	10 C10
Charlton (Upavon) **77**	11 E6
Cherhill **712**	8 D4
Cheverell Magna **539**	10 C6
Cheverell Parva **176**	10 D6
Chicklade **71**	10 C8
Chilmark **425**	10 C8
Chilton Foliat **299**	9 G4
Chippenham **25,794**	8 C3
Chirton **409**	10 E6
Chisbury	9 G4
Chiseldon **2,651**	9 F3
Chitterne **289**	10 D7
Chittoe	8 C4
Cholderton **200**	11 F7
Christian Malford **681**	8 C3
Church End	8 D3
Chute (Upr. & Lwr.) **309**	11 G6
Chute Forest **146**	*
Clarendon Park **269**	*
Clench Common	9 F4
Clevancy	8 D3
Cleverton (with Lea) **766**	8 D2
Cliffe Pypard **323**	9 E3
Coate (Devizes)	8 D5
Coate (Swindon)	9 F2
Codford St Mary	10 C8
Codford St Peter	10 C7
Colerne **1,250**	8 B4
Collingbourne Ducis **802**	11 G6
Collingbourne Kingston **454**	11 F6
Compton	11 E6
Compton Bassett **271**	8 D4
Compton Chamberlayne **85**	10 D9
Coombe Bissett **653**	11 E9
Corsham **10,549**	8 B4
Corsley **731**	10 B7
Corsley Heath	10 B7
Corston	8 C2
Corton	10 C7
Covingham **4,128**	*
Cricklade **4,099**	9 E1
Crockerton	10 B7
Crudwell **948**	8 C1
Dauntsey **471**	8 D2
Deptford	10 D8
Derry Hill	8 C4
Devizes **11,250**	8 D5
Dilton Marsh **1,924**	10 B6
Dinton **536**	10 D9
Donhead St Andrew **422**	10 C9
Donhead St Mary **981**	10 C9
Downton **2,784**	11 F10
Durley	9 F5
Durrington **6,926**	11 F7
East Chisenbury	11 E6
Eastcott	10 D6
East Coulston **151**	10 C6
Eastcourt	8 D1
Easterton **591**	10 D6
East Grafton (with West) **603**	9 G5
East Grimstead (with West) **514**	11 F9
East Kennett **100**	9 E4
East Knoyle **645**	10 B9
Easton Grey **70**	8 B2
Easton Royal **260**	9 F5
East Tytherton	8 C3
Ebbesbourne Wake **198**	10 D9

Edington **716**	10 C6
Elcombe	9 E3
Enford **655**	11 E6
Erlestoke **285**	10 C6
Etchilhampton **162**	8 D5
Everleigh **249**	11 F6
Farley (with Pitton) **704**	11 F9
Figheldean **675**	11 E7
Firsdown **611**	*
Fittleton **370**	11 E6
Fonthill Bishop **112**	10 C8
Fonthill Gifford **108**	10 C9
Ford	8 B3
Fosbury	9 G5
Fovant **641**	10 D9
Foxham	8 D3
Foxley	8 C2
Froxfield **356**	9 G4
Fyfield **191**	9 E4
Garsdon	8 C2
Gastard	8 B4
Goatacre	8 D3
Great Bedwyn **1,093**	9 G5
Great Durnford **405**	11 E8
Great Hinton **212**	8 C5
Great Somerford **734**	8 C2
Great Wishford **360**	11 E8
Green Hill	8 D2
Grittenham	8 D2
Grittleton **373**	8 B3
Ham **175**	9 H5
Hanging Langford	10 D8
Hankerton **314**	8 C1
Hannington **228**	9 F1
Hannington Wick	9 F1
Hardenhuish	8 C3
Hatch	10 C9
Hawkeridge	10 B6
Haydon Wick **7,417**	9 E2
Heddington **364**	8 D4
Heytesbury **643**	10 C7
Heywood **459**	10 B6
Highway	8 D3
Highworth **8,668**	9 F1
Hilmarton **798**	8 D3
Hilperton **2,632**	8 B5
Hindon **493**	10 C8
Hinton Parva	9 F2
Holt **1,458**	8 B5
Homington	11 E9
Hook	9 E2
Horningsham **418**	10 B7
Horton	8 D5
Huish **54**	9 E5
Hullavington **1,122**	8 B2
Idmiston **2,177**	11 F8
Imber	10 C7
Inglesham **117**	9 F1
Keevil **404**	8 C5
Kilmington **282**	10 A8
Kingston Deverill **267**	10 B8
Kington Langley **718**	8 C3
Kington St Michael **695**	8 C3
Knook **61**	10 C7
Lacock **1,068**	8 C4
Lake	11 E8
Landford **1,195**	11 G10
Landford Manor	11 G10
Langley Burrell **412**	8 C3
Larkhill	11 E7
Latton **372**	9 E1
Laverstock **3,029**	11 F9

Place	Pop.	Ref.
Lea (with Cleverton) **766**		8 C2
Leigh **283**		8 D1
Leigh Delamere		8 B3
Liddington **343**		9 F2
Limpley Stoke **627**		9 A5
Little Bedwyn **286**		9 G4
Little Langford		10 D8
Little Somerford **416**		8 C2
Littleton Drew		8 B3
Littleton Pannell		10 D6
Lockeridge		9 E4
Longbridge Deverill **851**		10 B7
Lopcombe Corner		11 F8
Lover		11 F10
Lower Stanton St Quintin		8 C3
Lower Woodford		11 E8
Luckington **508**		8 B2
Ludgershall **3,379**		11 G6
Ludwell		10 C10
Lydiard Millicent **1,203**		9 E2
Lydiard Tregoze **382**		*
Lyneham **4,747**		8 D3
Maiden Bradley **328**		10 A8
Malmesbury **3,999**		8 C2
Manningford Bohune		9 E5
Manningford Bruce		9 E5
Manton		9 F4
Marden **155**		9 E5
Market Lavington **1,858**		10 D6
Marlborough **6,788**		9 E4
Marston **142**		8 C5
Marston Meysey **209**		9 E1
Marten		9 G5
Melksham **12,788**		8 C5
Mere **2,257**		10 B8
Middle Winterslow		11 F8
Middle Woodford		11 E8
Mildenhall **472**		9 F4
Mile Elm		8 D4
Milston **126**		11 F7
Milton Lilbourne **484**		9 F5
Minety **1,325**		8 D1
Monkton Deverill		10 B8
Monkton Farleigh **478**		8 B4
Morgan's Vale		11 F10
Neston		8 B4
Netheravon **1,146**		11 E6
Netherhampton **158**		11 E9
Netherstreet		8 D4
Nettleton **569**		8 B3
Newton Toney **373**		11 F8
Newtown		10 C9
Normansland		11 F10
Norrington Common		8 B5
North Bradley **1,770**		10 B6
North Newnton **414**		9 E5
North Tidworth **5,813**		11 F6
North Wraxall **360**		8 B3
North Wroughton		9 F2
Norton **114**		8 B2
Norton Bavant **109**		10 C7
Norton Ferris		10 A8
Notton		8 C4
Nunton		11 E9
Oaksey **443**		8 D1
Oare		9 F5
Odstock **548**		11 E9
Ogbourne Maizey		9 F4
Ogbourne St Andrew **262**		9 F4
Ogbourne St George **399**		9 F3
Orcheston **282**		10 D7
Oxenwood		9 G5
Patney **149**		8 D5
Pewsey **2,831**		9 F5
Pitton (with Farley) **704**		11 F9
Plaitford		11 G10
Porton		11 F8
Potterne **1,590**		8 D5
Potterne Wick		8 D5
Poulshot **352**		8 C5
Preshute **160**		*
Preston		8 D3
Purton **3,879**		9 E2
Purton Stoke		9 E1
Quidhampton **363**		11 E9
Ramsbury **1,877**		9 G4
Redlynch **3,158**		11 F10
Ridge		10 C8
Rivar		9 G5
Rockley		9 E4
Rodbourne		8 C2
Roundway **1,633**		8 D5
Rowde **1,294**		8 C5
Rushall **114**		10 E6
St Edith's Marsh		8 D5
Salisbury **36,890**		11 F9
Sandridge		8 C4
Sandy Lane		8 C4
Savernake **194**		*
Sedgehill & Semley **584**		10 B9
Seend **1,089**		8 C5
Seend Cleeve		8 C5
Sells Green		8 C5
Semington **803**		8 C5
Sevenhampton		9 F1
Shalbourne **550**		9 G5
Shaw		8 B4
Sherrington **70**		10 C8
Shear Cross		10 B7
Sherston **1,372**		8 B2
Shrewton **1,780**		10 D7
Sopworth **81**		8 B2
South Marston **703**		9 F2
South Newton **696**		11 E8
Southwick **1,971**		10 B6
South Wraxall **397**		8 B5
Spirthill		8 D3
Stanton Fitzwarren **211**		9 F1
Stanton St Bernard **141**		9 E5
Stanton St Quintin **747**		8 C3
Stapleford **249**		11 E8
Startley		8 C2
Staverton **306**		8 B5
Steeple Ashton **955**		8 C5
Steeple Langford **517**		10 D8
Stert **167**		8 D5
Stibb Green		9 F5
Stockley		8 D4
Stockton **192**		10 C8
Stoford		11 E8
Stourton **201**		10 A8
Stratford Toney **70**		11 E9
Stratton St Margaret **13,383**		9 F2
Studley		8 C4
Sutton Benger **904**		8 C3
Sutton Mandeville **215**		10 D9
Sutton Veny **585**		10 C7
Swallowcliffe **184**		10 C9
Swindon **127,348**		9 E2
Teffont Evias		10 D9
Teffont Magna **216**		10 D8
The Common		11 F8
The Green		10 B9
Thickwood		8 B4
Tidcombe (with Fosbury) **105**		9 G5
Tilshead **343**		10 D7
Tisbury **1,836**		10 C9
Tockenham **221**		8 D3
Tockenham Wick		8 D3
Tollard Royal **106**		10 C10
Trowbridge **25,279**		8 B5
Trowle Common		8 B5
Tytherington		10 C7
Uffcott		9 E3
Upavon **1,241**		11 E6
Upper Inglesham		9 F1
Upper Minety		8 D1
Upper Seagry **270**		8 C3
Upper Upham		9 F3
Upper Woodford **447**		11 E8
Upton Lovell **144**		10 C7
Upton Scudamore **250**		10 B7
Urchfont **977**		8 D5
Wanborough **1,478**		9 F2
Warminster **16,267**		10 B7
Wedhampton		8 D5
West Ashton **387**		10 B6
Westbury. **9,939**		10 B6
Westbury Leigh		10 B6
West Dean **220**		11 G9
West Grafton (with East) **603**		9 F5
West Grimstead (with East) **514**		11 F9
West Harnham		11 E9
West Kennett		9 E4
West Kington		8 B3
West Knoyle **139**		10 B8
West Lavington **1,076**		10 D6
West Overton **629**		9 E4
West Stowell		9 E5
West Tisbury **577**		*
West Tytherton		8 C3
Westwood **1,195**		8 B5
Wexcombe		9 G5
Whaddon		11 F9
Whiteparish **1,313**		11 F10
Whittonditch		9 G4
Wick		11 F10
Wilcot **549**		9 E5
Wilsford (Amesbury) **120**		11 E8
Wilsford (Upavon) **82**		10 E6
Wilton (Marlborough)		9 G5
Wilton (Salisbury) **3,717**		11 E9
Wingfield **385**		10 B6
Winsley **1,834**		8 B5
Winterbourne Bassett **123**		9 E3
Winterbourne Dauntsey		11 F8
Winterbourne Earls **1,266**		11 F8
Winterbourne Gunner		11 F8
Winterbourne Monkton **161**		9 E4
Winterbourne Stoke **193**		11 E7
Winterslow **1,836**		11 F8
Woodborough **264**		9 E5
Woodfalls		11 F10
Woodminton		10 D10
Woodsend		9 F3
Wootton Bassett **10,524**		9 E2
Wootton Rivers **271**		9 F5
Worton **601**		8 C5
Wroughton. **7,111**		9 E3
Wylye **409**		10 D8
Yatesbury		8 D4
Yatton Keynell **656**		8 B3
Zeals **636**		10 A9

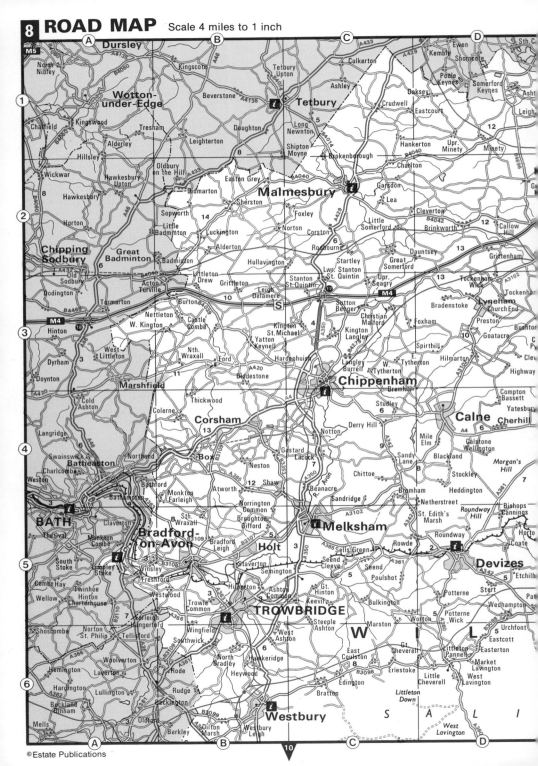

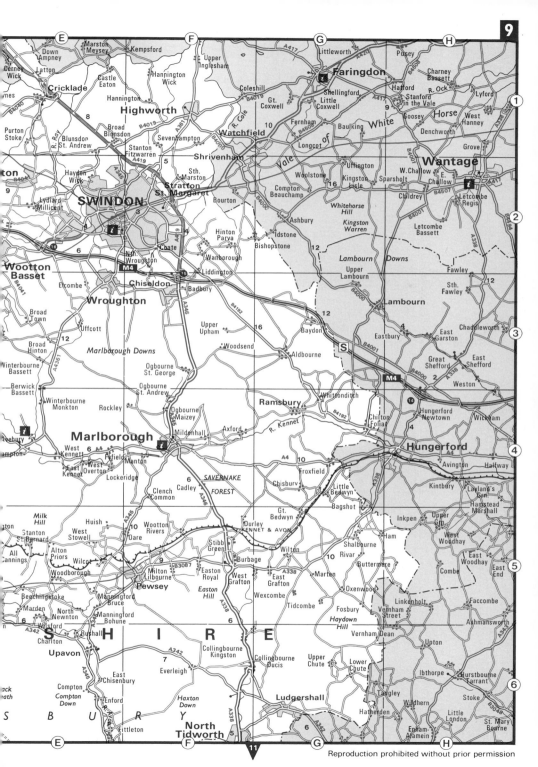

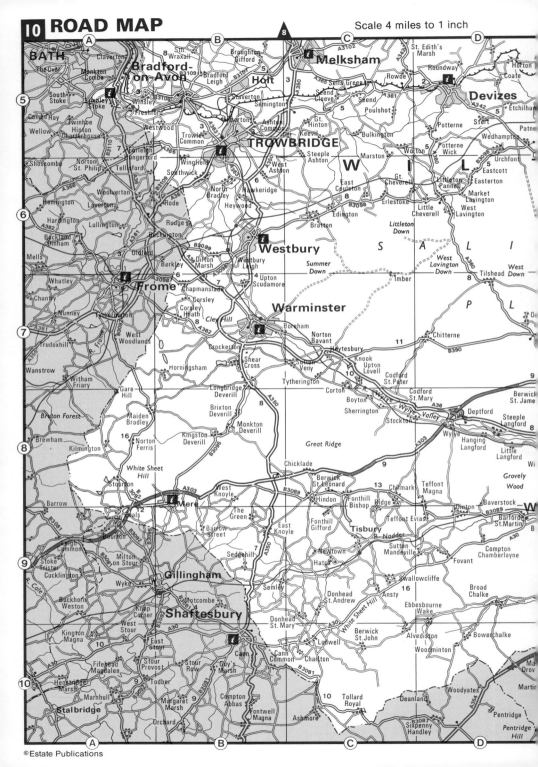

10 ROAD MAP

Scale 4 miles to 1 inch

©Estate Publications

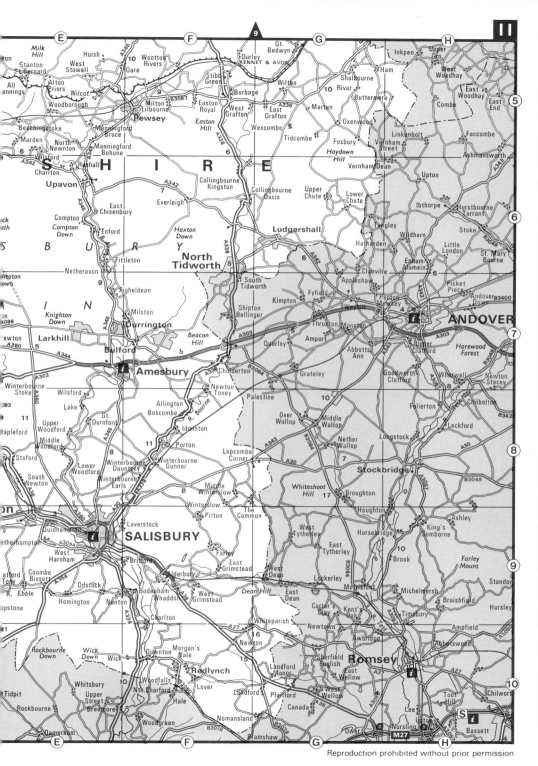

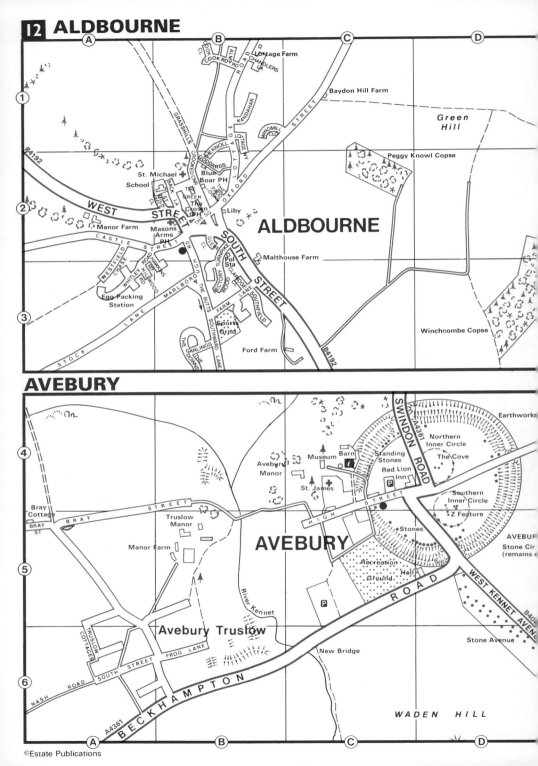

12 ALDBOURNE

A · B · C · D

1

COOK RD · YR RD
ALL · CHANDLERS LA
Cottage Farm

KANDAHAR

COTTAGE WAY

Baydon Hill Farm

Green Hill

GRASSHILLS

WINDMILL CLO

STREET

Peggy Knowl Copse

THE KNOLL
GODDARDS
CROOKED LA

St. Michael
School

Blue
Boar PH

BACK LA

FOXFORD

COTTAGE

THE GREEN

THE SQ

2

WEST STREET

The Crown PH

Liby

ALDBOURNE

Manor Farm

Masons Arms PH

CASTLE STREET

WESTFIELD CLOSE

WHITLEY RD
HAWKINS

SOUTH STREET

HIGH ST

GLEBE

Pol Sta

THE LADDE

Malthouse Farm

Egg Packing Station

MARLBORO RD

VICTORY WOOD
TURNPIKE
GLEBE
LAGGE LANE
SOUTHFIELD

THE BUTTS

3

STOCK LANE

FARM

SOUTHWARD LANE

Sports Grnd

Winchcombe Copse

THE GARLINGS
THE DOWNS

Ford Farm

B4192

AVEBURY

A · B · C · D

4

SWINDON ROAD
A4361

Earthworks

Museum
Barn

Standing Stones

Northern Inner Circle

The Cove

Avebury Manor

Red Lion Inn

St. James

Southern Inner Circle

Z Feature

AVEBUR

Bray Cottage

BRAY STREET

STREET

Truslow Manor

HIGH STREET

AVEBURY

Stones

Stone Cir (remains o

5

BRAY ST

Manor Farm

River Kennet

Recreation Ground

Hall

ROAD

WEST KENNET AVEN

B4

Stones

TRUSLOW COTTAGE

Avebury Truslow

FROG LANE

New Bridge

Stone Avenue

6

NASH ROAD

SOUTH STREET

A4361 BECKHAMPTON

WADEN HILL

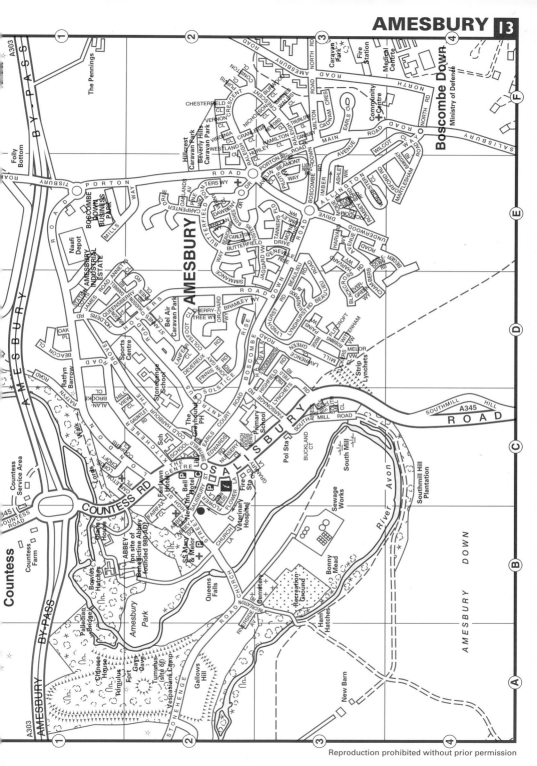

AMESBURY 13

Countess

Boscombe Down

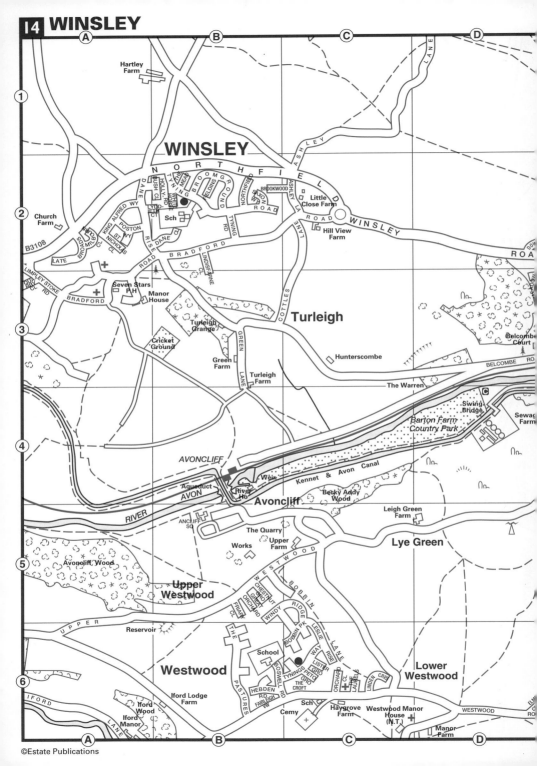

WINSLEY

Turleigh

Hartley Farm

Church Farm

B3108

LIMPLEY STOKE RD

BRADFORD

Seven Stars P.H.

Manor House

Cricket Ground

Turleigh Grange

Green Farm

Turleigh Farm

KING ALFRED WY

ST NICHOLAS CL

POSTON WY

BUSH CL

HOLLY RD

THE MEAD

TYNING

FIELDINGS

BROOMGROUND

NORTHFIELD

BRADFORD ROAD

TYNING RD

LINDISFARNE

COTTLES LANE

GREEN LANE

ASHLEY LANE

ASHLEY LA

Brookwood

Little Close Farm

Hill View Farm

WINSLEY ROAD

ROAD

Huntferscombe

The Warren

BELCOMBE RO

Belcombe Court

Swing Bridge

Barton Farm Country Park

Sewage Farm

AVONCLIFF

Weir

Aqueduct

AVON

River Ho

Kennet & Avon Canal

Becky Addy Wood

Avoncliff

Leigh Green Farm

Lye Green

RIVER

ANCLIFF SQ

The Quarry

Upper Farm

Works

Avoncliff Wood

Upper Westwood

Reservoir

UPPER

WESTWOOD

CHESTNUT CREST

ORCHARD CREST

FRIARY CL

WINDY RIDGE

BOBBIN PK

BOBBIN LN

LESLIE RISE

WAY

LISTER CL

PETO

GRO

THE CROFT

ORCHARD CL

LAUREL

LINDEN CRES

Lower Westwood

School

TYNINGS

THE PASTURES

HEBDEN RD

FAIRLEIGH VW

BOSWELL RD

Cemy

Haygrove Farm

Sch

Westwood Manor House (N.T.)

WESTWOOD

Manor Farm

Westwood

Iford Wood

Iford Lodge Farm

Iford Manor

IFORD LANE

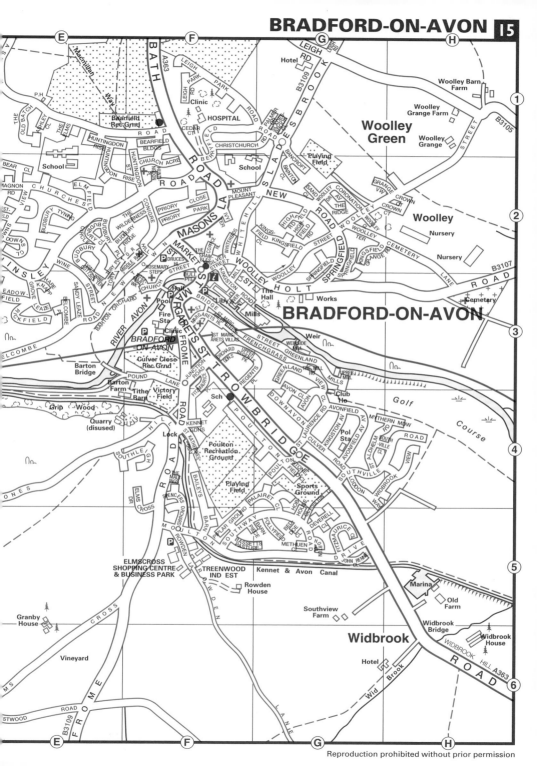

BRADFORD-ON-AVON `15`

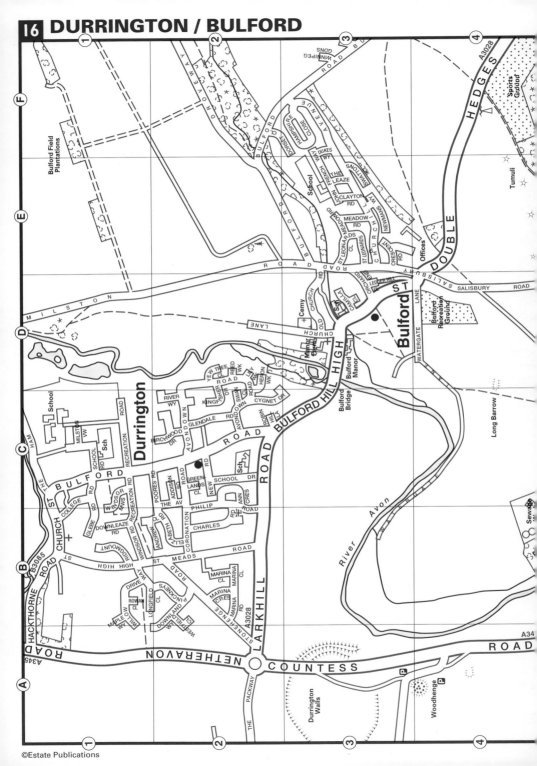

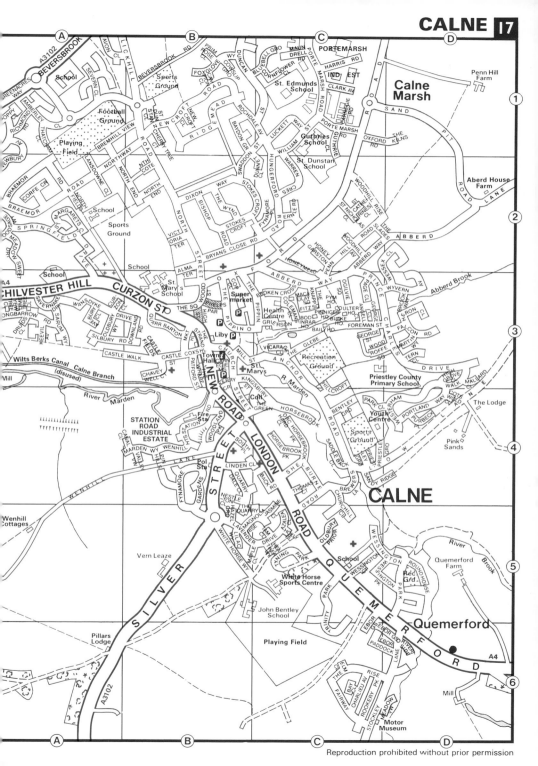

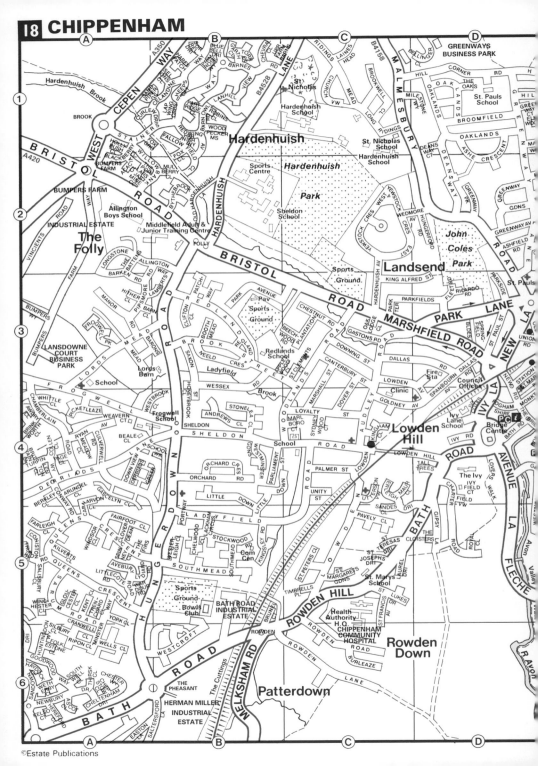

18 CHIPPENHAM

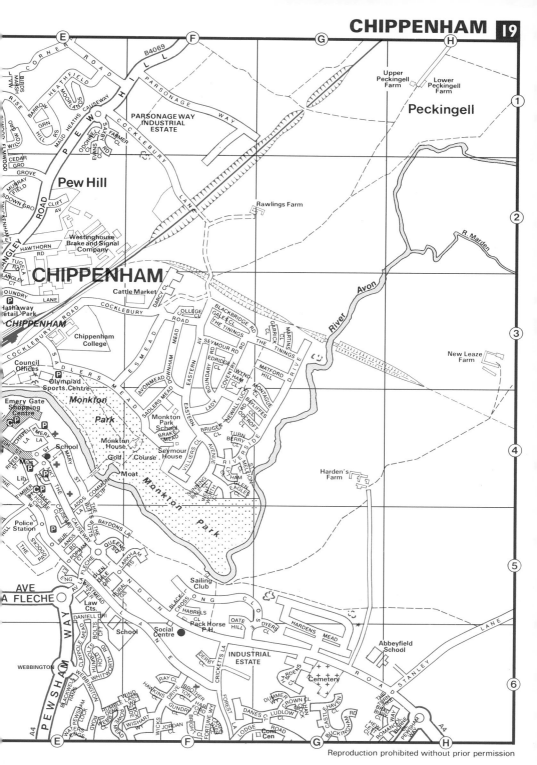

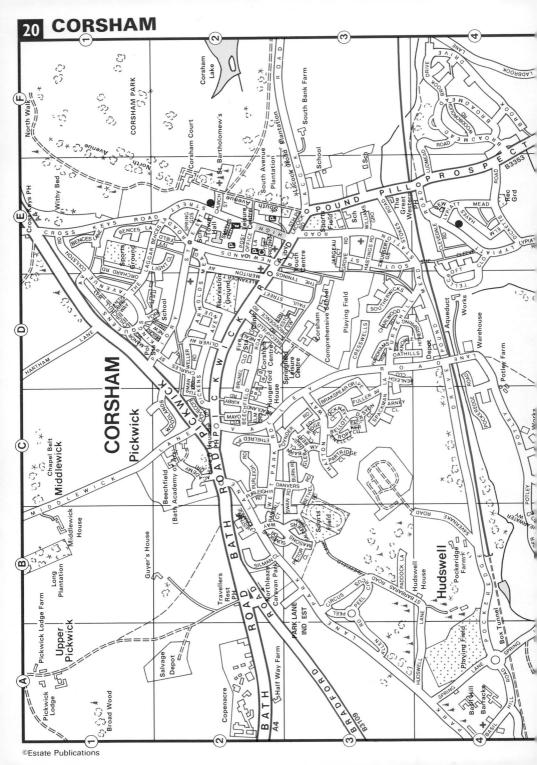

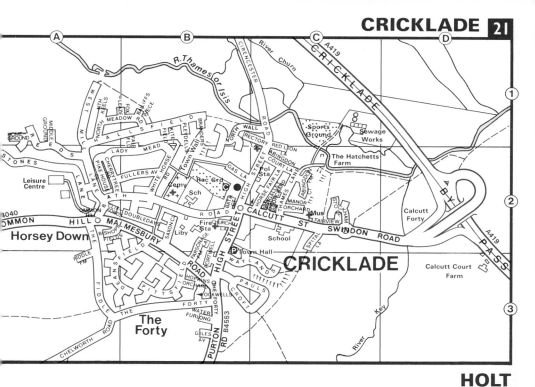

HOLT

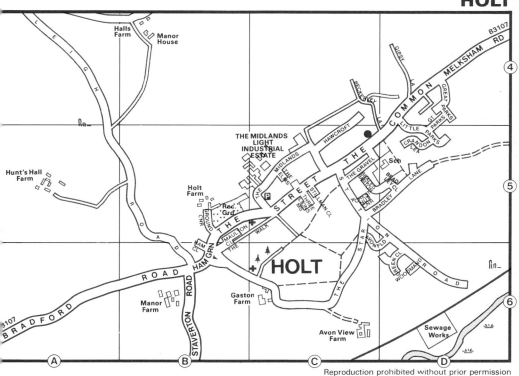

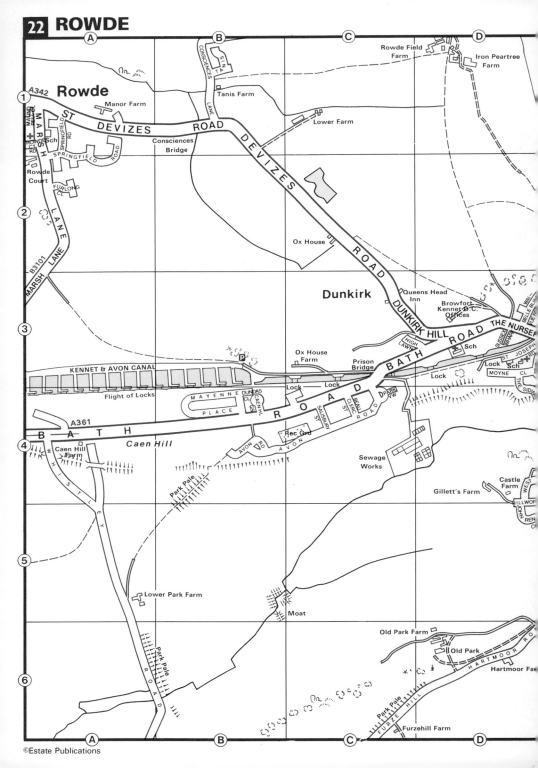

A342 **Rowde**

MARSH ST

Manor Farm

DEVIZES ROAD

Sch

SPRINGFIELD RD

Rowde Court

FURLONG CL

CONSCIENCES LANE

Tanis Farm

ST A

Consciences Bridge

Lower Farm

DEVIZES

Ox House

ROAD

Rowde Field Farm

Iron Peartree Farm

Dunkirk

Queens Head Inn

Browfort Kennet D.C. Offices

DUNKIRK HILL

BELLE WAL

SUSSEX WHARF

THE NURSER

HIGH LAWN

Sch

BATH ROAD

JOSEPH

Lock

MOYNE CL

THE SIDING

B3101

MARSH LANE

KENNET & AVON CANAL

P

Flight of Locks

Ox House Farm

Prison Bridge

Lock — Lock

Lock

Sch

Lock

Lock

MAYENNE PLACE

DUNDAS CL

CAEN HILL CL

ROAD

CLERC ST

BELL

SALISBURY RD

OLD

A361

BATH

Caen Hill

Caen Hill Farm

WHISTLEY

AVON RD

AVON

Rec Grd

Sewage Works

Gillett's Farm

Castle Farm

LILLWORT

JOHN REN

WEST

Park Pale

Lower Park Farm

Moat

Old Park Farm

Old Park

HARTMOOR RD

Hartmoor Far

Park Pale ROAD

Park Pale

FURZE HILL

Furzehill Farm

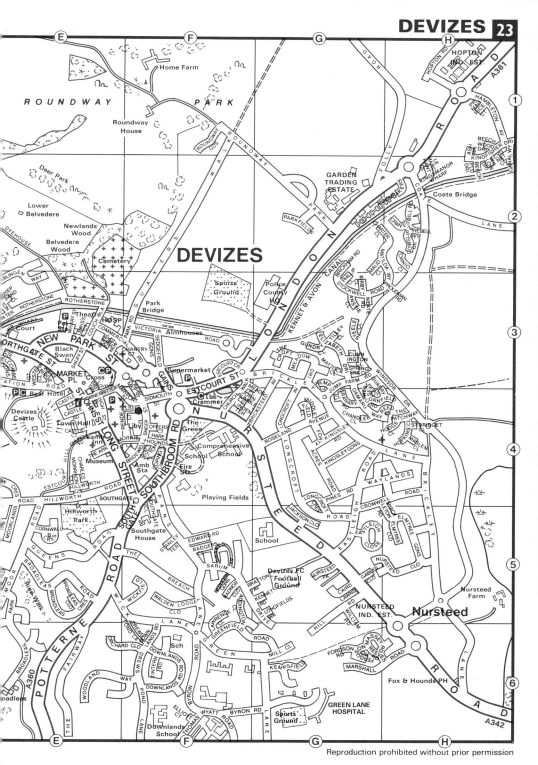

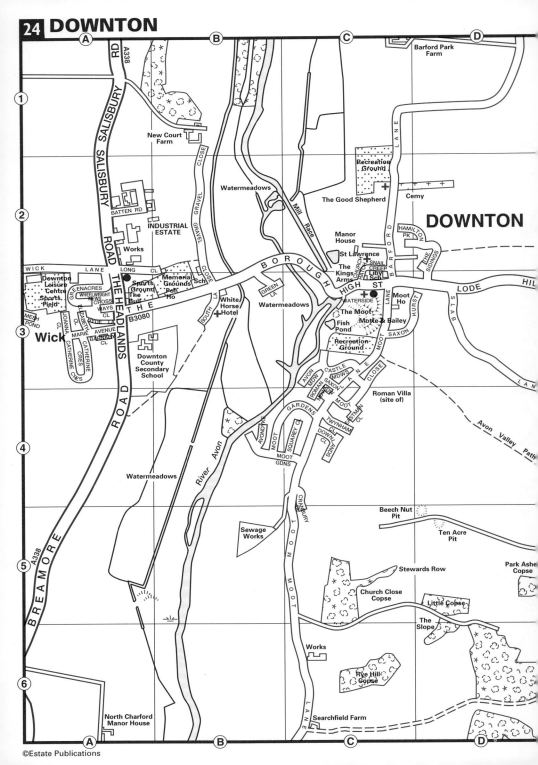

DOWNTON

Barford Park Farm

New Court Farm

Recreation Ground

The Good Shepherd

Cemy

INDUSTRIAL ESTATE

Works

Watermeadows

Manor House

St Lawrence

The Kings Arms

WICK LANE

Downton Leisure Centre Sports Field

Sports Ground

The Bull

Memorial Grounds Poll Ho

White Horse Hotel

Watermeadows

WATERSIDE

The Moot

Motte & Bailey

Moot Ho

MESH POND

Wick

Downton County Secondary School

Fish Pond

Recreation Ground

Roman Villa (site of)

Watermeadows

River Avon

MOOT GDNS

Sewage Works

Beech Nut Pit

Ten Acre Pit

Stewards Row

Church Close Copse

Park Ashe Copse

Little Copse

The Slope

Works

Rye Hill Copse

North Charford Manor House

Searchfield Farm

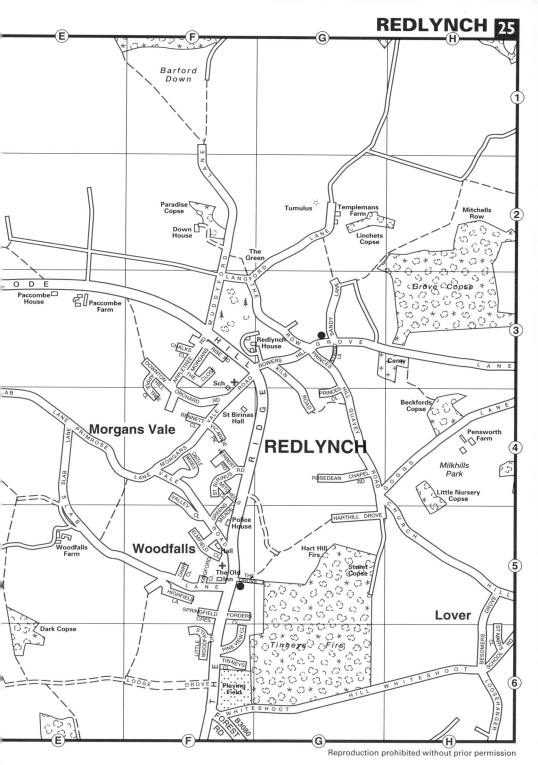

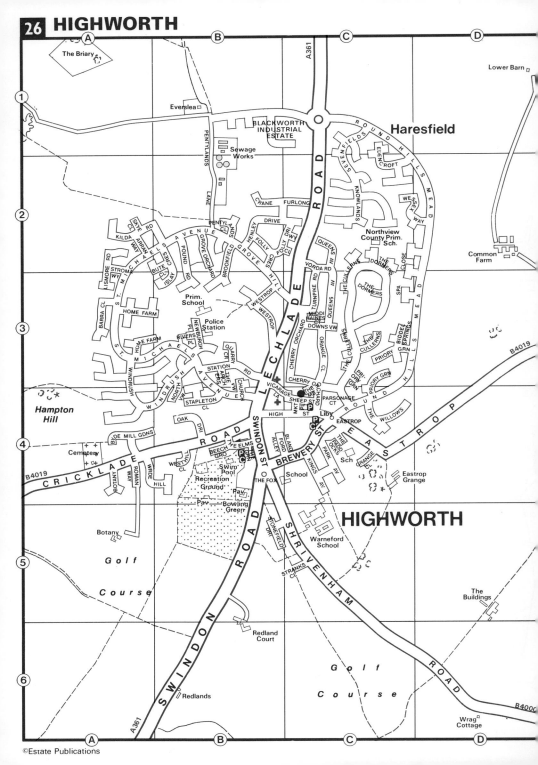

The Briary

Lower Barn

Everslea

A361

BLACKWORTH INDUSTRIAL ESTATE

Sewage Works

Haresfield

PENTYLANDS LANE

ROUND HILLS MEAD

SEVENFIELDS

KNOWLANDS

EVENCROFT

WESSEX WAY

Common Farm

CRANE FURLONG

PENTYLA CL

HENLEY

DRIVE

FOLLY DRI

FOLLY DRI

SKYE RD

KILDA

ADRIAN

TWY

AVENUE

GROVE ORCHARD

BROOKFIELD

LECHLADE ROAD

GROVE HILL

WESTROP

QUEENS

RD

VORDA RD

TURNPIKE RD

QUEENS AV

VW

Northview County Prim. Sch.

THE DORMERS

THE DORMERS

CLOSE

SPA

POUND RD

STROM WY

BUTE CRES

ISLAY

ST. MICHAELS

LISMORE RD

BARRA CL

HOME FARM

HOME FARM

ST.

Prim. School

NEWBURGH PL

RIVERSMEAD

WESTROP

CHERRY ORCHARD

MIDDL HAINES

DOWNS VW

ORANGE CL

THE CULLERNS

THE CULLERNS

THE CULLERNS

BIDDEL SPRINGS

PRIORY

HILLS MEAD

B4019

Police Station

WINDRUSH

ST.

MICHAELS

NORTH

AVENUE

STATION RD

QUARRY CRT

CHURCH

STAPLETON CL

VICARAGE LA

SHEEP ST

MKT PL

HIGH

CHERRY ORCHARD

CHERRY OR CHARD

PARSONAGE CT

PRIORY GRN

PRIORY GRN

THE WILLOWS

EASTROP

Lib

P

P

P

Hampton Hill

OAK DRI

WEST MILL

HILL

CL

DE MILL GDNS

BEECH GRO

THE ELMS

P

Cemetery

BOTANY WAY

ROMAN WAY

WRDE CL

Swim Pool

BLAND FORD ALLEY

BREWERY ST

KINGS ST

PARK AV

THE FOX

School

KINGS AV

ORANGE

Sch

EASTROP

Eastrop Grange

CRICKLADE B4019

SWINDON ST

Recreation Ground

Pav.

Pav.

Bowling Green

School

STONEFIELD DRI

Warneford School

HIGHWORTH

SWINDON ROAD

SHRIVENHAM ROAD

STRANKS CL

Golf

Course

Redland Court

The Buildings

A361

Redlands

Golf Course

Wrag Cottage

B400

ROAD

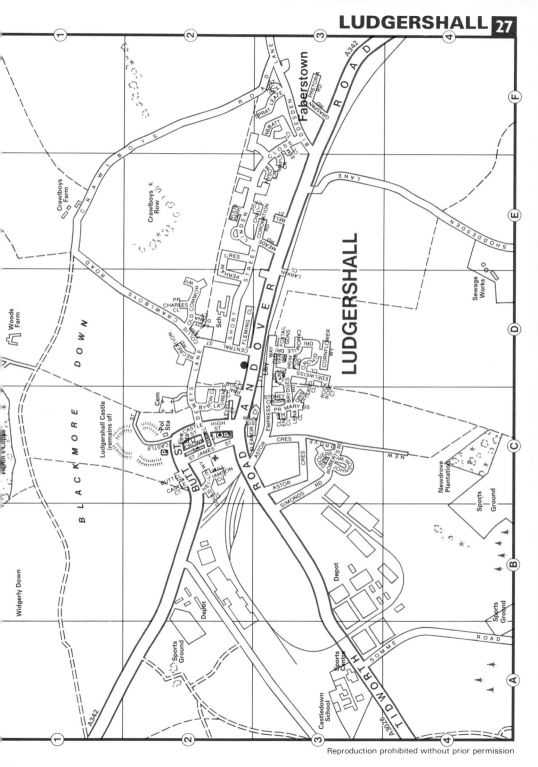

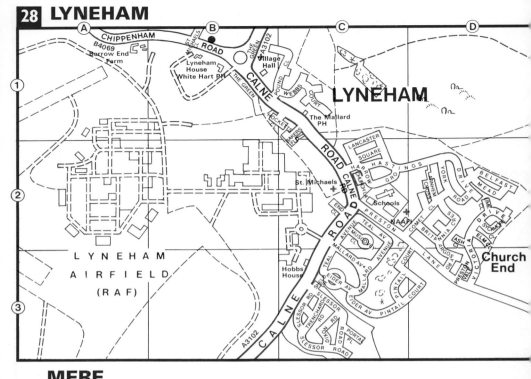

MERE

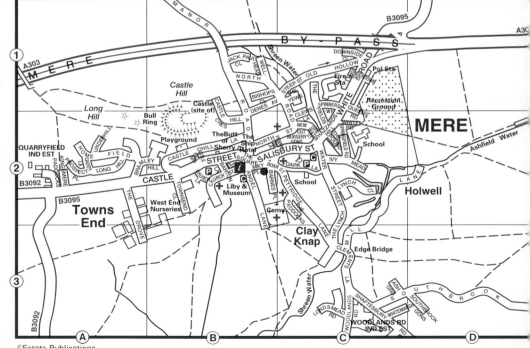

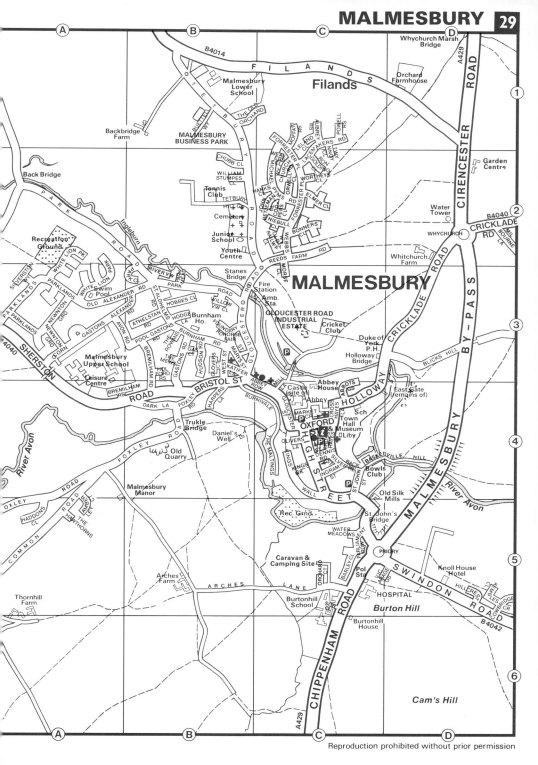

MARLBOROUGH

Barton Down
(Training Course)

Barton Copse

Marlborough Common

Club Ho.

Golf Course

FREES

Wedgwood Field

St. John's Close

Observatory

Cricket Ground

Rifle Range

Playing Field

Cricket Ground

SWINDON RD

PORT HILL

A346

THE THORNS

ROGERS MDW FIELD

BAILEY ACRE
FRANCKLYN ACRE
LAWRENCE ACRE
NEWBY ACRE
PURLYN ACRE

NORTH VIEW PL

BLOWHORN

THE COMMON

LAINE

HERD ST

ALEXANDR TERR

SILVERLESS

KINGSBURY STREET

BLACKWELL PATH

ST DAVIDS WAY

CROSS

OXFORD

THE GREEN

NEW RD

Town Hall

Bear Hotel

PARADE

IRONMONGER LANE

Merchants House

Castle & Ball Hotel

Jubilee Centre
The Priory

MARKET

HIGH

SCHO

ALMA PL

CHESTNUT

Leisure Centre

Liby.

St. Peters

FIGGINS

RUSSELL

i

Council Offices

Van Drenan Sch

DUCKS MEADOW

MARLBOROUGH

EDWARDS MDW

SASSOON

FALKNER CL

LYNES VW

SHIRLEY

MACNEICE DRI

AUBREY

DANDO DRI

MORRIS RD

STENN YSON CL

BENSON CL

THOMSON

JEFFERIES

FIRMING

SHAKE-SPEARE DRI

FIELDS

COLLEGE

HAWKINS MDW

AVE

GOLDING

HUGHES

DAVES

BETJEMAN RD

FARRAR DRI

MANTON

MANTON HOLLOW

A4

BATH ROAD

Manton Mill

Manton

R Kennet

BRIDGE ST

PRESHUTE LANE

HIGH ST

Manton Weir Farm

Manton Grange

Preshute House

The Mount
(Castle Mound)

MARLBOROUGH COLLEGE

St. Nicholas Chapel
(site of)

Treacle Bolly

River Park

BRIDEWELL ST

PEWSEY RD

GEORGE

GRANHAM CL

LWR
CH FLD

St. Johns School

UPP

Preshute

Sports Ground

Preshute White Horse

Red Cow Down

Granham Hill

Granham Hill

ROAD

PEWSEY (GRANHAM HILL)

A345

Pantawick

MANTON DROVE

Granham Farm

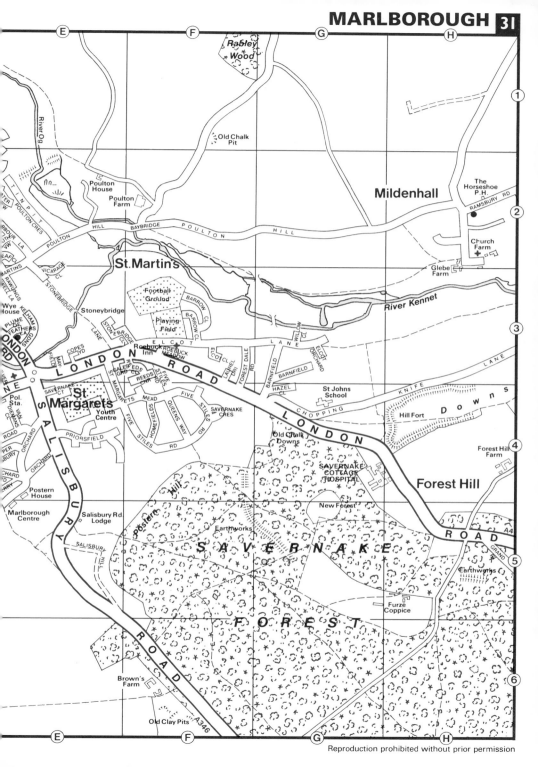

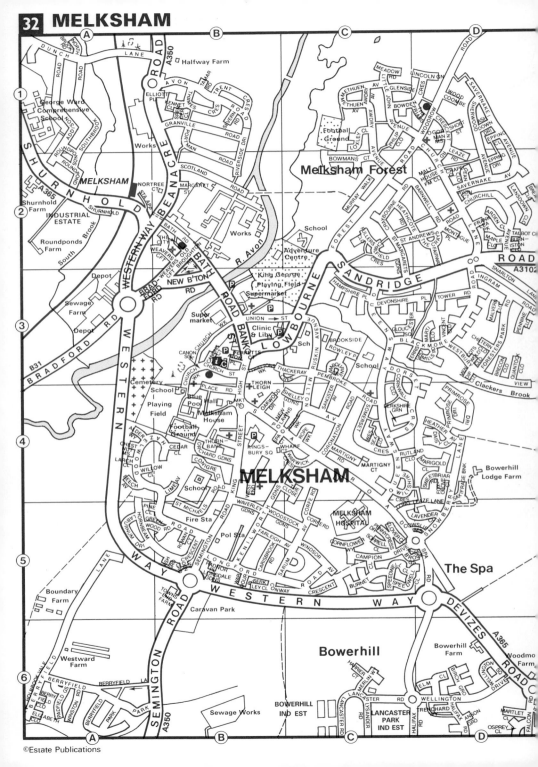

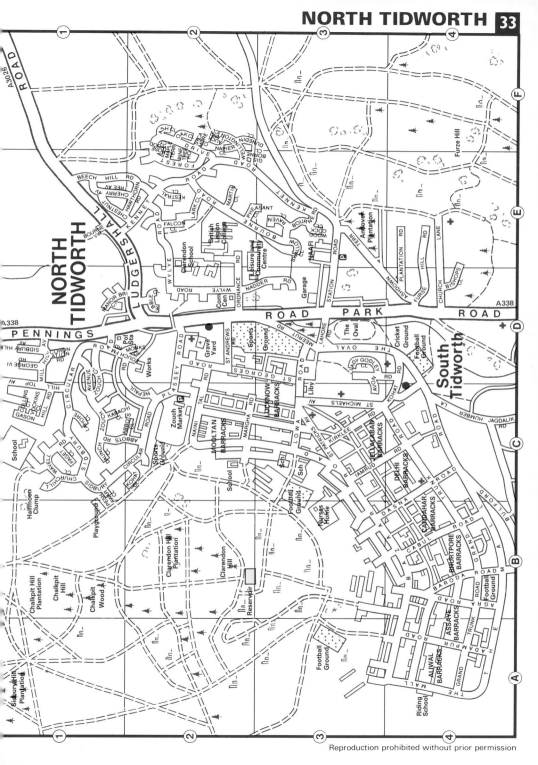

NORTH TIDWORTH

South Tidworth

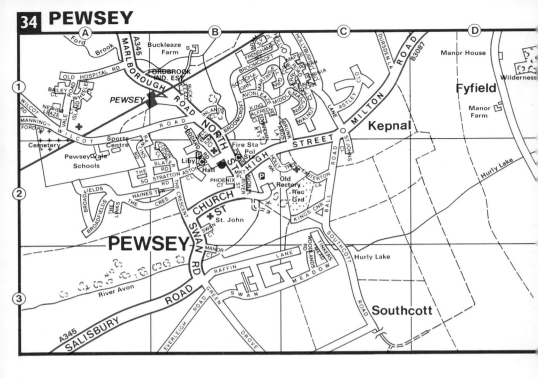

POTTERNE

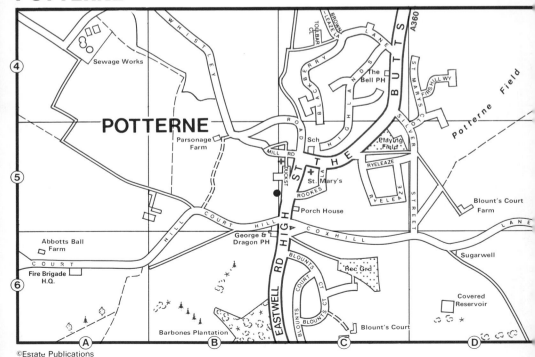

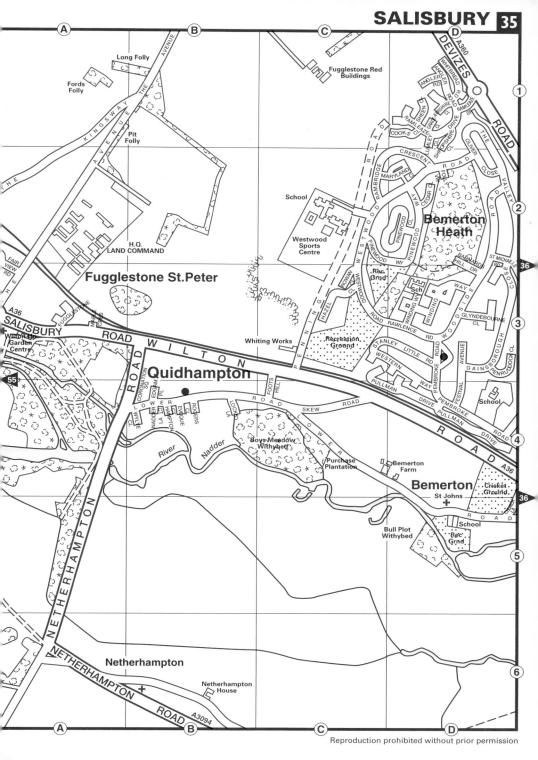

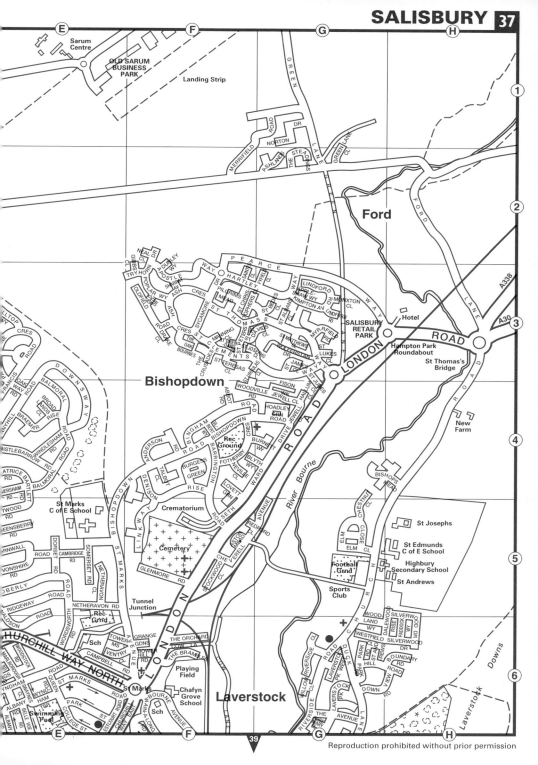

Sarum Centre

OLD SARUM BUSINESS PARK

Landing Strip

Ford

A338

A30

Bishopdown

SALISBURY RETAIL PARK

Hotel

Hampton Park Roundabout

St Thomas's Bridge

LONDON ROAD

New Farm

BISHOPS ROAD

Rec Ground

St Josephs

St Edmunds C of E School

Highbury Secondary School

St Andrews

Crematorium

River Bourne

St Marks C of E School

Cemetery

Football Grnd

Sports Club

Tunnel Junction

Rec Grnd

Sch

THE ORCHARD

THE BRAMBLES

CHURCHILL WAY NORTH

Playing Field

St Marks

Chafyn Grove School

Sch

Swimming Pool

Laverstock

Laverstock Downs

39

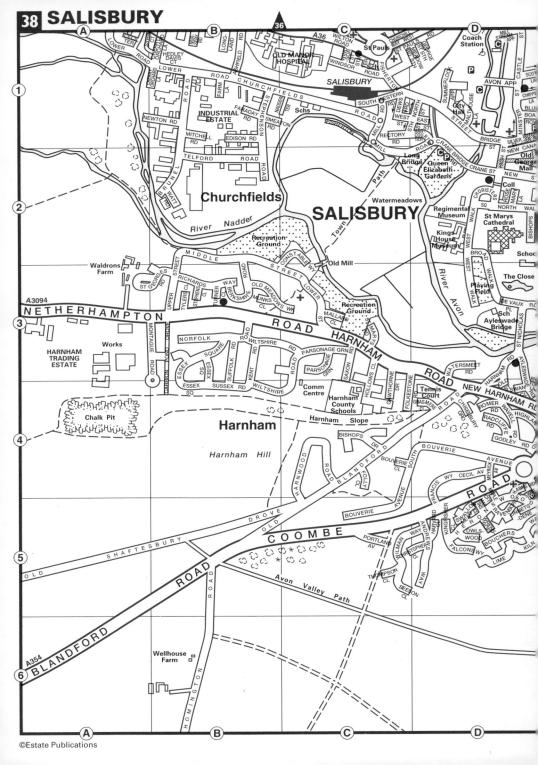

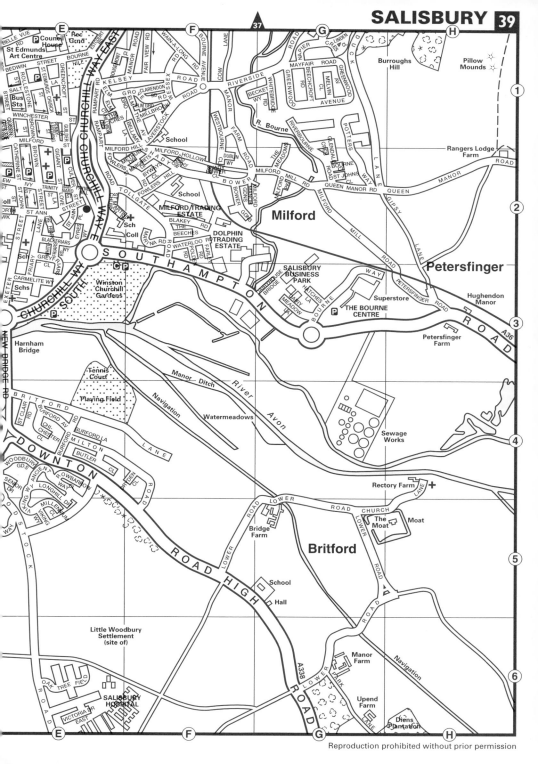

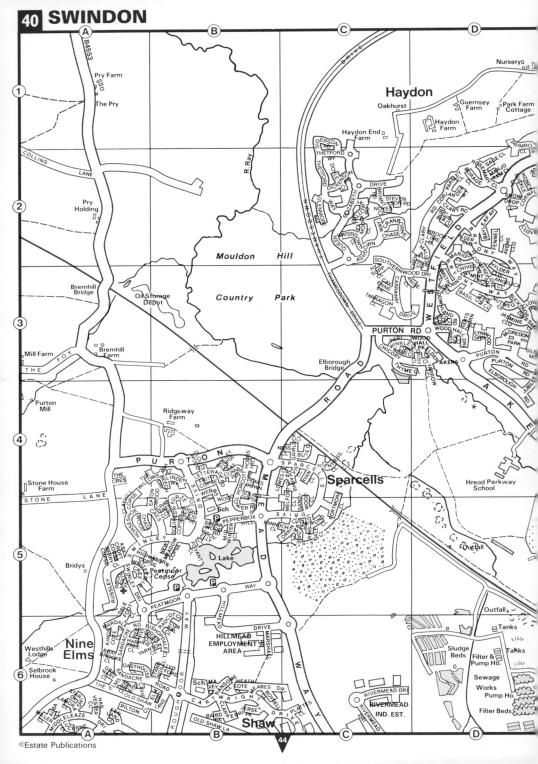

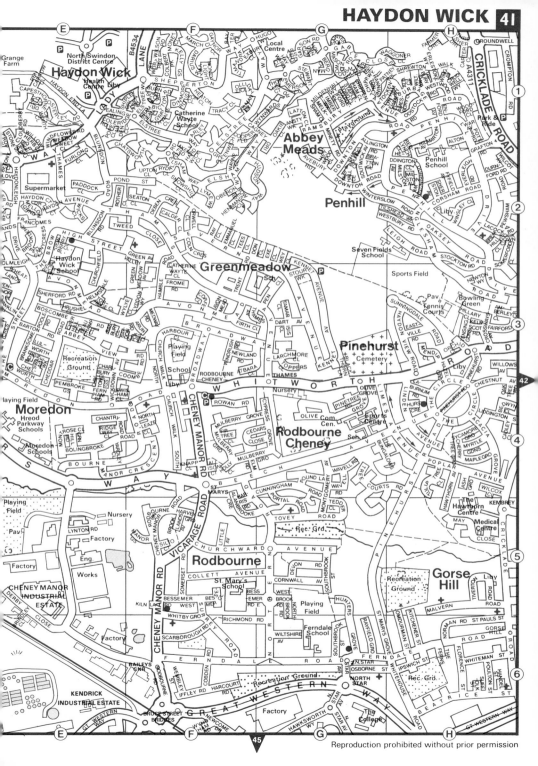

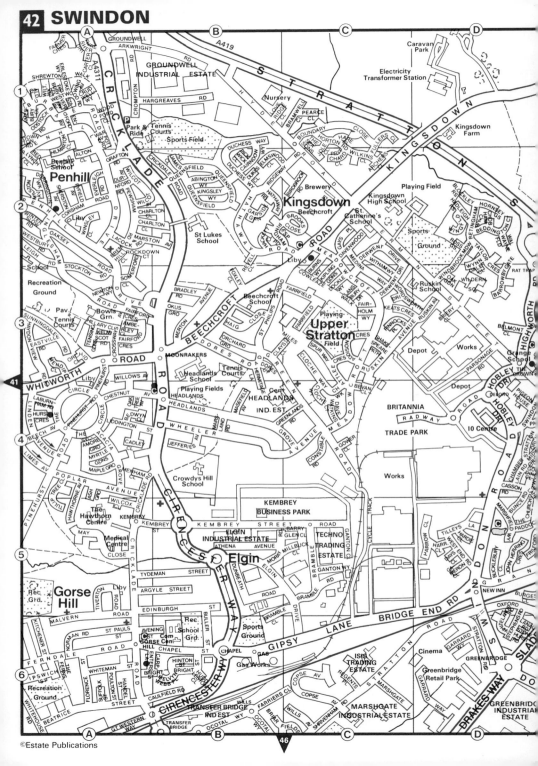

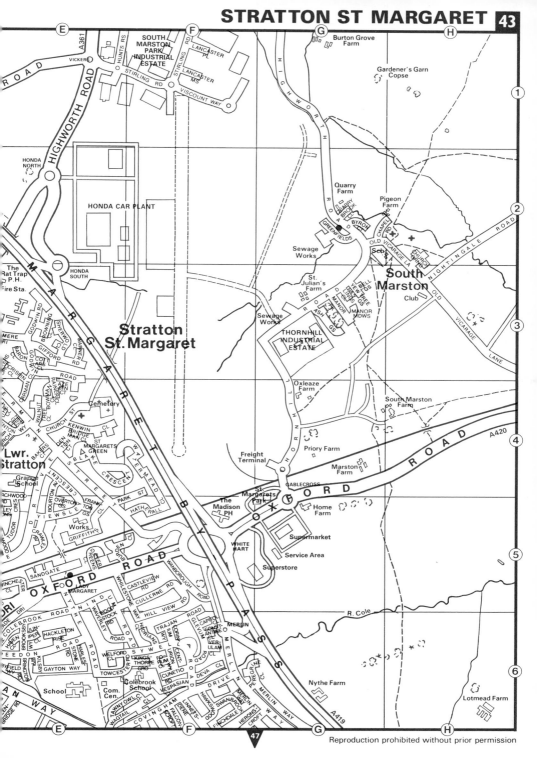

Grid references: E F G H (top), 1 2 3 4 5 6 (right side), E F G (bottom)

HIGHWORTH ROAD A361

SOUTH MARSTON PARK INDUSTRIAL ESTATE

HUNTS RD
VICKERS
STIRLING RD
LANCASTER PL
LANCASTER MS
VISCOUNT WAY

HIGHWORTH ROAD

Burton Grove Farm

Gardener's Garn Copse

HONDA NORTH

HONDA CAR PLANT

Quarry Farm

Pigeon Farm

HONDA SOUTH

The Rat Trap P.H.
Fire Sta.

Sewage Works

GREENFIELDS

QUARRY BROOK ROAD

BYRON

CHAPEL RD

OLD VICARAGE LA
Sch.
CHURCH

South Marston

NIGHTINGALE ROAD

OLD VICARAGE LANE

St. Julian's Farm

Club

MARGARET ROAD

Stratton St. Margaret

Sewage Works

THORNHILL INDUSTRIAL ESTATE

MANOR
BELL
YEW TREE
ASH GS
MANOR MDWS

Oxleaze Farm

South Marston Farm

Cemetery

CHURCH
KENWIN CL
BRIDGE
MANOR
MARGARETS GREEN
BLAKE
CRESCENT

WATERMEAD

HORN
ROAD

Lwr. Stratton

Grange School

DEN
STREET
OVERTON GS
FRANK CL
PARK ST
HATH HALL
CRESCENT

Freight Terminal

Priory Farm

Marston Farm

GABLECROSS

Home Farm

St. Margarets Park

The Madison PH

OXFORD ROAD A420

WHITE HART

Supermarket

Service Area

Superstore

OXFORD ROAD

SANDGATE
LADY MARGARET

BY PASS

CASTLEVIEW RD
CULLERNE RD
HILL VIEW RD

WANBOROUGH ROAD

WELSTONE WAY

R. Cole

MERLIN

TRAJAN WAY
CORIN CT
WEBULAM
UNION RD
PLUM CL
DEVA CL
VESPASIAN

MERLIN WAY

MERLIN WAY

MERLIN DRIVE

School
Com. Cen.

Colebrook School

Nythe Farm

A419

Lotmead Farm

WAY

WNY OWL
WAGTAIL
SWANBROOK
COVINGHAM
HERONS CROFT
FINCHDALE
FALCON

A419

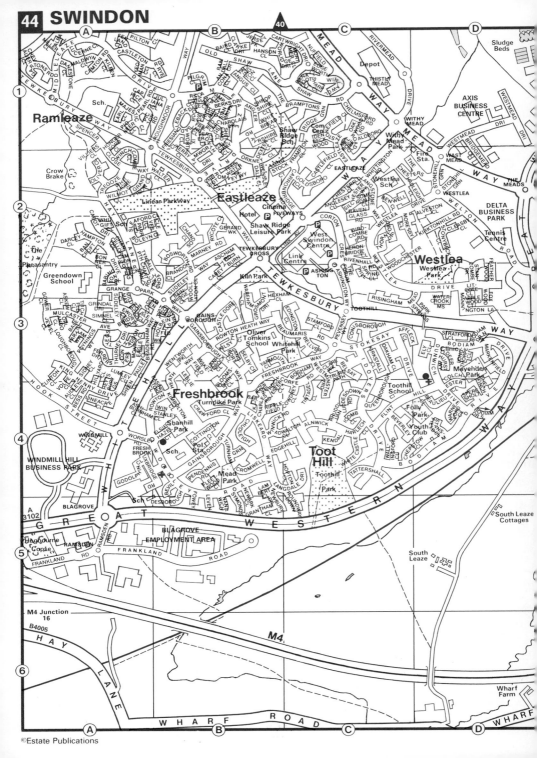

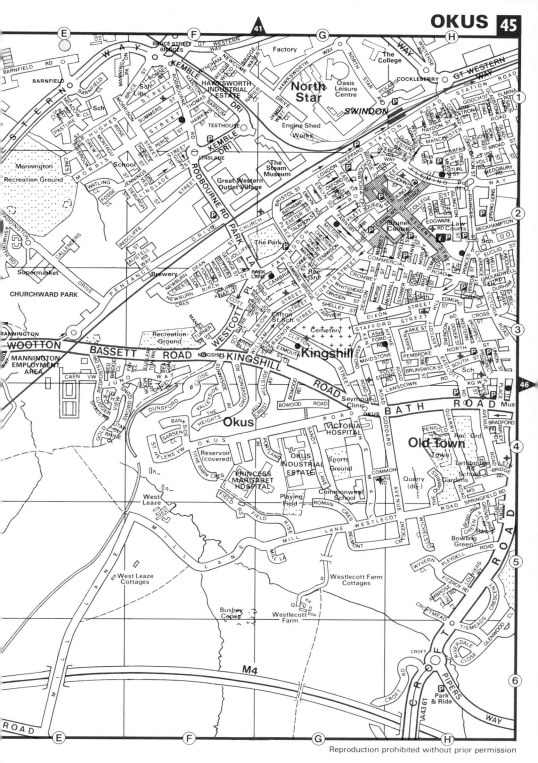

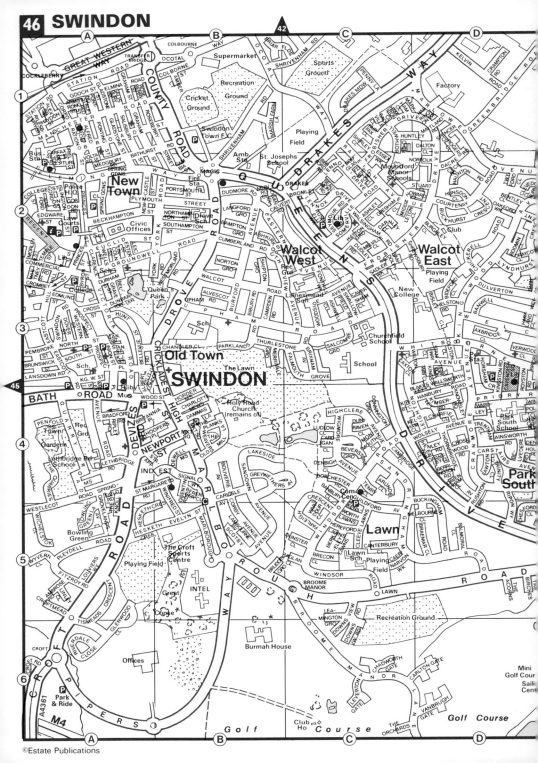

43

E F G H

Covingham

Covingham
Park School

School
Nythe

PICCADILLY

Kingfisher

Rousset

Stormwater
Lagoon

Dorcan
School

Pool

FARADAY
PARK

The Poplars

Wanborough
House

Park
North
& Sch

ark
orth

Bowleymead

Warehouse

FARADAY
RD

DORCAN

Dorcan

INDUSTRIAL

ISLANDSMEAD

STUBS
MEAD

Eldene

Eldene
School

EDISON

EDISON   RD

Factory

ESTATE

Marsh Farm

WHEATSTONE RD

Inlands
Cottages

Inlands Farm

SNODSHILL

Liden
School

GRUNDYS

Liden

Post House
Hotel

Great Moor
Leaze Farm

Little Moor
Leaze Farm

COATE

MARLBOROUGH

Jefferies
Museum

Coate

WOODBINE   TERR

ROAD

Pump
House

Weirs

Wokingham
Lodge

The Retreat

PURLEY

Boat
House

Paddling
Pool

Day
House

Day House
Copse

COMMON
HEAD

ROAD

Coate Water
Country Park

Hospital
(under construction)

A419

B4192

E F G H

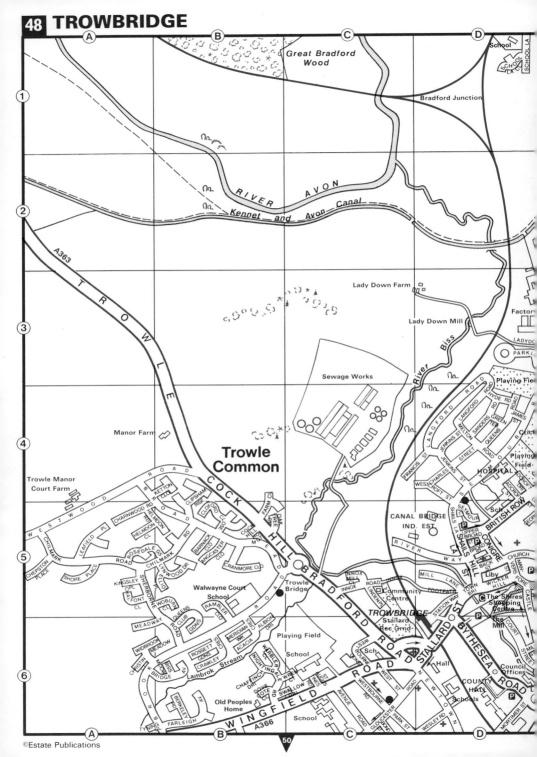

A   B   C   D

School
SCHOOL LA

Great Bradford Wood

Bradford Junction

RIVER AVON

Kennet and Avon Canal

Lady Down Farm

Lady Down Mill

Factory

LADYDO
PARK

River Biss

Playing Fie

Sewage Works

ROAD
LANGFORD
HYDE RD
JAMES
Playing Field
HOSPITAL

Manor Farm

Trowle Common

FRANCIS ST
JENKINS ST
MELTON
SANDERS GREEN
QUEENS
WESTCROFT ST
CHARLES ST
SHAILS LA
SEYMOUR
BRITISH ROW

Trowle Manor
Court Farm

WESTWOOD ROAD
CHILMARK
CHEPSTON PLACE
SHORE PLACE
LEASFIELD PL
CHARNWOOD RD
HELMDON CL
KETTON CLO
CLIPSHAM RISE
CLIFORD CLOSE
BARNACK CLO
ANGCASTER CLO
COCKHILL
CANAL BRIDGE IND. EST.
UPPER BROAD
SHAILS HILL
CONGRE
BACK ST
CHURCH
LIBY

ROSEDALE RD
CHILMARK
LINWOOD DR
CRANMORE CLO
FARM CL
OAK TREE
RIVER
WAY
MILL LANE
WICKER HILL
FORE
CASTLE
The Shires
Shopping Centre

KINGSLEY
SHERBORN
FONT
WOBURN CL
QUEENS
CLUB GDNS
RAMBLER
MEADWAY
WIDBROOK
MEADOW
CHRISTIN
BISS BRIDGE
Walwayne Court School
MERIDIAN WK
ALBION DRI
ACACIA
WARBLER
WREN
Trowle Bridge
BRADFORD ROAD
Community Centre
FOOTPATH
TROWBRIDGE
Stallard Rec. Grnd.
STATION WAY
STALLARD ST
TOWN BRI
The Mill
COURT STREET
Council Offices

ROSSETT GDNS
CRAWLEY
CHAFFINCH
NIGHTINGALE
DOTE
SWALLOW
Playing Field
School
WEST ST
Sch
BOURNE RD
S.32M
Hall
NEWTOWN
BYTHESEA ROAD
COUNTY HALL
Schools
MORTIMER ST

BERKELEY AV
TYNING
FARLEIGH
Old Peoples Home
WINGFIELD ROAD
A366
School
WESTBOURNE RD
AVENUE
GLOUCESTER RD
PARK ST
WESLEY RD
COUNTY ROAD

A   B   C   D

50

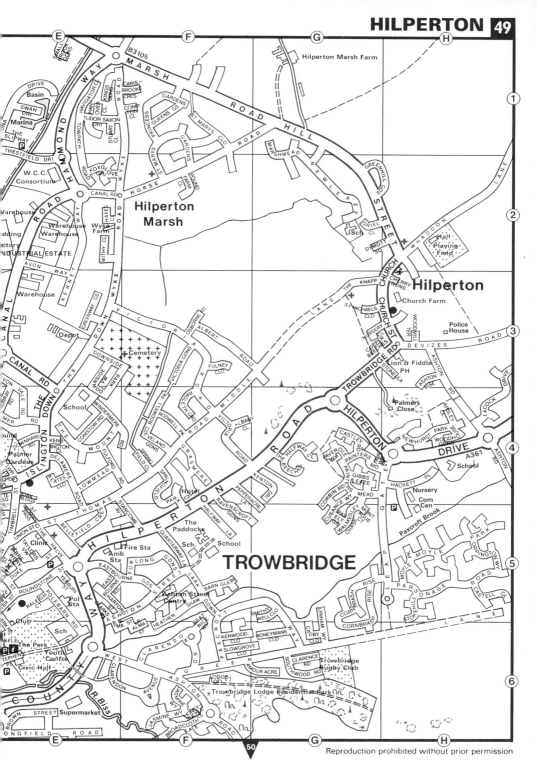

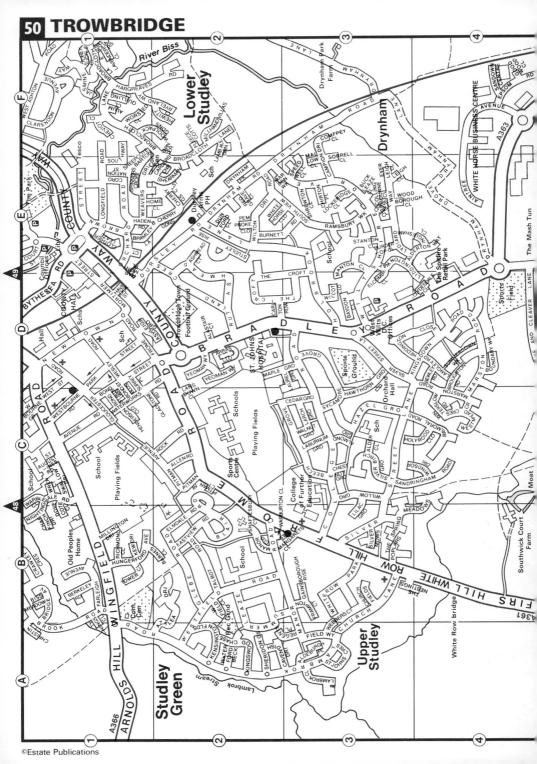

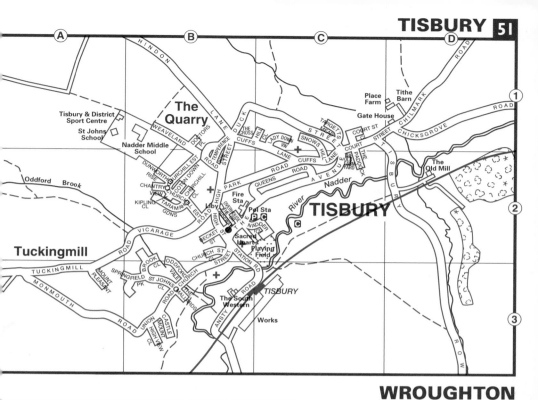

WROUGHTON

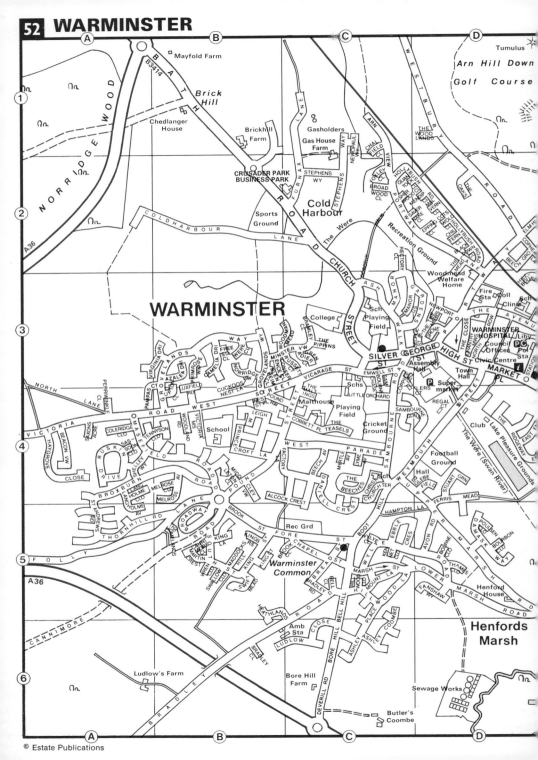

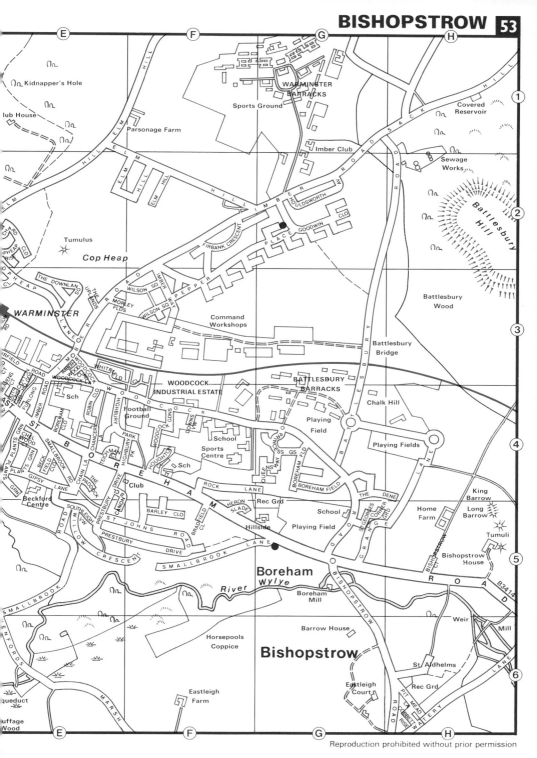

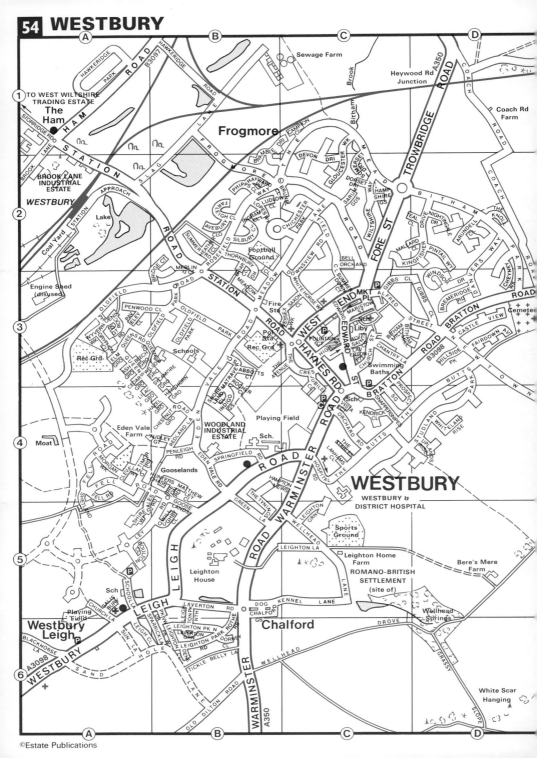

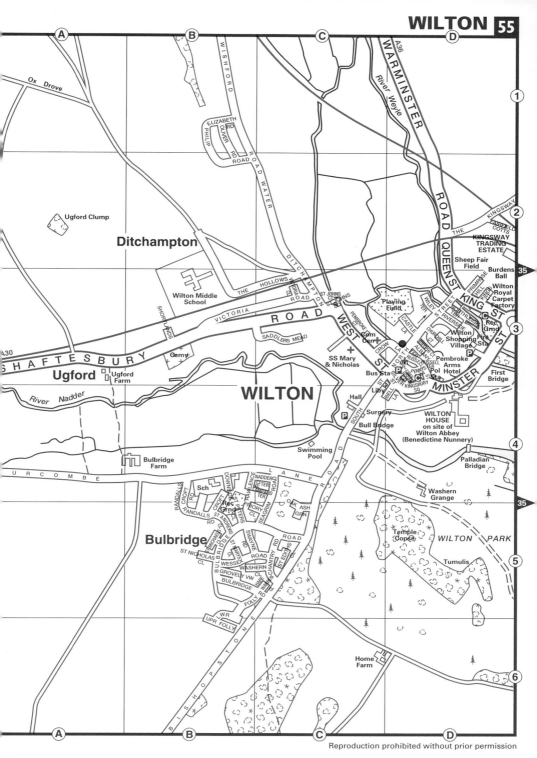

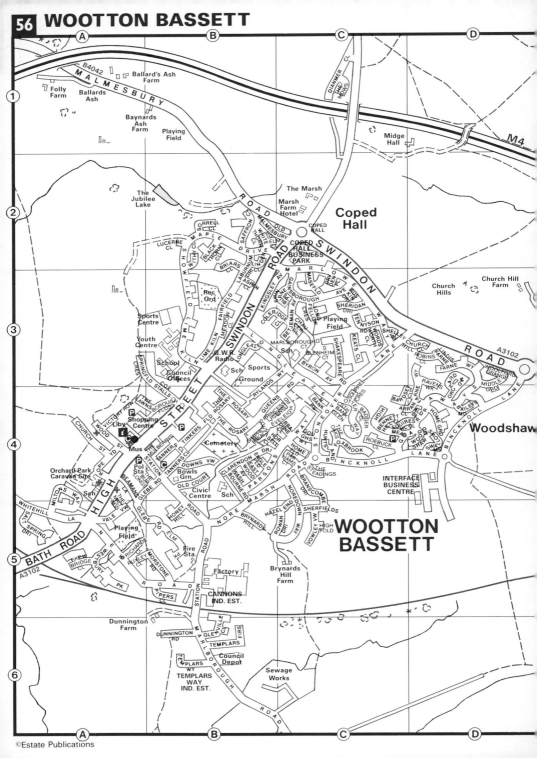

A - Z INDEX TO STREETS
with Postcodes

The Index includes some names for which there is insufficient space on the maps. These names are preceded by an * and are followed by the nearest adjoining thoroughfare.

ALDBOURNE

Alma Rd. SN8 12 B1
Back La. SN8 12 B2
Castle St. SN8 12 A2
Chandlers La. SN8 12 B1
Claridge Clo. SN8 12 B3
Cook Clo. SN8 12 B1
Cook Rd. SN8 12 B1
Crooked Corner. SN8 12 B2
Farm La. SN8 12 B3
Glebe Clo. SN8 12 B2
Goddards La. SN8 12 B2
Grasshills. SN8 12 B1
Hawkins Rd. SN8 12 B3
Hillwood Rd. SN8 12 A3
Kandahar. SN8 12 B1
Lottage Rd. SN8 12 B1
Lottage Way. SN8 12 B1
Marlborough Rd. SN8 12 B3
Oxford St. SN8 12 B2
Rectory Wood. SN8 12 B3
St Michaels Clo. SN8 12 B2
South St. SN8 12 B2
Southfield. SN8 12 B3
Southward La. SN8 12 B3
Stock La. SN8 12 A3
The Butts. SN8 12 B3
The Downs. SN8 12 B3
The Garlings. SN8 12 B3
The Green. SN8 12 B2
The Knoll. SN8 12 B1
The Paddocks. SN8 12 B2
The Square. SN8 12 B2
Turnpike. SN8 12 B2
West St. SN8 12 A2
Westfield Chase. SN8 12 A2
Whitley Rd. SN8 12 A3
Windmill Clo. SN8 12 B1

AMESBURY

Abbess Clo. SP4 13 C3
Abbey La. SP4 13 B2
Abbey Sq. SP4 13 B2
Alanbrooke Clo. SP4 13 C1
Allington Way. SP4 13 E3
Amesbury By Pass. SP4 13 A1
Amesbury Rd. SP4 13 F3
Annets Clo. SP4 13 D1
Antrobus Rd. SP4 13 C2
Aragon Clo. SP4 13 D1
Ashley Walk. SP4 13 E3
Avon Bldgs. SP4 13 C2
Avonstoke Clo. SP4 13 C3
Barnes Wallis Clo. SP4 13 F3
Bawdsey Rd. SP4 13 E4
Beacon Clo. SP4 13 D1
Beamont Way. SP4 13 E3
Beauchamp Dri. SP4 13 E2
Beaulieu Rd. SP4 13 D3
Beger Rd. SP4 13 E4
Blackcross Rd. SP4 13 D3
Boscombe Down Rd. SP4 13 D2
Bramley Way. SP4 13 D2
Buckland Ct. SP4 13 C3
Burwood Clo. SP4 13 F3
Butterfield Dri. SP4 13 E2
Cadnam Cres. SP4 13 F3
Canbury Clo. SP4 13 F3
Carleon Clo. SP4 13 E2
Carleton Pl. SP4 13 C2
Carpenters Dri. SP4 13 E2
Chambers Av. SP4 13 D3
Cherrytree Way. SP4 13 D2
Chesterfield Clo. SP4 13 F2
Church La. SP4 13 B2
Church St. SP4 13 B2
Coach House Mews. SP4 13 C2
Cold Harbour. SP4 13 C2
Coltsfoot Clo. SP4 13 D2
Coniston Clo. SP4 13 F2
Coopers Clo. SP4 13 C2
Countess Rd. SP4 13 B1
Cranleigh Clo. SP4 13 F2
Darrell Rd. SP4 13 D1
Dawbeny Dri. SP4 13 E2
Devereux Rd. SP4 13 D2
Diddledown Rd. SP4 13 E3
Earls Clo. SP4 13 F3
Earls Court Rd. SP4 13 C2
Edwards Rd. SP4 13 C2
Evergreen Way. SP4 13 D3
Fairfax Clo. SP4 13 C2
Finnis Rd. SP4 13 D2
Flitcroft. SP4 13 D3
Flower La. SP4 13 B2
Fosters Bushes. SP4 13 E2
Gauntlet Rd. SP4 13 C2
Geneville Rise. SP4 13 E3
Hamilton Clo. SP4 13 F3
Harvard Way. SP4 13 E3
Haywain. SP4 13 D3
Heyford Clo. SP4 13 F3
High St. SP4 13 B2
Highfield Rd. SP4 13 C3
Hillview Clo. SP4 13 C1
Holders Rd. SP4 13 D2
Hudson Rd. SP4 13 D2
Hurley Clo. SP4 13 F2
Imber Av. SP4 13 E3
INDUSTRIAL & RETAIL:
Amesbury Ind Est. SP4 13 D1
Boscombe Down Business Park. SP4 13 E1
Jaggard View. SP4 13 D3
James Rd. SP4 13 D1
Javelin Clo. SP4 13 E3
John Gay Rd. SP4 13 D2
Kickdom Clo. SP4 13 E3
Kitchener Rd. SP4 13 C2
Lanes Clo. SP4 13 D2
Lanfear Clo. SP4 13 D2
Lawrence Clo. SP4 13 D3
Leonard Cheshire Clo. SP4 13 E3
Lightning Rd. SP4 13 E3
London Rd. SP4 13 C2
Lords Croft. SP4 13 C1
Lumley Walk. SP4 13 E3
Lynchets Rd. SP4 13 C3
Lynchfield Rd. SP4 13 D3
Lyndhurst Rd. SP4 13 D3
McKie Rd. SP4 13 E3
Main Rd. SP4 13 F3
Martlesham Rd. SP4 13 E4
Melor Vw. SP4 13 D3
Millgreen Rd. SP4 13 D3
Mills Way. SP4 13 E1
Milton Rd. SP4 13 F3
Moyne Gdns. SP4 13 E3
Nicolson Clo. SP4 13 F2
North Rd. SP4 13 F3
Nursery Clo. SP4 13 C2
Oak Pl. SP4 13 D1
Oaklands Av. SP4 13 E2
Old Granary La. SP4 13 C2
Orchard Way. SP4 13 D2
Orford Rd. SP4 13 E4
Pains Way. SP4 13 D3
Parsonage Rd. SP4 13 C3
Pilots Vw. SP4 13 E3
Pine Walk. SP4 13 E2
Pointers Way. SP4 13 E2
Porton Rd. SP4 13 E3
Purvis Clo. SP4 13 F2
Queensberry Rd. SP4 13 D1
Raleigh Cres. SP4 13 E2
Ratfyn Rd. SP4 13 C1
Recreation Rd. SP4 13 B3
Ringwood Av. SP4 13 D3
Riverside Av. SP4 13 A2
Robbins Ridge. SP4 13 D3
Romsey Rd. SP4 13 E3
St Annes Clo. SP4 13 D2
Salisbury Rd, Amesbury. SP4 13 C2
Salisbury Rd, Boscombe Down. SP4 13 F4
Salisbury St. SP4 13 B2
School La. SP4 13 C2
Simmance Way. SP4 13 D2
Smithfield St. SP4 13 C2
Solstice Rise. SP4 13 C2
South Mill Clo. SP4 13 C3
South Mill Rd. SP4 13 C3
Southmill Hill. SP4 13 C4
Station Cotts. SP4 13 D1
Stockbarrow. SP4 13 D3
Stonehenge Rd. SP4 13 A2
Tanners Field. SP4 13 E3
Tempest Rd. SP4 13 E3
The Centre. SP4 13 C2
The Drove. SP4 13 C2
Thurlow Clo. SP4 13 F3
Tisbury Rd. SP4 13 E1
Tuckers Clo. SP4 13 D3
Underwood Dri. SP4 13 E3
Vernon Clo. SP4 13 F2
Verny Clo. SP4 13 E2
Virginia Clo. SP4 13 F2
Westland Clo. SP4 13 F2
Whelan Way. SP4 13 E2
Wilcot Clo. SP4 13 F3
Winchester Clo. SP4 13 E3
Wittenham Vw. SP4 13 D3

AVEBURY

Beckhampton Rd. SN8 12 A6
Bray St. SN8 12 A5
Frog La. SN8 12 B6
High St. SN8 12 C5
Nash Rd. SN8 12 A6
South St. SN8 12 A6
Swindon Rd. SN8 12 C4
Truslow Cottages. SN8 12 A6
West Kennet Av. SN8 12 D5

BRADFORD-ON-AVON

Ancliff Sq. BA15 14 B5
Ashley Clo. BA15 15 E1
Ashley La. BA15 14 C2
Ashley Rd. BA15 15 E1
Avon Clo. BA15 15 G3
Avonfield Av. BA15 15 G4
Baileys Barn. BA15 15 F4
Bainton Clo. BA15 15 G2
Bancroft. BA15 15 G1
Barn Piece. BA15 15 G5
Barton Orchard. BA15 15 E3
Bassetts Pasture. BA15 15 F5
Bath Rd. BA15 15 F1
Bear Clo. BA15 15 E2
Bearfield Bldgs. BA15 15 F1
Beddoe Clo. BA15 15 G5
Belcombe Pl. BA15 15 E3
Belcombe Rd. BA15 15 E3
Berryfield Rd. BA15 15 F2
Bobbin La. BA15 14 C5
Bobbin Pk. BA15 14 C6
Boswell Rd. BA15 14 B6
Bradford Rd. BA15 14 A3
Bridge St. BA15 15 F3
Brookwood. BA15 14 B2
Broomground. BA15 14 B2
Budbury Clo. BA15 15 E2
Budbury Circ. BA15 15 E2
Budbury Pl. BA15 15 E2
Budbury Ridge. BA15 15 E2
Budbury Tyning. BA15 15 E2
Bull Pit. BA15 15 F3
Cedar Ct. BA15 15 F1
Cemetery La. BA15 15 H2
Chestnut Gro. BA15 14 B5
Christchurch Rd. BA15 15 F1
Church Acre. BA15 15 F2
Church St. BA15 15 F3
Churches. BA15 15 E2
Conigre Hill. BA15 15 F2
Coppice Hill. BA15 15 F2
Coronation Av. BA15 15 G2
Cottles La. BA15 14 B3
Crown Ct. BA15 15 H2
Culver Rd. BA15 15 G4
Dane Clo. BA15 14 B2
Dane Rise. BA15 14 A2
Deverell Clo. BA15 15 G5
Downavon. BA15 15 G4
Downs Clo. BA15 15 E2
Downs View. BA15 15 E2
Druces Hill. BA15 15 F2
Elmfield. BA15 15 E2
Elms Cross.BA15 15 E6
Elms Cross Dri. BA15 15 F4
Fairleigh View. BA15 14 B6
Fieldins. BA15 14 B2
Fitzmaurice Clo. BA15 15 G5
Fitzmaurice Pl. BA15 15 F4
Follyfield. BA15 15 G5
Frenchgrass. BA15 15 G3
Friary Clo. BA15 14 B5
Frome Rd. BA15 15 F3
Grange View. BA15 15 G2
Great Orchard. BA15 14 B5
Green La. BA15 14 B3
Greenland Mills. BA15 15 G3
Greenland View. BA15 15 G3
Grove Leaze. BA15 15 E3
Hare Knapp. BA15 15 E3
Hebden Rd. BA15 14 B6
Highfield Rd. BA15 15 G2
Hob House Clo. BA15 15 G5
Holly Bush Clo. BA15 14 B2
Holt Rd. BA15 15 G3
Horton Clo. BA15 15 G5
Huntingdon Pl. BA15 15 F2
Huntingdon Rise. BA15 15 E1
Huntingdon St. BA15 15 F1
Iford La. BA15 14 A6
INDUSTRIAL & RETAIL:
Elmscross Shopping Centre & Business Pk. BA15 15 E5
Treenwood Ind Est. BA15 15 F5
Ivy Ter. BA15 15 F2
John Rennie Clo. BA15 15 G5
Jones Hill. BA15 15 E4
Junction Rd. BA15 15 F3
Kennet Gdns. BA15 15 F4
King Alfred Way. BA15 14 A2
Kingsfield. BA15 15 G2
Kingsfield Clo. BA15 15 G2
Kingsfield Grange Rd. BA15 15 G2
Kingston Av. BA15 15 G4
Kingston Rd. BA15 15 F2
Late Broads. BA15 14 A2
Leigh Park Rd. BA15 15 F1
Leigh Rd. BA15 15 G1
Leslie Rise. BA15 14 C6
Limpley Stoke Rd. BA15 14 A2
Linden Cres. BA15 14 C6
Lindisfarne Clo. BA15 14 B2
Lister Gro. BA15 14 C6
Lodden Way. BA15 15 G4
Lyddieth Ct. BA15 14 A2
Magnon Rd. BA15 15 E2
Market St. BA15 15 F2
Masons La. BA15 15 F2
Meadowfield. BA15 15 E3
Methuen Clo. BA15 15 G5
Middle Rank. BA15 15 F2
Mill La. BA15 15 F3
Millbourn Clo. BA15 14 A2
Moulton Dri. BA15 15 F5
Mount Pleasant. BA15 15 F2
Mythern Mdw. BA15 15 G4
New Rd. BA15 15 G2
Newtown. BA15 15 E3
Northfield. BA15 14 B2
Orchard Clo. BA15 14 C6
Orchard Gdns. BA15 15 F3
Palairet Clo. BA15 15 F4
Palmer Dri. BA15 15 G1
Peto Gro. BA15 14 C6
Piplar Ground. BA15 15 F5
Poston Way. BA15 14 A2
Poulton. BA15 15 G4
Poulton La. BA15 15 G4
Pound La. BA15 15 F3
Priory Clo. BA15 15 F2
Priory Park. BA15 15 F2
Quarry Clo. BA3 14 A3
Regents Pl. BA15 15 F3
Rickfield. BA15 15 E3
River Ct. BA15 15 F3
Rosemary Steps. BA15 15 F2
Rosemary Wk. BA15 15 F3
Rowden La. BA15 15 F5
St Aldhelm Rd. BA15 15 G4
St Katherines Quay . BA15 15 F4
St Laurence Rd. BA15 15 G4
St Margarets Hill. BA15 15 F3
St Margarets St. BA15 15 F2
St Margarets Steps. BA15 15 F3
St Margarets Villas. BA15 15 F3
St Nicholas Clo. BA15 14 A2
Sand Clo. BA15 15 G2
Sandy Leaze. BA15 15 E3
Saxon Way. BA15 14 B2
Silver St. BA15 15 F2
Sladesbrook. BA15 15 G1
Sladesbrook Clo. BA15 15 G2
Southleigh. BA15 15 E4
Southville Clo. BA15 15 G4
Southville Rd. BA15 15 G4
Southway Rd. BA15 15 H5
Spencers Orchard. BA15 15 F5
Springfield. BA15 15 G3
Stonefield Clo. BA15 15 G4
The Old Batch. BA15 15 E1
The Elms. BA15 14 E1
The Croft. BA15 14 C6
The Laurels. BA15 14 C6
The Maltings. BA15 15 F4
The Mead. BA15 14 B2
The Mill Ho. BA15 15 G3
The Pastures. BA15 14 B6
The Ridge. BA15 15 G2
The Shambles. BA15 15 F2
The Wilderness. BA15 15 F2
Tory. BA15 15 E3
Tory Pl. BA15 15 E3
Trowbridge Rd. BA15 15 F3
Tyning Rd. BA15 14 B2
Tynings Way. BA15 14 C6
Upper Mill. BA15 15 G3
Upper Regents Park. BA15 15 F3
Upper Westwood. BA15 14 A6
Vine Cotts. BA15 15 E2
Wellside Mill. BA15 15 G3
Westfield. BA15 14 D2
Westwood Rd. BA15 14 D6
White Hill. BA15 15 F2
White Horse Rd. BA15 14 B2
Whiteheads La. BA15 15 F2
Widbrook Hill. BA15 15 H6
Widbrook Vw. BA15 15 G4
Windy Ridge. BA15 14 B5
Wine St. BA15 15 E2
Wine St Ter. BA15 15 E2
Winsley Rd. BA15 15 C2
Woolley Clo. BA15 15 G2
Woolley Dri. BA15 15 G2
Woolley St. BA15 15 F2
Woolley Ter. BA15 15 G2

BULFORD/ DURRINGTON

Addison Sq. SP4 16 B2
Alberta Gdns. SP4 16 F3
Andrew Clo. SP4 16 B2
Ann Cres. SP4 16 B2
Avondown Rd. SP4 16 C2
Birchwood Dri. SP4 16 C2
Bowdich Clo. SP4 16 C1
Bulford Driveway. SP4 16 E2
Bulford Droveway. SP4 16 D3
Bulford Hill. SP4 16 C3
Bulford Rd, Bulford. SP4 16 E2
Bulford Rd, Durrington. SP4 16 B1
Camellia Clo. SP4 16 D3
Charles Rd. SP4 16 B2
Church La. SP4 16 D3

Church St. SP4 16 B1
Churchill Av. SP4 16 D3
Clayton Rd. SP4 16 E3
College Rd. SP4 16 B1
Coronation Rd. SP4 16 B2
Countess Rd. SP4 16 A3
Crescent Rd. SP4 16 D3
Cygnet Dri. SP4 16 C2
Dorset Clo. SP4 16 E3
Double Hedges. SP4 16 D4
Downland Way. SP4 16 A2
Downleaze. SP4 16 B1
Dukes Way. SP4 16 B2
Elizabeth Rd. SP4 16 B2
Glebe Rd. SP4 16 C2
Glendale Rd. SP4 16 C2
Greenland Clo. SP4 16 B2
Hackthorn Rd. SP4 16 A1
Hampshire Clo. SP4 16 E3
Herons Walk. SP4 16 C2
High St, Bulford. SP4 16 D3
High St,
  Durrington. SP4 16 B1
John French Way. SP4 16 E3
Kingfisher Dri. SP4 16 C2
Larkhill Rd. SP4 16 A2
Latchmere Lodge. SP4 16 C2
Ledger Hill Clo. SP4 16 D3
Lily Walk. SP4 16 C2
Longfield Clo. SP4 16 A1
Mackenzie Gdns. SP4 16 F3
Maple Way. SP4 16 A2
Marina Clo. SP4 16 B2
Marina Cres. SP4 16 A2
Marina Rd. SP4 16 A2
Meadow Rd. SP4 16 E3
Meads Rd. SP4 16 B2
Milston Rd. SP4 16 D1
Milston Vw. SP4 16 C1
Netheravon Rd. SP4 16 A2
New Rd. SP4 16 B2
Newmans Way. SP4 16 B1
Old Barns Way. SP4 16 B1
Old Coach Rd. SP4 16 D3
Old Ward Rd. SP4 16 F3
Ontario Gdns. SP4 16 F3
Orchard End. SP4 16 D3
Philip Rd. SP4 16 A2
Pinckneys Way. SP4 16 A2
Poores Rd. SP4 16 C1
Recreation Rd. SP4 16 C1
Reed Walk. SP4 16 C2
Ridgmount. SP4 16 B1
River Way. SP4 16 C2
Robin Hill La. SP4 16 C2
St Leonards Clo. SP4 16 D3
Salisbury Rd. SP4 16 D4
School Dri. SP4 16 B2
School Rd. SP4 16 C1
Station Ter. SP4 16 D4
Stonehenge Rd. SP4 16 A2
Swan Clo. SP4 16 C2
Swattons Clo. SP4 16 E3
The Avenue. SP4 16 B2
The Ham. SP4 16 B1
The Leaze. SP4 16 E3
Vancouver Gdns. SP4 16 F3
Water St. SP4 16 D3
Watergate La. SP4 16 C4
Westfield Clo. SP4 16 A2
Willow Dri. SP4 16 A1
Wiltshire Clo. SP4 16 F3
Windsor Mews. SP4 16 B1
Windsor Rd. SP4 16 B1
Winnipeg Gdns. SP4 16 F3
Yew Tree Clo. SP4 16 C2

CALNE

Abberd La. SN11 17 D2
Abberd Way. SN11 17 C3
Alma Ter. SN11 17 B2
Amberley Clo. SN11 17 A1
Anchor Rd. SN11 17 C3
Angell Clo. SN11 17 C3
Avebury Clo. SN11 17 A3
Avon Clo. SN11 17 A1
Azalea Clo. SN11 17 C5
Back Rd. SN11 17 C4
Baily Ho. SN11 17 C3
Bay Clo. SN11 17 C6
Baydon Gro. SN11 17 B1
Bentley Gro. SN11 17 C4
Beversbrook. SN11 17 A1
Beversbrook Rd. SN11 17 B1

Bishop Rd. SN11 17 B2
Blake Ho. SN11 17 C3
Bluebell Gro. SN11 17 C1
Bodinrar Ho. SN11 17 C3
Braemor Rd. SN11 17 A2
Bremhill Vw. SN11 17 A1
Brewers La. SN11 17 C4
Broken Cross. SN11 17 C3
Brookway. SN11 17 D3
Bryans Close Rd. SN11 17 B2
Campion Clo. SN11 17 B4
Canal Clo. SN11 17 B4
Carnegie Mews. SN11 17 B3
Carnegie Rd. SN11 17 C1
Castle St. SN11 17 B3
Castle Walk. SN11 17 A3
Castlefields. SN11 17 B3
Charlieu Av. SN11 17 C6
Chavey Well Ct. SN11 17 B1
Cherry Tree Ct. SN11 17 B1
Chilvester Hill. SN11 17 A3
Church St. SN11 17 B3
Churchill Clo. SN11 17 C4
Clark Av. SN11 17 C1
Colemans Clo. SN11 17 C3
Cop Clo. SN11 17 B3
Corfe Cres. SN11 17 A2
Cornflower Clo. SN11 17 C1
Coulter Ho. SN11 17 C3
Cowslip Gro. SN11 17 B1
Coxs Hill. SN11 17 B3
Curzon Clo. SN11 17 A3
Curzon St. SN11 17 A3
Dixon Way. SN11 17 B2
Downland Rd. SN11 17 A3
Druids Clo. SN11 17 A3
Duncan St. SN11 17 B1
Dunnet Clo. SN11 17 C2
Ebor Gdns. SN11 17 C6
Ebor Paddock. SN11 17 C6
Elm Clo. SN11 17 C6
Ernle Rd. SN11 17 C2
Fairway. SN11 17 C6
Falcon Rd. SN11 17 D3
Fitz Sq. SN11 17 C3
Foreman St. SN11 17 C4
Foxglove Way. SN11 17 B1
Fynamore Gdns. SN11 17 B4
Fynamore Pl. SN11 17 C2
George Clo. SN11 17 C3
George St. SN11 17 C3
Greenacres Way. SN11 17 A1
Grierson Clo. SN11 17 C1
Guthrie Rd. SN11 17 C1
Harris Rd. SN11 17 C1
Hazel Gro. SN11 17 B5
Heather Way. SN11 17 C5
Heron Clo. SN11 17 D3
High St. SN11 17 B3
Highgrove Clo. SN11 17 D3
Hillcroft. SN11 17 C2
Holly Clo. SN11 17 C5
Honey Garston. SN11 17 C2
Honeymead. SN11 17 C2
Horsebrook. SN11 17 C4
Horsebrook Pk. SN11 17 C4
Hungerford Rd. SN11 17 C2
INDUSTRIAL & RETAIL:
Portemarsh Ind Est.
  SN11 17 C1
Station Rd Ind Est.
  SN11 17 B4
Jasmine Clo. SN11 17 C5
Keevil Av. SN11 17 A3
Kerry Cres. SN11 17 B3
Kingsbury St. SN11 17 B3
Lansdowne Clo. SN11 17 A2
Lickhill Rd. SN11 17 B1
Lilac Way. SN11 17 B5
Lime Tree Clo. SN11 17 A3
Linden Clo. SN11 17 B4
*Lodge Clo,
  Longbarrow Rd. SN11 17 A3
London Rd. SN11 17 C4
Longbarrow Rd. SN11 17 C4
Low La. SN11 17 C4
Luckett Way. SN11 17 C1
Macaulay Sq. SN11 17 C3
Magnolia Rise. SN11 17 B5
Mallard Clo. SN11 17 C4
Maple Clo. SN11 17 C5
Marden Way. SN11 17 A3
Market Hill. SN11 17 B3
Martin Way. SN11 17 C3
Maundrell Rd. SN11 17 C1
Meadow Vw. SN11 17 D6

Meadow Sweet Dri.
  SN11 17 A2
Mill St. SN11 17 B3
Nestleton Clo. SN11 17 B4
New Rd. SN11 17 B3
Newbury Av. SN11 17 A2
Newcroft Clo. SN11 17 B1
Newcroft Rd. SN11 17 B1
North End. SN11 17 A2
North Fields. SN11 17 A2
North St. SN11 17 B2
Northcote. SN11 17 B2
Northway. SN11 17 A2
Ogilvie Sq. SN11 17 C3
Oldbury Prior. SN11 17 C5
Oldbury Way. SN11 17 A3
Orchard Clo. SN11 17 C4
Oxford Rd. SN11 17 B3
Page Clo. SN11 17 C3
Park Clo. SN11 17 D4
Patford St. SN11 17 B3
Penn Hill Rd. SN11 17 C2
Phelps Par. SN11 17 B3
Pinnhills. SN11 17 B4
Pinniger Ho. SN11 17 C3
Poppy Clo. SN11 17 A1
Porte Marsh Rd. SN11 17 C1
Portland Way. SN11 17 D4
Priestley Gro. SN11 17 C1
Primrose Clo. SN11 17 B1
Prince Charles Dri.
  SN11 17 C3
Purbeck Pl. SN11 17 A3
Pym Ho. SN11 17 C3
Quarr Barton. SN11 17 B3
Quarry Dale Clo. SN11 17 C4
Quemerford. SN11 17 C5
Richmond Rd. SN11 17 A1
Ridgemead. SN11 17 B1
Riverside. SN11 17 D6
Rochdale Av. SN11 17 B1
Rookery Pk. SN11 17 C6
Roundhouse. SN11 17 D5
Saddle Back Clo. SN11 17 C4
St Catherines Clo. SN11 17 C2
St Dunstan Clo. SN11 17 A3
St Margarets Clo. SN11 17 A2
St Nicholas Clo. SN11 17 C2
Sand Pit Rd. SN11 17 D1
Sandy Ridge. SN11 17 C4
Sarum Way. SN11 17 A3
Savernake Dri. SN11 17 A3
Severn Clo. SN11 17 A1
Shelburne Rd. SN11 17 C4
Silbury Rd. SN11 17 A3
Silver St. SN11 17 B5
South Pl. SN11 17 B4
Springfield Dri. SN11 17 A2
Station Rd. SN11 17 B4
Stockley La. SN11 17 C6
Stokes Croft. SN11 17 C2
Swaddon St. SN11 17 B2
Tamarisk Clo. SN11 17 C5
Tern Clo. SN11 17 D3
Thatcham Clo. SN11 17 A1
The Glebe. SN11 17 C3
The Green. SN11 17 C4
The Kilns. SN11 17 D1
The Knapp. SN11 17 C3
The Pippin. SN11 17 B3
The Quarry. SN11 17 B5
The Rise. SN11 17 C6
The Slades. SN11 17 C2
The Square. SN11 17 B3
The Strand. SN11 17 B3
The Wharf. SN11 17 B2
The Wynd. SN11 17 C4
Thomas Ct. SN11 17 C4
Trinity Pk. SN11 17 C5
Tyning Pk. SN11 17 C5
Valley View. SN11 17 B4
Vicarage Clo. SN11 17 C3
Victoria Ter. SN11 17 C3
*Walter Sutton Clo,
  Longbarrow Rd. SN11 17 A3
Wansdyke Dri. SN11 17 A3
Warren Cres. SN11 17 C2
Wenhill Heights. SN11 17 B4
Wenhill La. SN11 17 B4
Wessex La. SN11 17 D3
Wessington Ct. SN11 17 V5
Wessington Pk. SN11 17 D5
Westerham Way. SN11 17 D4
White Horse Way.
  SN11 17 B5
William St. SN11 17 C1
Wood St. SN11 17 B3

Woodhill Av. SN11 17 C2
Woodhill Rise. SN11 17 C2
Woodland Pk. SN11 17 B4
Woodroffe Sq. SN11 17 C3
Woodsage Way. SN11 17 B3
Wyvern Av. SN11 17 D3
Yew Tree Clo. SN11 17 A3

CHIPPENHAM

Acacia Clo. SN14 18 A2
Allington Way. SN14 18 A2
Andrews Clo. SN14 18 B4
Applewood Clo. SN14 18 C3
Arundel Clo. SN14 18 A4
Ascot Clo. SN14 18 A6
Ashe Cres. SN14 18 D1
Ashfield Rd. SN15 18 D2
Audley Rd. SN14 18 C4
Avebury Rd. SN14 18 A5
Avenue la Fleche.
  SN15 18 D4
Avonmead. SN15 19 F3
Awdry Clo. SN14 19 F6
Bakehouse Clo. SN15 19 E4
Barken Rd. SN14 18 A2
Barn Clo. SN14 18 A3
Barn Owl Clo. SN14 18 B1
Barnes Rd. SN14 18 B1
Barons Mead. SN14 18 A3
Barrow Grn. SN15 19 E1
Bath Rd,
  Hungerdown. SN14 18 A6
Bath Rd,
  Lowden. SN15 18 C5
Baydons La. SN15 19 E5
Bayliffes Clo. SN15 19 G4
Beale Clo. SN14 18 A4
Beechwood Rd. SN14 18 C3
Bellinger Clo. SN15 18 D1
Berkley Clo. SN14 18 A4
Birch Gro. SN15 18 D2
Birds Marsh Vw. SN15 19 E1
Blackberry Clo. SN14 18 B1
Blackbridge Rd. SN15 19 F3
Blackcross. SN15 19 F5
Blackwell Hams. SN15 19 E6
Bluebell Dri. SN14 18 B1
Bolts Croft. SN15 19 E6
Boothmead. SN14 18 B3
Borough Par. SN15 18 D4
Boundary Rd. SN15 19 F4
Bradbury Clo. SN15 19 G6
Brake Mead. SN15 19 F4
Bright Clo. SN15 19 F6
Brinkworth Clo. SN14 18 A4
Bristol Rd. SN14 18 A1
Brittain Clo. SN14 18 A4
Brook St. SN14 18 B3
Brookwell Clo. SN15 18 C1
Broomfield. SN15 18 D1
Brotherton Clo. SN15 19 F4
Bruges Clo. SN15 19 F4
Brunel Ct. SN14 18 B5
Buckingham Rd. SN15 19 G6
Bulls Hill. SN15 19 E5
Bumpers Farm Way.
  SN14 18 A3
Burlands Rd. SN15 19 E6
Burleaze. SN15 18 C6
Bythebrook. SN14 18 B2
Canterbury St. SN14 18 B3
Carnarvon Clo. SN14 18 A5
Carpenter Clo. SN15 19 F6
Castlehaven Clo. SN15 19 G6
Causeway Clo. SN15 19 E1
Cedar Gro. SN15 19 E2
Celandine Way. SN14 18 B1
Chamberlain Rd. SN14 18 A4
Chapel La. SN15 19 E4
Charter Rd. SN15 19 E6
Cheltenham Dri. SN14 18 A6
Chelwood Clo. SN14 18 B5
Chepstow Clo. SN14 18 A5
Chester Way. SN14 18 A6
Chestnut Rd. SN14 18 C3
Cheval Clo. SN14 18 B1
Church View. SN15 18 C1
Claypole Mead. SN15 19 E6
Clift Av. SN15 19 E2
Clift Ho. SN15 18 D2
Clifton Clo. SN14 18 B3
Clover Dean. SN14 18 A4
Cocklebury La. SN15 19 E1
Cocklebury Rd. SN15 19 E3

Colborne Clo. SN15 19 H6
College Clo. SN15 19 F3
Collen Clo. SN14 18 A4
Common Slip. SN15 19 E4
Coniston Rd. SN14 18 A5
Conway Rd. SN14 18 A4
Cranwell Clo. SN14 18 A6
Cricketts La. SN15 19 F6
Crown Clo. SN15 19 G6
Culverwell Rd. SN14 18 A4
Curlew Clo. SN14 18 A1
Dallas Rd. SN15 18 C3
Danes Clo. SN15 19 F6
Daniell Dri. SN15 19 F3
Darcy Clo. SN15 19 F3
Deansway. SN15 18 D1
Deansway Ct. SN15 18 D1
Derby Clo. SN15 19 F6
Derriads Grn. SN14 18 A4
Derriads La. SN14 18 A4
Dover St. SN14 18 C4
Down View. SN14 18 A4
Downham Mead. SN15 19 F3
Downing St. SN14 18 C3
Dummer Way. SN15 19 G6
Dyers Clo. SN15 19 G6
Eastern Av. SN15 19 F3
Easton La. SN14 18 A6
Edridge Clo. SN15 18 D1
Elmwood. SN15 18 D1
Emery La. SN15 19 E4
Erleigh Dri. SN15 18 C4
Esmead. SN15 19 F3
Evans Clo. SN15 19 E2
Fairfoot Clo. SN14 18 B1
Fallow Field Clo. SN14 18 B1
Farleigh Clo. SN14 18 A4
Farmer Clo. SN15 19 E1
Field Vw. SN15 18 D4
Fleet Rd. SN15 18 D3
Fogham Shire. SN15 18 D4
Folkestone Clo. SN14 18 A6
Forest La. SN15 19 F6
Fortune Way. SN15 19 F6
Foundry La. SN15 19 E3
Fox Clo. SN14 18 B1
Foxgrove. SN14 18 A1
Frogwell. SN14 18 A3
Frogwell Pk. SN14 18 A3
Gales Clo. SN15 19 F3
Garrick Clo. SN15 19 G3
Garth Clo. SN14 18 B1
Gascelyn Clo. SN14 18 A4
Gastons Rd. SN14 18 C3
Gipsy La. SN15 18 D5
Gladstone Rd. SN15 18 D4
Glendale Dri. SN15 19 E5
Gleneagles Clo. SN15 19 F4
Gloucester Clo. SN14 18 A5
Goldney Av. SN15 18 C4
Goodwood Way. SN14 18 A6
Greenway Av. SN15 18 D2
Greenway Ct. SN15 18 D1
Greenway Gdns. SN15 18 D1
Greenway La. SN15 18 D1
Greenway Pk . SN15 18 D2
Gundry Clo. SN15 19 F6
Habrels Clo. SN15 19 F5
Hancock Clo. SN15 19 G6
Hardenhuish Av. SN14 18 C3
Hardenhuish La. SN14 18 B2
Hardens Mead. SN15 19 G6
Hares Patch. SN14 18 B1
Harford Clo. SN15 19 F6
Harnish Way. SN15 18 B1
Hawkins Clo. SN15 19 F6
Hawthorn Rd. SN15 19 E2
Haydock Clo. SN14 18 A6
Heathfield. SN15 19 E1
Hereford Clo. SN14 18 A6
Hewlett Clo. SN15 19 G6
High St. SN15 19 E4
Hill Corner Rd. SN15 18 D1
Hill Rise. SN15 19 E1
Hither Clo. SN14 18 A3
Hollybush Clo. SN14 18 A1
Honeybrook Clo. SN14 18 B3
Humboldts Hold. SN15 19 E6
Hungerdown La. SN14 18 A6
Hungerford Rd. SN15 18 D2
INDUSTRIAL & RETAIL:
Bath Rd Ind Est. SN14 18 B5
Bumpus Farm
  Ind Est. SN14 18 A4
Greenways Business
  Park. SN15 18 D1

Herman Miller Ind Est. SN14 18 B6
Lansdowne Ct Business Park. SN14 18 A3
Parsonage Way Ind Est. SN15 19 F1
Ivy Cotts. SN15 18 D4
Ivy La. SN15 18 D4
Ivy Rd. SN15 18 D4
Ivyfield Ct. SN15 18 D4
Jasmine Clo. SN14 18 A2
Jordan Clo. SN15 19 F6
Kelso Ct. SN14 18 A6
Kent Clo. SN14 18 A5
Kilverts Clo. SN14 18 A5
King Alfred St. SN14 18 C3
Kingham Clo. SN14 18 C4
Kingsley Rd. SN14 18 B5
Lackham Circus. SN14 18 B5
Ladds La. SN15 19 E5
Lady Coventry Rd. SN15 19 F4
Ladyfield Rd. SN14 18 B5
Laines Head. SN15 18 C1
Lamberts. SN14 18 B3
Langley Ct. SN15 19 E3
Langley Rd. SN15 19 E2
Lanhill Vw. SN14 18 B1
Lansdown Gro. SN15 19 E2
Lapwing Cres. SN15 18 B1
Laurel Dri. SN15 18 C5
Lenton Clo. SN14 18 A4
Little Down. SN14 18 B4
Little Englands. SN15 19 E5
Littlecote Rd. SN14 18 A5
Lockside. SN15 19 F6
Lodge Rd. SN15 19 G6
London Rd. SN15 19 E5
Long Clo. SN15 19 F5
Long Ridings. SN15 18 C1
Longstone. SN14 18 A2
Lords Mead. SN14 18 A3
Lovers Walk. SN15 18 D4
Lowden. SN15 18 C5
Lowden Av. SN15 18 C3
Lowden Hill. SN15 18 C4
Loyalty St. SN14 18 C4
Ludlow Clo. SN15 19 G6
Lydiard Rd. SN14 18 A5
Lytham Clo. SN15 19 F4
Malmesbury Rd. SN15 18 C1
Manor Rd. SN14 18 A3
Maple Way. SN15 18 D1
Market Pl. SN15 19 E4
Marlborough Ct. SN14 18 C4
Marshall St. SN14 18 C4
Marshfield Rd. SN14 18 C3
Martins Clo. SN15 19 G3
Matford Hill. SN15 19 G3
Maud Heaths Causeway. SN15 19 E1
Maur Clo. SN15 18 C4
Meadow Clo. SN14 18 A4
Melksham Rd. SN14 18 B6
Milestone Way. SN15 18 D1
Minster Way. SN14 18 A6
Monkton Hill. SN15 18 D4
Montague Clo. SN15 19 G4
Moorlands. SN15 19 E1
Mulberry Clo. SN14 18 B2
Murrayfield. SN15 19 E2
Neeld Cres. SN14 18 B3
New La. SN15 18 D3
New Rd. SN15 18 D3
Newall Tuck Rd. SN4 19 F4
Newbury Dri. SN14 18 A6
Northwood. SN15 19 E1
Oak Lodge Clo. SN15 18 C3
Oaklands. SN15 18 D1
Oate Hill. SN15 19 F5
Odcroft Clo. SN15 19 F4
O'Donnell Clo. SN15 19 E1
Old Hardenhuish La. SN14 18 B2
Old Rd. SN15 18 D3
Orchard Cres. SN14 18 B4
Orchard Rd. SN14 18 B4
Page Clo. SN14 18 A4
Palmer St. SN14 18 C4
Park Av. SN14 18 B3
Park La. SN15 18 D3
Park Ter. SN14 18 C3
Parkfields. SN14 18 C3
Parkside. SN15 18 D3
Parliament St. SN14 18 B4
Parsonage Way. SN15 19 F1
Partridge Clo. SN15 18 B1
Patchway. SN14 18 B3
Pavely Clo. SN15 18 C5
Pew Hill. SN15 19 E1
Pewsham Lock. SN15 19 E6
Pewsham Way. SN15 19 E6
Pewsham Way. SN15 19 H6
Picketleaze. SN14 18 A4
Pipsmore Rd. SN14 18 A3
Plantation. SN14 18 C3
Popham Ct. SN15 19 E5
Portway. SN14 18 B5
Primrose Way. SN14 18 B1
Queens Cres. SN14 18 A5
Queens Sq. SN15 19 E5
Ray Clo. SN15 19 F6
Redland. SN14 18 B3
Redwing Av. SN14 18 B1
Ricardo Rd. SN15 18 D3
Ridings Mead. SN15 18 C1
Ripon Clo. SN14 18 A6
River St. SN15 19 E4
Riverside Dri. SN15 19 G4
Robins Clo. SN15 18 B1
Roman Way. SN15 19 G6
Rowden Hill. SN15 18 C5
Rowden La. SN15 18 C6
Rowden Rd. SN15 18 C6
Rowe Mead. SN15 19 E6
Royal Clo. SN15 18 D5
Rumble Dene. SN15 19 E6
Rural Gdns. SN15 19 E5
Ryan Av. SN14 18 A4
Sadlers Mead. SN15 19 E3
St Clements Ct. SN14 18 C3
St Francis Av. SN15 18 C5
St Josephs Dri. SN15 18 C5
St Lukes Dri. SN15 18 C5
St Margarets Gdns. SN15 18 C5
St Mary St. SN15 19 E4
St Marys Pl. SN15 18 D3
St Mellion Clo. SN15 19 F2
St Paul St. SN15 18 D3
St Peters Clo. SN15 18 C5
St Teresa's Dri. SN15 18 C5
Salisbury Clo. SN14 18 A5
Saltersford La. SN14 18 A6
Sandes Clo. SN15 18 C4
Sandown Dri. SN14 18 A6
Sandpiper Gdns. SN14 18 A1
Sarum Rd. SN14 18 A5
Saxby Rd. SN15 19 E1
Saxon St. SN14 18 B3
School Walk. SN14 18 A4
Selions Clo. SN14 18 B1
Seymour Rd. SN15 19 F3
Sheepscroft. SN14 18 B1
Sheldon Rd. SN14 18 B4
Silbury Clo. SN14 18 A6
Sorrel Dri. SN14 18 B1
Southmead. SN14 18 B5
Southwell Clo. SN14 18 A6
Spanbourn Av. SN15 18 D4
Spinney Clo. SN14 18 A5
Springfields Bldgs. SN15 18 D3
Stainers Way. SN14 18 A1
Stanley La. SN15 19 H6
Station Hill. SN15 18 D3
Stockwood Rd. SN14 18 B5
Stonelea Clo. SN14 18 B4
Sunningdale Clo. SN15 19 F4
Sydney Wood Ct. SN14 18 C4
Tall Trees. SN15 18 D3
The Battens. SN14 18 A2
The Bridge. SN15 18 D4
The Butts. SN15 19 E5
The Causeway. SN15 19 E4
The Cloisters. SN15 18 D5
The Firs. SN14 18 A5
The Hamlet. SN15 18 D2
The Oaks. SN15 18 D1
The Paddocks. SN15 19 E5
The Poplars. SN14 18 A2
The Tinings. SN15 19 F3
The Turnpike. SN15 19 H6
Thirsk Clo. SN14 18 A6
Timber St. SN15 19 E4
Timbrells Pl. SN15 18 C5
Torr Clo. SN14 18 B1
Truro Walk. SN14 18 A5
Tugela Rd. SN15 19 E2
Turnberry Clo. SN15 19 F4
Turpin Way. SN14 18 A4
Twickenham Way. SN15 19 E2
Union Rd. SN15 18 D3
Unity St. SN14 18 C4
Upper Farm Barns. SN14 18 B1
Utterson View. SN15 18 C4
Villiers Clo. SN15 19 F4
Vincients Rd. SN14 18 A2
Wardour Rd. SN14 18 A5
Waters Edge. SN15 19 E6
Weavern Ct. SN14 18 A4
Webb Clo. SN15 19 E6
Webbington Rd. SN15 19 E6
Wedmore Av. SN15 18 D2
Wells Clo. SN14 18 A6
Wentworth Clo. SN15 19 F4
Wessex Rd. SN14 18 B3
West Cepen Way. SN4 18 A1
Westbrook Clo. SN14 18 A4
Westcroft. SN14 18 B6
Westerleigh Clo. SN14 18 B5
Westmead La. SN15 18 D5
Westmead Ter. SN15 19 E5
Westminster Gdns. SN14 18 B4
Wetherby Clo. SN14 18 A6
Whittle Clo. SN14 18 A4
Whitworth Rd. SN15 19 E6
Wicks Dri. SN15 19 F6
Willow Gro. SN15 19 E1
Willowbank. SN14 18 B2
Winchester Clo. SN14 18 A5
Windlass Way. SN15 19 F6
Windsor Clo. SN14 18 A5
Wishart Way. SN15 19 F6
Wood La. SN15 19 E5
Woodlands Rd. SN14 18 C4
Woodpecker Clo. SN14 18 B1
Wyndham Clo. SN15 19 F3
Yewstock Cres East. SN15 18 C2
Yewstock Cres West. SN15 18 C2
York Clo. SN14 18 A5

CORSHAM

Academy Dri. SN13 20 C2
Alexander Ter. SN13 20 D2
Allen Rd. SN13 20 A3
Arney Clo. SN13 20 C3
Arnolds Mead. SN13 20 D2
Barn Clo. SN13 20 C3
Basil Hill Rd. SN13 20 A4
Bath Rd. SN13 20 A2
Beechfield Rd. SN13 20 C2
Bellott Dri. SN13 20 C3
Bences La. SN13 20 E1
Bethel Rd. SN13 20 C3
Bradford Rd. SN13 20 A3
Brakspear Dri. SN13 20 C3
Broadmead. SN13 20 F4
Brook Dri. SN13 20 F4
Brunel Clo. SN13 20 D2
Burn Rd. SN13 20 C3
Charles St. SN13 20 D2
Charlwood Rd. SN13 20 D3
Chestnut Grange. SN13 20 B2
Church St. SN13 20 E2
Churchill Way. SN13 20 D1
Clevedale Rd. SN13 20 E4
Coulston Rd. SN13 20 E1
Cresswells. SN13 20 D3
Cross Keys Rd. SN13 20 E1
Curl Croft Rd. SN13 20 B4
Danvers Rd. SN13 20 C2
Dew Clo. SN13 20 E4
Dickens Av. SN13 20 C2
Dicketts Rd. SN13 20 E4
Dovecote Dri. SN13 20 C2
Edridge Pl. SN13 20 C3
Elm Gro. SN13 20 C2
Elm Hayes. SN13 20 E4
Erneston Vw. SN13 20 D2
Ethelred Pl. SN13 20 C2
Fuller Av. SN13 20 C3
Furzehill. SN13 20 D3
Glebe Way. SN13 20 C3
Grove Rd. SN13 20 E3
Hardhams Rise. SN13 20 D3
Hartham La. SN13 20 D1
Hastings Rd. SN13 20 E3
Hatton Way. SN13 20 C3
High St. SN13 20 E2
Hitherspring. SN13 20 D4
Hudswell La. SN13 20 A4
Hulbert Clo. SN13 20 C3
INDUSTRIAL & RETAIL:
Park La Ind Est. SN13 20 A3
Ivy Field. SN13 20 E2
Jargeau Ct. SN13 20 E3
Kings Av. SN13 20 D1
Kirby Rd. SN13 20 C2
Lacock Rd. SN13 20 E3
Ladbrook La. SN13 20 F4
Light Clo. SN13 20 E2
Ludmead Rd. SN13 20 E4
Lypiatt Mead. SN13 20 E4
Lypiatt Rd. SN13 20 E4
Manor Rd. SN13 20 D1
Masons Way. SN13 20 B3
Mayo Clo. SN13 20 C2
Meadland. SN13 20 C2
Meriton Av. SN13 20 E2
Methuen Way. SN13 20 D1
Middlewick La. SN13 20 C1
Neale Clo. SN13 20 D2
Newlands Rd. SN13 20 E2
Nursery Gdns. SN13 20 E3
Oathills. SN13 20 D3
Oliver Av. SN13 20 D2
Orchard Rd. SN13 20 D1
Paddock La. SN13 20 B3
Park La. SN13 20 A4
Partridge Clo. SN13 20 C3
Paul St. SN13 20 D3
Peel Circus. SN13 20 B3
Penleigh Clo. SN13 20 D3
Pickwick Rd. SN13 20 C2
Pictor Clo. SN13 20 B3
Pockeredge Dri. SN13 20 A4
Pockeredge Rd. SN13 20 C4
Post Office La. SN13 20 E2
Potley La. SN13 20 C4
Pound Hill Prospect. SN13 20 E3
Pound Mead. SN13 20 D4
Poynder Rd. SN13 20 C3
Priory New Rd. SN13 20 D2
Priory St. SN13 20 D2
Providence Rd. SN13 20 D2
Purleigh Rd. SN13 20 C2
Queens Av. SN13 20 D1
Randall Ct. SN13 20 B2
St Barbaras Rd. SN13 20 B3
Saunders Gro. SN13 20 B3
Savernake Rd. SN13 20 B4
Shearwater Way. SN13 20 B4
Sheffield La. SN13 20 B3
Silman Clo. SN13 20 B2
Smiths Yd. SN13 20 E2
South Pl. SN13 20 E3
South St. SN13 20 E3
Southerwicks. SN13 20 D3
Spackman La. SN13 20 C3
Spring Gdns. SN13 20 E2
Spring La. SN13 20 A4
Station Rd. SN13 20 E3
Stokes Rd. SN13 20 E3
Sumsions Dri. SN13 20 B3
Swan Rd. SN13 20 C3
Syon Clo. SN13 20 C3
Tacker Clo. SN13 20 C3
Tellcroft Clo. SN13 20 D4
The Cleeve. SN13 20 E4
The Knowle. SN13 20 D3
The Laggar. SN13 20 D1
The Precinct. SN13 20 E2
The Tynings. SN13 20 D3
Tropenell Clo. SN13 20 C3
Tupman Rd. SN13 20 C2
Upper Potley. SN13 20 B4
Valley Rd. SN13 20 C2
Weller Rd. SN13 20 D2
West Park Rd. SN13 20 C2
Williams Gro. SN13 20 E3
Woodborough Rd. SN13 20 F4
Woodlands. SN13 20 C2
Yockney Clo. SN13 20 C3
York Clo. SN13 20 D1

CRICKLADE

Abingdon Ct Farm. SN6 21 C2
Abingdon Ct La. SN6 21 C2
Bailiffs Piece. SN6 21 B1
Bath Ct. SN6 21 B2
Bath Rd. SN6 21 A2
Bishopsfields. SN6 21 A2
Branders. SN6 21 B1
Calcutt St. SN6 21 C2
Chelworth Rd. SN6 21 A3
Cherrytree Rd. SN6 21 A2
Church La. SN6 21 B2
Cirencester Rd. SN6 21 B1
Cliffords. SN6 21 A2
Common Hill. SN6 21 A2
Cricklade By-Pass. SN6 21 C1
Deansfield. SN6 21 A3
Doubledays. SN6 21 B2
Fairfield. SN6 21 B1
Fairview. SN6 21 C2
Fiddle Farm. SN6 21 A3
Foxleaze. SN6 21 B1
Fullers Av. SN6 21 B2
Galley Orchard. SN6 21 C2
Gas La. SN6 21 B2
Giles Av. SN6 21 B3
Hallsfield. SN6 21 A1
Hammonds. SN6 21 C2
High St. SN6 21 B2
Homeground. SN6 21 A1
Hopkins Orchard. SN6 21 B3
Horse Fair La. SN6 21 C2
Kitefield. SN6 21 B1
Lady Mead. SN6 21 A2
Malmesbury Rd. SN6 21 A2
Manor Orchard. SN6 21 C2
Middle Ground. SN6 21 A1
North Keels. SN6 21 A1
North Meadow Rd. SN6 21 A1
North Wall. SN6 21 B1
Ockwells. SN6 21 B3
Parsonage Farm La. SN6 21 B3
Pauls Croft. SN6 21 B3
Pike House Clo. SN6 21 A2
Pittsfield. SN6 21 B3
Pleydells. SN6 21 B1
Portwell. SN6 21 B3
Purton Rd. SN6 21 B3
Rectory La. SN6 21 C1
Red Lion La. SN6 21 C1
Reeds. SN6 21 A1
Saxon Clo. SN6 21 B2
Spital La. SN6 21 C2
Stones La. SN6 21 A2
Swindon Rd. SN6 21 C2
Thames La. SN6 21 C2
The Fiddle. SN6 21 A2
The Forty. SN6 21 B3
*The Mannings, Parsonage Farm La. SN6 21 B2
Water Furlong. SN6 21 B3
Waylands. SN6 21 B3
West Mill La. SN6 21 A1
White Horse Rd. SN6 21 B2

DEVIZES

Addington Clo. SN10 23 F5
Anstie Clo. SN10 23 G3
Ash Walk. SN10 23 H1
Avon Rd. SN10 22 B4
Avon Ter. SN10 23 E3
Badgers Clo. SN10 23 F5
Bath Rd. SN10 22 A4
Beau Clerc St. SN10 22 C4
Beechfield Dri. SN10 23 H2
Beechwood Dri. SN10 23 H1
Belle Vue Rd. SN10 22 D3
Bratton Av. SN10 23 G5
Brickham Rd. SN10 23 G3
Brickley La. SN10 23 G3
Bricksteed Av. SN10 23 G4
Bridewell St. SN10 23 F4
Broadleas Clo. SN10 23 E5
Broadleas Cres. SN10 23 E5
Broadleas Pk. SN10 23 E6
Broadleas Rd. SN10 23 E5
Byron Rd. SN10 23 F6
Caen Hill Gdns. SN10 22 B4
Caird Lawns. SN10 23 G5
Canal Way. SN10 23 H2
Castle Ct. SN10 23 E4
Castle La. SN10 23 E4
Castle Rd. SN10 23 E4
Chandler Clo. SN10 23 G4
Chantry Ct. SN10 23 F3
Charles Morrison Clo. SN10 23 E4
Charter Clo. SN10 23 G2
Church Walk. SN10 23 F4

Church Yard. SN10 23 E4
Coate La. SN10 23 H2
Colston Rd. SN10 23 E3
Commercial Rd. SN10 23 E3
Consciences La. SN10 22 B1
Coping Clo. SN10 23 F4
Cornfield Rd. SN10 23 G4
Cornwall Cres. SN10 23 E5
Couch La. SN10 23 E3
Cowslip Clo. SN10 23 H2
Cranesbill Rd. SN10 23 H2
Cromwell Rd. SN10 23 G4
Cunnington Clo. SN10 23 G3
Cygnet Clo. SN10 23 H2
Devizes Rd. SN10 22 A1
Downlands Rd. SN10 23 F6
Drakes Av. SN10 23 F5
Drews Pond La. SN10 23 F6
Dundas Clo. SN10 22 B4
Dunkirk Hill. SN10 22 C3
Dyehouse La. SN10 23 E2
Eastleigh Clo. SN10 23 G5
Eastleigh Rd. SN10 23 G5
Edward Rd. SN10 23 F5
Elcombe Gdns. SN10 23 E3
Elizabeth Dri. SN10 23 G3
Elliott Ct. SN10 23 F6
Elmtree Clo. SN10 23 H5
Elmtree Gdns. SN10 23 H5
Estcourt Cres. SN10 23 F3
Estcourt Hill. SN10 23 E4
Estcourt St. SN10 23 F3
Ferguson Rd. SN10 23 G6
Folly Rd. SN10 23 G2
Fordson Rd. SN10 23 G6
Forty Acres Rd. SN10 23 G4
Furlong Clo. SN10 22 A2
Furze Hill. SN10 22 C6
Gables Clo. SN10 23 G5
Gains La. SN10 23 F3
Granary Clo. SN10 23 G4
Granary Rd. SN10 23 G4
Great Western Clo. SN10 23 E3
Green La. SN10 23 F6
Greenfield Rd. SN10 23 F6
Gundry Clo. SN10 23 G3
Hambleton Av. SN10 23 H1
Hare & Hounds St. SN10 23 F4
Harebell Way. SN10 23 H2
Hartfield. SN10 23 E5
Hartmoor Rd. SN10 22 D6
High Lawn. SN10 22 C3
High St, Devizes. SN10 23 E4
High St, Rowde. SN10 22 A1
Hill Rd. SN10 23 G6
Hillworth Gdns. SN10 23 E4
Hillworth Rd. SN10 22 E4
Hodge Clo. SN10 23 H4
Hopkins Clo. SN10 23 H4
Hopton Rd. SN10 23 H1
INDUSTRIAL & RETAIL:
Garden Trading Est. SN10 23 G2
Hopton Ind Est. SN10 23 H1
Nursteed Ind Est. SN10 23 G5
Jackson Clo. SN10 23 G5
John Rennie Clo. SN10 22 D5
John Rumble Ct. SN10 23 F4
Jump Farm Rd. SN10 23 G3
Kemp Clo. SN10 23 G3
Kempsfield. SN10 23 G6
Kennet Rd. SN10 23 G5
Kingfisher Dri. SN10 23 H1
Kingsley Gdns. SN10 23 G4
Kingsley Rd. SN10 23 G4
Kingsmanor Wharf. SN10 23 H2
Kirby Clo. SN10 23 G3
*Lansdowne Gro, Sheep St. SN10 23 F4
*Lansdowne Ter, Sheep St. SN10 23 F4
Lawrence Clo. SN10 23 F6
Le Marchant Clo. SN10 23 H2
Lewis's Ct. SN10 23 E3
Linden Ter. SN10 23 F4
Little Brittox. SN10 23 E3
London Rd. SN10 23 G3
Long St. SN10 23 E4
Longcroft Av. SN10 23 G4
Longcroft Cres. SN10 23 G4
Longcroft Rd. SN10 23 G4
Longfields Walk. SN10 23 G5
Lower Wharf. SN10 23 E3
Market Pl. SN10 23 E3
Marsh La. SN10 22 A1
Marshall Rd. SN10 23 G6
Maryport St. SN10 23 F4
Maslen Clo. SN10 23 H4
Massey Rd. SN10 23 G6
Matilda Way. SN10 23 G2
Mattock Clo. SN10 23 G3
Maud Clo. SN10 23 G2
Maundrell Clo. SN10 22 A1
Mayenne Pl. SN10 22 B4
Meadow Dri. SN10 23 G3
Meads Pl. SN10 23 F4
Middle Field Clo. SN10 23 G4
Mill Clo. SN10 23 G6
Monday Market St. SN10 23 F3
Moonrakers. SN10 23 H2
Morris La. SN10 23 F4
Moyne Clo. SN10 22 D3
Neate Rd. SN10 23 G3
New Park Rd. SN10 23 E3
New Park St. SN10 23 E3
Northgate Gdns. SN10 23 E3
Northgate St. SN10 23 E3
Nursteed Clo. SN10 23 H5
Nursteed Pk. SN10 23 G5
Nursteed Rd. SN10 23 F4
Oamaru Way. SN10 23 G4
Offers Ct. SN10 23 F4
Orchard Clo. SN10 23 F6
Pans La. SN10 23 F4
Park Vw. SN10 22 C4
Parkfields. SN10 23 G2
Phillip Clo. SN10 23 G3
Pines Rd. SN10 23 G4
Potterne Rd. SN10 23 E6
Prince Maurice Ct. SN10 23 H1
Proudman Rd. SN10 23 H3
Quakers Walk. SN10 23 F3
Quarry Clo. SN10 23 G4
Queens Rd. SN10 23 E5
Radnor Clo. SN10 23 F5
Redhorn Gdns. SN10 23 F5
Reed Clo. SN10 23 H4
Reeves Rd. SN10 23 G6
Rendells Ct. SN10 23 F4
Roseland Av. SN10 23 G4
Rotherstone. SN10 23 E3
Roundway Gdns. SN10 23 F1
Roundway Pk. SN10 23 F1
Rowde Court Rd. SN10 22 A1
Royal Oak Ct. SN10 23 E3
St Bridget Clo. SN10 23 H4
*St Johns Ct Church Yd. SN10 23 E4
St Johns St. SN10 23 E4
St Josephs Rd. SN10 22 D3
Salisbury St. SN10 22 C4
Sarum Dri. SN10 23 F5
Sedgefield Gdns. SN10 23 F3
Shackleton Rd. SN10 23 H5
Sheep St. SN10 23 F4
Sheppard Clo. SN10 23 E3
Sidmouth St. SN10 23 F4
Snuff St. SN10 23 E3
Southbroom Rd. SN10 23 F4
Southgate. SN10 23 F5
Southgate Clo. SN10 23 F5
Springers Clo. SN10 23 G3
Springfield Rd. SN10 22 A1
Stanley Ter. SN10 23 F5
Station Rd. SN10 22 E3
Steele Clo. SN10 23 G3
Stockwell Rd. SN10 23 G3
Sussex Wharf. SN10 22 D3
Sutton Pl. SN10 23 F4
Tanis. SN10 22 B1
The Ark. SN10 23 E4
The Breach. SN10 23 F5
The Brittox. SN10 23 E4
The Croft. SN10 23 G3
The Fairway. SN10 23 E6
The Moorlands. SN10 23 E5
The Nursery. SN10 22 D3
The Patchway. SN10 23 H4
The Sidings. SN10 22 D4
Thomas Wyatt Rd. SN10 23 F6
Tilley Clo. SN10 23 G3
Tintern Rd. SN10 23 F6
Tornio Clo. SN10 23 H2
Victoria Rd. SN10 23 F3
Waiblingen Way. SN10 22 D3
Walden Lodge Clo. SN10 23 F5
Waylands. SN10 23 G4
Wessex Clo. SN10 23 G4
Westridge. SN10 23 E3
West View Cres. SN10 22 D4
Wharf St. SN10 23 E3
Whistley Rd. SN10 22 A4
Wick La. SN10 23 E5
Wickfield. SN10 23 F5
William Rd. SN10 23 G5
Willow Dri. SN10 23 H2
Windsor Dri. SN10 23 G3
Wine St. SN10 23 E4
Woodland Way. SN10 23 E6

DOWNTON & REDLYNCH

Apple Tree Clo. SP5 25 F3
Appletree Rd. SP5 25 F3
Avon Meadow. SP5 24 C3
Avondyke. SP5 24 B4
Barford La. SP5 24 C2
Barnaby Clo. SP5 24 A3
Batten Rd. SP5 24 A2
Bennett Clo. SP5 25 F4
Besomers Drove. SP5 25 H6
Bowers Hill. SP5 25 G3
Breamore Rd. SP5 24 A5
Castle Meadows. SP5 24 C3
Castle Woods. SP5 25 F4
Catherine Cres. SP5 24 A3
Chalks Clo. SP5 25 F3
Chapel Rd. SP5 25 G4
Church Hatch. SP5 24 C3
Church Hill. SP5 25 H4
Cranbury Clo. SP5 24 C4
Crossways Clo. SP5 24 A3
Dairy Clo. SP5 25 F5
Downlands Clo. SP5 24 C4
Downton Hill. SP5 25 F3
Eastmans Clo. SP5 24 C4
Elizabeth Clo. SP5 24 A3
Elmfield Clo. SP5 25 F5
Forders Clo. SP5 25 F5
Forest Rd. SP5 25 F6
Goggs La. SP5 25 H4
Gravel Clo. SP5 24 B2
Green La. SP5 24 B3
Greenacres. SP5 24 A2
Greens Meade. SP5 25 F4
Grove La. SP5 25 G3
Hamilton Park. SP5 24 C2
Harthill Drove. SP5 25 G4
Herbert Rd. SP5 25 F4
High St. SP5 24 C3
Highfield La. SP5 25 F5
Hyde La. SP5 24 A3
INDUSTRIAL & RETAIL:
Batten Rd Ind Est. SP5 24 A2
Joanna Clo. SP5 24 A3
Kiln Rd. SP5 25 G3
Kingford Clo. SP5 25 F5
Langford La. SP5 25 F3
Little Woodfalls Dri. SP5 25 F6
Lode Hill. SP5 24 D2
Lodge Drove. SP5 25 F6
Long Clo. SP5 24 A2
Loosehanger. SP5 25 H6
Marie Av. SP5 24 A3
Mesh Pond. SP5 24 A3
Mitchells Clo. SP5 25 F4
Moot Clo. SP5 24 C4
Moot Gdns. SP5 24 B4
Moot La. SP5 24 C3
Morgans Rise Rd. SP5 25 F3
Morgans Vale Rd. SP5 25 F4
Muddyford La. SP5 25 F3
Orchard Rd. SP5 25 F4
Petticoat La. SP5 25 G3
Pine View Clo. SP5 25 F6
Primrose La. SP5 25 E4
Princes Clo. SP5 25 G4
Princes Hill. SP5 25 G3
Quavey Rd. SP5 25 G4
Roman Meadow. SP5 24 C4
Rosedene. SP5 25 G4
St Birinus Rd. SP5 25 F4
St Marys Clo. SP5 25 H6
Salisbury Rd. SP5 24 A1
Sandy La. SP5 25 G2
Saxon Hurst. SP5 24 C3
Saxon Meadow. SP5 24 C3
School Rd. SP5 25 H6
Slab La. SP5 24 D3
Snail Creep. SP5 24 C2
South La. SP5 24 B3
Springfield Cres. SP5 25 F5
Squarey Clo. SP5 24 C4
The Borough. SP5 24 A2
The Close. SP5 25 F3
The Drove. SP5 25 F5
The Headlands. SP5 24 A3
The Ridge. SP5 25 F6
The Row. SP5 25 F3
The Sidings. SP5 24 D2
Tinneys Clo. SP5 25 F6
Twynham Clo. SP5 24 C4
Vale Rd. SP5 25 F4
Valley Clo. SP5 25 F4
Vicarage Pk. SP5 25 F4
Waterside. SP5 24 C3
Wheelwright Mews. SP5 24 A3
Whiteshoot. SP5 25 H6
Whiteshoot Hill. SP5 25 F6
Wick La. SP5 24 A2

HIGHWORTH

Arran Way. SN6 26 A2
Barra Clo. SN6 26 A3
Beech Gro. SN6 26 B4
Biddel Springs. SN6 26 C3
Blandford Alley. SN6 26 B4
Botany. SN6 26 A4
Brewery St. SN6 26 B4
Brookfield. SN6 26 B2
Bute Clo. SN6 26 B2
Byde Mill Gdns. SN6 26 A4
Cherry Orchard. SN6 26 C3
Church Vw. SN6 26 B4
Crane Furlong. SN6 26 B2
Cricklade Rd. SN6 26 A4
Downs View. SN6 26 C3
Eastrop. SN6 26 C4
Edencroft. SN6 26 C2
Folly Clo. SN6 26 C2
Folly Cres. SN6 26 B2
Folly Dri. SN6 26 B2
Folly Way. SN6 26 C2
Grange Clo. SN6 26 C4
Grove Hill. SN6 26 B2
Grove Orchard. SN6 26 B2
Henley Dri. SN6 26 B2
High St. SN6 26 B4
Home Farm. SN6 26 A3
INDUSTRIAL & RETAIL:
Blackworth Ind Est. SN6 26 B1
Islay Cres. SN6 26 B3
Kilda Rd. SN6 26 A2
Kings Av. SN6 26 C4
Knowlands. SN6 26 C2
Lechlade Rd. SN6 26 B4
Lismore Rd. SN6 26 A3
Market Pl. SN6 26 C4
Middi Haines Ct. SN6 26 C3
Newburgh Pl. SN6 26 B3
North Vw. SN6 26 B4
Oak Dri. SN6 26 B4
Orange Clo. SN6 26 C3
Park Av. SN6 26 C4
Parsonage Ct. SN6 26 C4
Pentylands Clo. SN6 26 B2
Pentylands La. SN6 26 B1
Pound Rd. SN6 26 B2
Priory Grn. SN6 26 C3
Quarry Cres. SN6 26 B3
Queens Av. SN6 26 C2
Red Lion Mews. SN6 26 C4
Rivers Pl. SN6 26 B3
Roman Way. SN6 26 A4
Round Hills Mead. SN6 26 C1
St Michaels Av. SN6 26 A3
Sevenfields. SN6 26 C2
Sheep St. SN6 26 C4
Shrivenham Rd. SN6 26 C5
Skye Clo. SN6 26 A2
Spa Clo. SN6 26 C3
Stapleton Clo. SN6 26 B4
Station Rd. SN6 26 B3
Stonefield Dri. SN6 26 B5
Stranks Clo. SN6 26 C5
Stroma Way. SN6 26 A2
Swindon Rd. SN6 26 B6
Swindon St. SN6 26 B4
The Archers. SN6 26 B3
The Cullerns. SN6 26 C3
The Dormers. SN6 26 C3
The Elms. SN6 26 B4
The Green. SN6 26 B4
The Mews. SN6 26 C4
The Paddocks. SN6 26 C4
The Retreat. SN6 26 B3
The Willows. SN6 26 C4
Turnpike Rd. SN6 26 C3
Vicarage La. SN6 26 B3
Vorda Rd. SN6 26 C2
Wessex Way. SN6 26 D2
Westhill Clo. SN6 26 B4
Westrop. SN6 26 B3
Windrush. SN6 26 A3
Wrde Hill. SN6 26 A4

HOLT

Avonfield. BA14 21 C5
Beales Barton. BA14 21 C5
Beckerley La. BA14 21 C4
Bradford Rd. BA14 21 A6
Bradley Clo. BA14 21 D5
Bradley La. BA14 21 C5
Chestnut Corner. BA14 21 C5
Crandon Lea. BA14 21 D5
Gipsy La. BA14 21 D4
Great Parks. BA14 21 D4
Green Clo. BA14 21 D6
Ground Corner. BA14 21 B5
Ham Clo. BA14 21 B6
Ham Grn. BA14 21 B6
Hawcroft. BA14 21 C5
INDUSTRIAL & RETAIL:
The Midlands Light Ind Est. BA14 21 C5
Leigh Rd. BA14 21 A4
Little Parks. BA14 21 D4
Maulton Clo. BA14 21 B5
Melksham Rd. BA14 21 D4
Station Rd. BA14 21 C5
Staverton Rd. BA14 21 B6
Stillman Clo. BA14 21 C5
The Common. BA14 21 C5
The Elms. BA14 21 C5
The Gravel. BA14 21 C5
The Midlands. BA14 21 C5
The Star. BA14 21 C6
The Street. BA14 21 B5
The Walk. BA14 21 B6
Three Lions Mws. BA14 21 C5
Woodmand. BA14 21 D6

LUDGERSHALL

Abbatt Clo. SP11 27 F3
Andover Rd. SP11 27 C2
Astor Cres. SP11 27 C3
Bell St. SP11 27 E3
Biddesden La. SP11 27 F3
Brydges Rd. SP11 27 C3
Butt Clo. SP11 27 C2
Byron Clo. SP11 27 C2
Camomile Dri. SP11 27 D3
Castle Ct. SP11 27 C2
Castle St. SP11 27 C2
Central St. SP11 27 D2
Challis Ct. SP11 27 E3
Chapel La. SP11 27 C2
Clarence Gdns. SP11 27 C3
Clover Gdns. SP11 27 D3
Collis Ter. SP11 27 D2
Cornflower Way. SP11 27 D3
Coronation Rd. SP11 27 E3
Crawlboys Rd. SP11 27 D2
Crown La. SP11 27 C2
Deweys La. SP11 27 C2
Drovers Vw. SP11 27 C3
Edelweiss Clo. SP11 27 D3
Eleanor Ct. SP11 27 C2
Elm Clo. SP11 27 E3
Empress Way. SP11 27 C3
Fleming Clo. SP11 27 D2
Foxtail Gdns. SP11 27 D3
Gould Clo. SP11 27 C2
Graspan Rd. SP11 27 F3
Hei-Lin Way. SP11 27 C2
High St. SP11 27 C2
Hyson Cres. SP11 27 E3
Johnson Way. SP11 27 C3
Lady Diana Ct. SP11 27 D2
Lady Jane Wk. SP11 27 D3
Larkin Clo. SP11 27 D3
Laurence Ct. SP11 27 C2

Lena Clo. SP11 27 C3
Levell Ct. SP11 27 C2
Linden Clo. SP11 27 E2
Maple Cres. SP11 27 E3
Meade Rd. SP11 27 E3
New Dri. SP11 27 C4
Old Common Way.
SP11 27 D2
Orchid Dri. SP11 27 D3
Perham Cres. SP11 27 D2
Pretoria Rd. SP11 27 F3
Primrose Rd. SP11 27 D3
Prince Charles Clo.
SP11 27 D2
Princess Mary Gdns.
SP11 27 C3
Queens Clo. SP11 27 C3
Rawlings Ct. SP11 27 C2
Recreation Rd. SP11 27 D2
Roberts Rd. SP11 27 C3
Rockrose Ct. SP11 27 C3
St James St. SP11 27 C2
St Nicholas Clo. SP11 27 F3
Shoddesden La. SP11 27 E4
Short St. SP11 27 D2
Simonds Rd. SP11 27 B3
Somme Rd. SP11 27 A3
Spray Leaze. SP11 27 F3
Station App. SP11 27 C2
Stoney Cross. SP11 27 C3
Teasel Clo. SP11 27 C3
Tidworth Rd. SP11 27 A4
Williamson Clo. SP11 27 C2
Wood Park. SP11 27 E2

LYNEHAM

Argosy Rd. SN15 28 D2
Arnhem Cross. SN15 28 D2
Ash Clo. SN15 28 D2
Bakers Field. SN15 28 C1
Belfast Mead. SN15 28 D2
Britannia Cres. SN15 28 D2
Calne Rd. SN15 28 B1
Chippenham Rd. SN15 28 A1
Church La. SN15 28 C2
Comet Clo. SN15 28 D2
Dixon Rd. SN15 28 C3
Eider Av. SN15 28 C3
Elm Clo. SN15 28 D2
End Clo. SN15 28 C2
Harrow Gro. SN15 28 C2
Hastings Dri. SN15 28 C2
Hocketts Clo. SN15 28 B1
Lancaster Sq. SN15 28 C2
Lime Clo. SN15 28 D2
Mallard Av. SN15 28 C3
Muscovey Clo. SN15 28 C2
Pintail Ct. SN15 28 C3
Portal Pl. SN15 28 C3
Pound Clo. SN15 28 C1
Preston La. SN15 28 C2
Preston Vale. SN15 28 D3
St Michaels Clo. SN15 28 B1
Sheld Dri. SN15 28 C3
Slessor Rd. SN15 28 C3
Sycamore Clo. SN15 28 D2
Teal Av. SN15 28 C2
The Green. SN15 28 B1
Trenchard Rd. SN15 28 C3
Victoria Dri. SN15 28 D3
Webbs Ct. SN15 28 C1
York Rd. SN15 28 D2

MALMESBURY

Abbey Row. SN16 29 B4
Abbots Gdns. SN16 29 C4
Alexander Rd. SN16 29 A3
Amberley Ct. SN16 29 A5
Arches La. SN16 29 B5
Athelstan Rd. SN16 29 B3
Aubrey Rise. SN16 29 C1
Avon Rd. SN16 29 A3
Back Hill. SN16 29 C4
Barley Clo. SN16 29 C5
Baskerville Hill. SN16 29 C4
Blicks Hill. SN16 29 D3
Bonners Clo. SN16 29 C2
Bremilham Rise. SN16 29 A4
Bremilham Rd. SN16 29 B3
Bristol St. SN16 29 B4
Buettell Way. SN16 29 B1

Burnham Rd. SN16 29 B3
Burnivale. SN16 29 B4
Chippenham Rd. SN16 29 C6
Chubb Clo. SN16 29 B2
Cirencester Rd. SN16 29 D2
Common Rd. SN16 29 A5
Coopers Clo. SN16 29 A3
Corn Gastons. SN16 29 A3
Cowbridge Cres. SN16 29 D5
Cricklade Rd. SN16 29 D2
Cross Hayes. SN16 29 C4
Cross Hayes La. SN16 29 C4
Dark La. SN16 29 B4
Elmer Clo. SN16 29 C2
Filands. SN16 29 B1
Forrester Pl. SN16 29 C1
Foundary Rd. SN16 29 C2
Foxley Rd. SN16 29 B4
Gas Ct. SN16 29 B3
Gastons Rd. SN16 29 B3
Gloucester Rd. SN16 29 B3
Gloucester St. SN16 29 C4
Glovers Ct. SN16 29 B3
Haddons Clo. SN16 29 A5
Hanks Clo. SN16 29 C2
Harpers La. SN16 29 B4
High St. SN16 29 C4
Hillcrest. SN16 29 D5
Hobbes Clo. SN16 29 B3
Hodge La. SN16 29 B3
Holford Rise. SN16 29 B3
Holloway. SN16 29 C4
Horse Fair. SN16 29 C4
Hudson Rd. SN16 29 B3
INDUSTRIAL & RETAIL:
Gloucester Rd Ind Est.
SN16 29 C3
Malmesbury Business
Pk. SN16 29 B3
Ingram St. SN16 29 C4
John Betjeman Clo.
SN16 29 C2
Katifer La. SN16 29 B3
Kembles Clo. SN16 29 D5
Kings Walk. SN16 29 C4
Kings Wall. SN16 29 C4
Lacemakers Rd. SN16 29 C2
Leland Clo. SN16 29 C1
Malmesbury By-Pass.
SN16 29 D5
Market Cres. SN16 29 C4
Michael Pyms Rd. SN16 29 C2
Milbourne La. SN16 29 D2
Mill La. SN16 29 C4
Moffatt Rise. SN16 29 C1
Morse Clo. SN16 29 C3
Newton Gro. SN16 29 A3
Niebull Clo. SN16 29 C2
Old Alexander Rd.
SN16 29 A3
Old Railway Clo. SN16 29 C2
Olivers La. SN16 29 C4
Orchard Ct. SN16 29 C5
Orwell Clo. SN16 29 C2
Oxford St. SN16 29 C4
Park Clo. SN16 29 B3
Park Mead. SN16 29 B3
Park Rd. SN16 29 A2
Parklands. SN16 29 A3
Parliament Row. SN16 29 C5
Pool Gastons Rd. SN16 29 B3
Powell Rise. SN16 29 C1
Reeds Farm Rd. SN16 29 C2
River View. SN16 29 B3
Ron Golding Clo. SN16 29 C2
St Aldhelms Rd. SN16 29 B3
St Dennis Rd. SN16 29 C4
St John St. SN16 29 C4
St Marys St. SN16 29 B3
School Clo. SN16 29 C5
Sherston Rd. SN16 29 A3
Silver St. SN16 29 C4
Silverston Way. SN16 29 A3
Swindon Rd. SN16 29 D5
Tetbury Hill Gdns.
SN16 29 B2
Tetbury Rd. SN16 29 B1
The Hawthorns. SN16 29 A5
The Maltings. SN16 29 B3
The Mews. SN16 29 B3
The Old Orchard. SN16 29 B1
The Rowans. SN16 29 B3
Twynnoy Clo. SN16 29 C1
Vicarage Gdns. SN16 29 C5
Water Meadows. SN16 29 B3
Weavers Clo. SN16 29 C2
Webbs Way. SN16 29 C2

West St. SN16 29 B3
White Lion Pk. SN16 29 A3
William Stumpes Clo.
SN16 29 B2
Willow View Clo. SN16 29 B3
Wortheys Clo. SN16 29 C2
Wychurch Rd. SN16 29 C2

MARLBOROUGH

Alexandra Ter. SN8 30 D2
Alma Pl. SN8 30 D3
Angel Yd. SN8 30 D3
Aubrey Clo. SN8 30 B4
Back La. SN8 30 C3
Bailey Acre. SN8 30 D2
Barn St. SN8 30 D2
Barnfield. SN8 31 G3
Barrow Gro. SN8 31 F3
Bath Rd. SN8 30 A4
Bay Water Vw. SN8 30 D2
Baybridge. SN8 31 F2
Benson Clo. SN8 30 B4
Betjeman Rd. SN8 30 A4
Blackwell Path. SN8 30 D3
Blowhorn St. SN8 30 D2
Bridewell St. SN8 30 C4
Bridge St. SN8 30 A4
Cardigan Rd. SN8 30 C3
Chantry La. SN8 30 D3
Cherry Orchard. SN8 31 E4
Chestnut Dri. SN8 30 D4
Chopping Knife La.
SN8 31 G4
Cold Harbour La. SN8 30 D2
College Fields. SN8 30 B3
Copes Yd. SN8 31 E3
Cross La. SN8 30 C2
Culvermead Clo. SN8 31 E3
Dando Dri. SN8 30 B3
Davies Clo. SN8 30 A4
Ducks Meadow. SN8 30 D4
Edwards Meadow. SN8 30 B3
Elcot Clo. SN8 31 F3
Elcot La. SN8 31 F3
Elcot Orchard. SN8 31 G3
Falkner Clo. SN8 30 B3
Farrar Dri. SN8 30 A4
Figgins La. SN8 30 D4
Five Stiles Rd. SN8 31 F4
Forest Dale Rd. SN8 31 F3
Francklyn Acre. SN8 30 D2
Frees Av. SN8 30 B1
Gales Gro. SN8 31 E3
George La. SN8 30 D4
Golding Av. SN8 30 A4
Grand Av. SN8 31 H5
Granham Clo. SN8 30 D4
Granham Hil. SN8 30 C6
Hawkins Meadow. SN8 30 B4
Hazel Clo. SN8 31 G4
Herd St. SN8 30 D2
High St, Manton. SN8 30 A4
High St,
Marlborough. SN8 30 D3
Hilliers Yd. SN8 30 D3
Homefields. SN8 31 F4
Hughenden Yd. SN8 30 D3
Hughes Clo. SN8 30 A4
Hyde La. SN8 30 C2
Ironmonger La. SN8 30 D3
Irving Way. SN8 30 C3
Isbury La. SN8 30 D4
Isbury Rd. SN8 30 D4
Jefferies Clo. SN8 30 B4
Kelham Gdns. SN8 31 E3
Kennet Mews. SN8 30 D3
Kennet Pl. SN8 30 D3
Kingsbury St. SN8 30 D3
Lainey's Clo. SN8 30 D2
Laurel Dri. SN8 31 F3
Lawrence Acre. SN8 30 D2
Leaf Clo. SN8 31 E2
Leaze Rd. SN8 30 C2
London Rd. SN8 31 E3
Lower Church Fld. SN8 30 C3
Lyne's View. SN8 30 C3
MacNeice Dri. SN8 30 A3
Manton Drove. SN8 30 A6
Manton Hollow. SN8 30 A3
Mayfield. SN8 31 E3
Morris Rd. SN8 30 B4
New Rd. SN8 30 D3
Newby Acre. SN8 30 D2
North View Pl. SN8 30 D2

Orchard Rd. SN8 31 E4
Oxford St. SN8 30 D3
Pewsey Rd. SN8 30 D4
Plume Of Feathers La.
SN8 31 E3
Port Field. SN8 30 D2
Port Hill. SN8 30 D1
Poulton Cres. SN8 31 E2
Poulton Hill. SN8 31 E2
Preshute La. SN8 30 A4
Priorsfield. SN8 31 E4
Purlyn Acre. SN8 30 D2
Queens Way. SN8 31 F4
Rabley Wood View.
SN8 30 D2
Ramsbury Rd. SN8 31 H2
Rawlings Well La. SN8 31 E3
Reeds Clo. SN8 31 F3
Reeds Cnr. SN8 31 F3
Riding School Yd. SN8 30 D3
River Park. SN8 30 A4
Roebuck Meadow. SN8 31 F3
Rogers Meadow. SN8 30 D1
Russel Sq. SN8 30 D3
St Davids Way. SN8 30 D2
St Johns Clo. SN8 30 C2
St Margarets Mead. SN8 31 E3
St Martins. SN8 30 D3
Salisbury Hill. SN8 31 E5
Salisbury Rd. SN8 31 E4
Sassoon Wk. SN8 30 B3
Savernake Court. SN8 31 E4
Savernake Cres. SN8 31 F4
Shakespeare Dri. SN8 30 C4
Silverless St. SN8 30 D2
Sorley Clo. SN8 30 B3
South View. SN8 31 E2
Stonebridge Clo. SN8 31 E3
Stonebridge La. SN8 31 E3
Swindon Rd. SN8 30 D2
Tennyson Clo. SN8 30 B4
The Common. SN8 30 D2
The Green. SN8 30 D3
The Parade. SN8 30 D3
The Thorns. SN8 30 D1
Thomson Way. SN8 30 B4
Tinpit. SN8 31 E2
Town Mill. SN8 30 D3
Upper Church Fld. SN8 30 D4
Upper Isbury. SN8 31 E4
Van Diemans Clo. SN8 31 E4
Vicarage Clo. SN8 31 E3
Willow Clo. SN8 31 G3

MELKSHAM

Addison Rd. SN12 32 A1
Alder Way. SN12 32 A4
Anson Gro. SN12 32 D6
Arden Clo. SN12 32 D2
Ash Gro. SN12 32 B5
Ashdown Dri. SN12 32 D1
Avon Ct. SN12 32 D2
Avon Pl. SN12 32 B3
Avon Rd. SN12 32 B1
Awdry Av. SN12 32 C1
Bank St. SN12 32 B3
Barnwell Rd. SN12 32 D2
Bath Rd. SN12 32 B2
Beanacre Rd. SN12 32 B2
Beech Av. SN12 32 A4
Berkley Clo. SN12 32 B5
Berkshire Green. SN12 32 C4
Berryfield La. SN12 32 A6
Berryfield Park. SN12 32 A6
Birch Gro. SN12 32 B2
Blackmore Rd. SN12 32 C3
Bowden Cres. SN12 32 C1
Bowmans Ct. SN12 32 C2
Bradford Rd. SN12 32 A3
Bream Clo. SN12 32 D2
Brecon Clo. SN12 32 D3
Brookside. SN12 32 C3
Burnet Clo. SN12 32 C5
Burniston Clo. SN12 32 D2
Campion Dri. SN12 32 C5
Canon Sq. SN12 32 B3
Canons Ct. SN12 32 B3
Carisbrook Rd. SN12 32 B5
Cedar Clo. SN12 32 B4
Chalfield Cres. SN12 32 C2
Chapel Clo. SN12 32 C1
Chestnut Mews. SN12 32 A4
Chiltern Clo. SN12 32 D3

Church La. SN12 32 D2
Church St. SN12 32 B3
Church Walk. SN12 32 B3
Churchill Av. SN12 32 D2
Clover Clo. SN12 32 C5
Conigre Clo. SN12 32 B4
Conway Cres. SN12 32 B5
Corfe Rd. SN12 32 C5
Cornflower Way. SN12 32 C5
Cornwall Clo. SN12 32 C4
Coronation Rd. SN12 32 C4
Cotswold Clo. SN12 32 D3
Cowslip Mews. SN12 32 C5
Craybourne Rd. SN12 32 C2
Crescent Rd. SN12 32 D1
Daisy Clo. SN12 32 D4
Dean Clo. SN12 32 D2
Devizes Rd. SN12 32 D5
Devonshire Pl. SN12 32 C3
Dorset Cres. SN12 32 C3
Dunch La. SN12 32 A1
Elizabeth Clo. SN12 32 A6
Elliott Pl. SN12 32 B1
Elm Clo. SN12 32 D6
Epping Clo. SN12 32 D1
Epping Dri. SN12 32 D2
Fairway. SN12 32 D2
Falcon Rd. SN12 32 D6
Farleigh Av. SN12 32 B5
Ferris Gro. SN12 32 C3
Forest Rd. SN12 32 C2
Foresters Park Rd.
SN12 32 D3
Foxglove Clo. SN12 32 D4
Franklea Pk. SN12 32 D2
Fullers Clo. SN12 32 C2
Fulmar Clo. SN12 32 D6
Glenside. SN12 32 C1
Gloucester Sq. SN12 32 C3
Granville Rd. SN12 32 B1
Green Wood Rd. SN12 32 A5
Halifax Rd. SN12 32 C6
Hampshire Pl. SN12 32 C3
Hardie Walk. SN12 32 C4
Harrier Ct. SN12 32 C6
Hazlewood Rd. SN12 32 A4
Heathcote Rd. SN12 32 C2
Heather Av. SN12 32 D4
High St. SN12 32 B3
Holbrook Vale. SN12 32 A6
Hornbeam Cres. SN12 32 A5
Ingram Rd. SN12 32 D2
Kenilworth Gdns. SN12 32 B5
Kennet Clo. SN12 32 B1
King St. SN12 32 B4
Kingsbury Sq. SN12 32 B4
Laburnum Dri SN12 32 A5
Lambourne Cres. SN12 32 C3
Lancaster Rd. SN12 32 C6
Lansdown Clo. SN12 32 D2
Larch Clo. SN12 32 A4
Lavender Clo. SN12 32 C5
Leaze Rd. SN12 32 D2
Lime Av. SN12 32 B4
Lincoln Grn. SN12 32 D1
Linden Gro. SN12 32 B5
Little John Av. SN12 32 C1
Longford Rd. SN12 32 B5
Lonsdale Gdns. SN12 32 B5
Lowbourne. SN12 32 B3
Loxley Clo. SN12 32 C1
Lysander Way. SN12 32 C6
Malthouse Farm Clo.
SN12 32 D2
Malvern Clo. SN12 32 D3
Maple Clo. SN12 32 D2
Margaret St. SN12 32 B2
Marigold Clo. SN12 32 D4
Market Pl. SN12 32 B4
Marti Clo. SN12 32 D3
Martigny Ct. SN12 32 C4
Martigny Rd. SN12 32 C4
Martlet Clo. SN12 32 D6
Meadow Rd. SN12 32 C1
Mendip Clo. SN12 32 D3
Merlin Way. SN12 32 C6
Methuen Av. SN12 32 C1
Mills Rd. SN12 32 D3
Milton Av. SN12 32 C4
Montague Pl. SN12 32 D2
Murray Walk. SN12 32 C2
New Broughton Rd.
SN12 32 B3
New Lawns. SN12 32 B4
North Brook Rd. SN12 32 A1
Nortree Ct. SN12 32 B2
Oakwood Dri. SN12 32 B4

O'Gorman Mews. SN12 32 D1
Old Broughton Rd. SN12 32 B2
Orchard Gdns. SN12 32 B4
Osprey Clo. SN12 32 D6
Padfield Gdns. SN12 32 A6
Pembroke Rd. SN12 32 C3
Pennine Clo. SN12 32 D3
Pennycress Dri. SN12 32 C5
Perretts Ct. SN12 32 B3
Philip Clo. SN12 32 C1
Pine Clo. SN12 32 A5
Place Rd. SN12 32 B1
Portman Rd. SN12 32 B1
Primrose Dri. SN12 32 D4
Quantock Clo. SN12 32 D3
Queensway. SN12 32 C3
Radnor Pl. SN12 32 B5
Riverside Dri. SN12 32 B2
Rope Walk. SN12 32 C4
Rosebrook Gdns. SN12 32 C4
Roundpond. SN12 32 A1
Rowan Ct. SN12 32 B5
Rowley Pl. SN12 32 C3
Ruskin Av. SN12 32 C3
Rutland Av. SN12 32 C4
St Andrews Rd. SN12 32 D2
St Margarets Gdns. SN12 32 C2
St Michaels Rd. SN12 32 B5
Sandridge Rd. SN12 32 C3
Sangster Av. SN12 32 C4
Sarum Av. SN12 32 B5
Savernake Av. SN12 32 D1
Saxifrage Bank. SN12 32 D4
Scotland Rd. SN12 32 B2
Semington Rd. SN12 32 B6
Severn Rd. SN12 32 B1
Shelley Gdns. SN12 32 C4
Sherwood Av. SN12 32 D1
Short St. SN12 32 D1
Shurnhold. SN12 32 A2
Snarlton La. SN12 32 D3
Snowberry La. SN12 32 D5
Somerset Cres. SN12 32 C4
Sorrell Clo. SN12 32 C5
Southbrook Rd. SN12 32 A1
Spa Ct. SN12 32 B4
Spa Rd. SN12 32 B4
Speedwell Clo. SN12 32 C5
Spencer Clo. SN12 32 B1
Station App. SN12 32 A2
Strattons Walk. SN12 32 B3
Sweetbriar Rd. SN12 32 D4
Talbot Clo. SN12 32 D2
Tamar Rd. SN12 32 B1
Thackeray Cres. SN12 32 C3
Thames Cres. SN12 32 B1
The City. SN12 32 B2
The Close. SN12 32 D2
The Crays. SN12 32 D2
The Friars. SN12 32 D1
Thornbank. SN12 32 B4
Thornleigh. SN12 32 B3
Tower Rd. SN12 32 D3
Townsend Farm. SN12 32 B5
Trenchard Way. SN12 32 D6
Trent Cres. SN12 32 B1
Union St. SN12 32 B3
Vincent Clo. SN12 32 D3
Wardour Pl. SN12 32 B5
Warwick Cres. SN12 32 B5
Waverley Gdns. SN12 32 B5
Weavers Croft. SN12 32 B2
Wellington Dri. SN12 32 D6
Wellington Sq. SN12 32 D6
Wessex Clo. SN12 32 C4
West End. SN12 32 B4
Westbury Vw. SN12 32 D3
Western Way. SN12 32 A3
Wharf Ct. SN12 32 B4
Willow Clo. SN12 32 A4
Wiltshire Cres. SN12 32 C4
Windsor Av. SN12 32 C5
Winston Rd. SN12 32 A6
Woodcoombe. SN12 32 D1
Woodrow Rd. SN12 32 D1
Woodstock Gdns. SN12 32 B5

MERE

Angel La. BA12 28 B5
Ash Gro. BA12 28 C6
Barnes Pl. BA12 28 B5
Barton La. BA12 28 B5

Bishops Clo. BA12 28 B4
Boar St. BA12 28 B5
Bramley Hill. BA12 28 A5
Caddy La. BA12 28 B5
Castle Hill App. BA12 28 B5
Castle Hill Cres. BA12 28 B4
Castle St. BA12 28 A5
Church La. BA12 28 B5
Church St. BA12 28 B5
Clements La. BA12 28 D6
Clews La. BA12 28 C5
Dark La. BA12 28 C5
Denes Av. BA12 28 B4
Downside Clo. BA12 28 C4
Hazzards Hill. BA12 28 C5
Home Field. BA12 28 A5
INDUSTRIAL & RETAIL:
Quarryfield Ind Est. BA12 28 A5
Woodlands Rd Ind Est. BA12 28 C6
Ivy Mead. BA12 28 C5
Jack Paul Clo. BA12 28 B4
Kingsmere Paddocks. BA12 28 A5
Long Hill. BA12 28 B4
Lordsmead Rd. BA12 28 C6
Lynch Clo. BA12 28 C5
Manor Rd. BA12 28 B4
Market Pl. BA12 28 C5
Mere By-Pass. BA12 28 A4
Mill La. BA12 28 C6
New Cut. BA12 28 C5
North Rd. BA12 28 B4
North St. BA12 28 B5
Nursery Gdns. BA12 28 C4
Old Hollow. BA12 28 C4
Penny Bank La. BA12 28 B5
Pettridge La. BA12 28 C5
Prospect Pl. BA12 28 A5
Queens Rd. BA12 28 C4
Salisbury St. BA12 28 B5
Shaftesbury Rd. BA12 28 C6
Southbrook. BA12 28 C6
Southbrook Gdns. BA12 28 D6
Spinners Way. BA12 28 C5
Springfield Rd. BA12 28 C5
Steep St. BA12 28 C4
The Drove. BA12 28 A5
The Fields. BA12 28 C5
The Lynch. BA12 28 C6
The Paddocks. BA12 28 C5
The Pound. BA12 28 C5
The Square. BA12 28 B5
The Yews. BA12 28 C4
Townsend Clo. BA12 28 B5
Underdown Mead. BA12 28 C4
Underhill. BA12 28 A5
Upper Water St. BA12 28 C5
Water St. BA12 28 C5
Wellhead. BA12 28 C5
White Rd. BA12 28 B5
Whitemarsh. BA12 28 C5
Woodlands Rd. BA12 28 C6

NORTH TIDWORTH

Abbots Clo. SP9 33 C2
Abbots Rd. SP9 33 C2
Adampur Rd. SP9 33 A4
Agra Rd. SP9 33 B4
Ash Clo. SP9 33 F2
Ashdown Ter. SP9 33 D4
Auckland Clo. SP9 33 F2
Avon Rd. SP9 33 C3
Baroda Rd. SP9 33 B4
Bazaar Rd. SP9 33 B4
Beech Hill Rd. SP9 33 E1
Bishops Clo. SP9 33 D4
Bourne Rd. SP9 33 E3
Bourne Vw. SP9 33 E1
Bulford Rd. SP9 33 B4
Cabul Rd. SP9 33 B4
Cherry Tree Av. SP9 33 E1
Chestnut Av. SP9 33 D4
Church La. SP9 33 D4
Churchill Clo. SP9 33 C1
Collins Ct. SP9 33 C1
Coronation Rd. SP9 33 C1
Dasna Rd. SP9 33 B3
Daunch Clo. SP9 33 C1

Dunedin Clo. SP9 33 F2
Ebble Clo. SP9 33 D2
Falcon Clo. SP9 33 E2
Forest Dri. SP9 33 E2
Furse Hill Rd. SP9 33 D4
Gason Hill Rd. SP9 33 C1
George VI Rd. SP9 33 D1
Gisborne Clo. SP9 33 E3
Grand Trunk Rd. SP9 33 A4
Hawthorn Rd. SP9 33 E2
Hill Top Av. SP9 33 C1
Humber La. SP9 33 C4
Iamrud Rd. SP9 33 C3
Jagdalik Rd. SP9 33 C4
Karachi Clo. SP9 33 C1
Kennet Rd. SP9 33 E2
Kestral Clo. SP9 33 E2
Kirklee Rd. SP9 33 C3
Kohat Clo. SP9 33 C2
Kohat Rd. SP9 33 C4
Lady Godley Clo. SP9 33 D3
Lahore Clo. SP9 33 C1
Lahore Rd. SP9 33 D3
Lark Clo. SP9 33 E2
Lowa Rd. SP9 33 C3
Ludgershall Rd. SP9 33 D2
Manor Bridge Ct. SP9 33 D1
Maple Ter. SP9 33 E2
Margha Rd. SP9 33 C2
Martin Clo. SP9 33 E2
Meerut Rd. SP9 33 C3
Mill Hill Av. SP9 33 D1
Monks Clo. SP9 33 D2
Nadder Rd. SP9 33 D2
Naini Tal Rd. SP9 33 C2
Napier Clo. SP9 33 F2
Nepaul Rd. SP9 33 C2
Oak Clo. SP9 33 F2
Ordnance Rd. SP9 33 D2
Paget Rd. SP9 33 C1
Park Rd. SP9 33 D3
Plantation Rd. SP9 33 D4
Pennings Rd. SP9 33 D1
Peshawar Clo. SP9 33 B1
Pheasant Clo. SP9 33 E2
Pinetree House. SP9 33 E2
Plassey Rd. SP9 33 C2
Raven Clo. SP9 33 E3
Rosewood Ct. SP9 33 E2
St Andrews Rd. SP9 33 D2
St Georges Rd. SP9 33 C3
St Michaels Av. SP9 33 C3
St Patricks Av. SP9 33 C3
Sidbury Circular Rd. SP9 33 C1
Sidbury Hill Av. SP9 33 D1
Station Rd. SP9 33 D3
Swallow Clo. SP9 33 E3
Sycamore Clo. SP9 33 F2
The Mall. SP9 33 A4
The Oval. SP9 33 D3
Vockins Clo. SP9 33 C1
Wavell Rd. SP9 33 C1
Wellington Rd. SP9 33 E2
Woodcock Clo. SP9 33 E3
Wylye Rd. SP9 33 D2
Zouch Av. SP9 33 C2
Zouch Clo. SP9 33 C2
Zouch Farm Rd. SP9 33 D2

PEWSEY

Astley Clo. SN9 34 C1
Aston Clo. SN9 34 B2
Avon Pl. SN9 34 B2
Avonleaze Rd. SN9 34 B1
Bailey Clo. SN9 34 A1
Ball Rd. SN9 34 C2
Bramley Clo. SN9 34 B1
Broadfields. SN9 34 A2
Broomcroft Rd. SN9 34 B1
Brunkards La. SN9 34 C1
Buckleaze La. SN9 34 B1
Cherry Clo. SN9 34 C1
Church St. SN9 34 B2
Coronation Clo. SN9 34 B2
Dursden La. SN9 34 C1
Easterton La. SN9 34 C2
Edwardian La. SN9 34 B1
Everleigh Rd. SN9 34 B3
Frensham Way. SN9 34 B1
Goddard Rd. SN9 34 B1
Green Dro. SN9 34 B3
Haines Ter. SN9 34 A2
Hawthorn Clo. SN9 34 C1

High St. SN9 34 B2
Holly Clo. SN9 34 C1
Holly Tree Wk. SN9 34 B2
Hollybush La. SN9 34 C1
INDUSTRIAL & RETAIL:
Fordbrook Ind Est. SN9 34 B1
Inlands Clo. SN9 34 B1
King Alfred Clo. SN9 34 B1
Kings Corner. SN9 34 C2
Lime Clo. SN9 34 C1
Little Island. SN9 34 C4
Manningford Rd. SN9 34 A1
Manor Ct. SN9 34 B2
Maple Clo. SN9 34 C1
Market Pl. SN9 34 B2
Marlborough Rd. SN9 34 A1
Martinsell Grn. SN9 34 B1
Middlemass Grn. SN9 34 B1
Millennium Ct. SN9 34 B1
Milton Rd. SN9 34 C1
Nether Leaze. SN9 34 A1
North St. SN9 34 B1
Old Hospital Rd. SN9 34 A1
Phoenix Ct. SN9 34 B2
Raffin La. SN9 34 B3
Rawlins Rd. SN9 34 A2
River St. SN9 34 B2
Robinia Clo. SN9 34 C1
Rowan Clo. SN9 34 C1
St Johns Clo. SN9 34 C2
Salisbury Rd. SN9 34 A3
Scotchel Grn. SN9 34 B1
Slater Rd. SN9 34 B2
Southcott Rd. SN9 34 C2
Stratton Rd. SN9 34 B2
Swan Ct. SN9 34 B2
Swan Meadow. SN9 34 B3
Swan Rd. SN9 34 B2
The Crescent. SN9 34 A2
The Links. SN9 34 A2
The Square. SN9 34 A2
Tinkers Mead. SN9 34 C3
Vale Rd. SN9 34 A1
Walnut Clo. SN9 34 C1
Wheeler Clo. SN9 34 A1
Wilcot Rd. SN9 34 A1
Woodlands Rd. SN9 34 C3

POTTERNE

Blackberry La. SN10 34 C4
Blounts Ct. SN10 34 C6
Brownleaze La. SN10 34 C4
Court Hill. SN10 34 A6
Coxhill La. SN10 34 C5
Duck St. SN10 34 C5
Eastwell Rd. SN10 34 C5
Firs Hill Way. SN10 34 D4
High St. SN10 34 C5
Highlands. SN10 34 C5
Mill Rd. SN10 34 B5
Rookes La. SN10 34 C5
Ryeleaze. SN10 34 D4
St Marys Clo. SN10 34 D4
Silver St. SN10 34 D5
The Butts. SN10 34 C5
Tollbar Clo. SN10 34 C5
Whistley Rd. SN10 34 B4

SALISBURY

Abbot Rd. SP1 37 F4
Albany Rd. SP1 37 F3
Aldworth Dri. SP1 37 F3
Alexandra Clo. SP2 36 A5
Alexandra Dri. SP2 36 A5
Ancient Way. SP2 39 E4
Anderson Rd. SP1 37 F5
Andrews Way. SP2 38 D5
Angler Rd. SP2 35 D1
Apostles Way. SP1 37 F3
Appleshaw Way. SP1 37 G3
Ash Cres. SP1 37 F3
Ashfield Rd. SP2 38 B1
Ashlands. SP4 37 G2
Ashley Rd. SP2 36 C6
Assisi Rd. SP1 36 D3
Aston Mead. SP1 37 F5
Attwood Rd. SP1 37 E5
Australian Av. SP2 36 A6
Avon App. SP1 38 D1
Avon Ter. SP2 36 C6

Ayleswade Rd. SP2 38 D3
Ayrshrie Clo. SP2 35 D1
Balmoral Rd. SP1 37 E4
Barnard St. SP1 39 E2
Barnards Hill Dri. SP2 35 D2
Barrington Rd. SP1 37 F4
Bartlett Rd. SP2 37 E4
Beatrice Rd. SP1 36 D4
Becket Way. SP1 39 F1
Bedford Rd. SP2 36 C6
Bedwin St. SP1 39 E1
Beechcroft Rd. SP1 39 G1
Beeson Clo. SP2 38 C5
Bellamy La. SP1 39 F1
Belle Vue Rd. SP1 37 E6
Berkshire Rd. SP2 38 B3
Bingham Rd. SP1 37 F4
Bishopdown Rd. SP1 37 E5
Bishops Dri. SP2 38 C4
Bishops Mead. SP1 37 G4
Bishops Walk. SP1 38 D2
Blackfriars Way. SP1 39 E2
Blakey Rd. SP1 39 F2
Blandford Rd. SP2 38 A6
Blue Boar Row. SP1 38 D1
Blyth Way. SP1 37 F4
Bouchers Way. SP2 38 D5
Boundary Rd. SP1 37 H6
Bourne Av. SP1 37 F6
Bourne Clo. SP1 39 G2
Bourne Hill. SP1 39 E1
Bourne Way. SP1 39 G3
Bouverie Av. SP2 38 D4
Bouverie Av Sth. SP2 38 C5
Bouverie Clo. SP2 38 C4
Bower Gdns. SP1 39 F2
Bower Hill Rd. SP1 37 F6
*Bowes Lyon Ct,
  Philip Ct. SP2 36 A5
Braemar Rise. SP1 37 E4
Brick La. SP2 36 A6
Bridge St. SP1 38 D1
Britford La. SP2 39 E4
Britford La W. SP2 38 D3
Broad Wk. SP1 38 D2
Broadlands Clo. SP1 37 E4
Brown St. SP1 39 E1
Brunel Rd. SP2 38 B2
Burford Av. SP2 39 E4
Burford La. SP2 39 E4
Burford Rd. SP2 39 E4
Burgess Grn. SP1 37 F4
Burnett Way. SP1 37 F4
Butcher Row. SP2 38 D1
Butler Clo. SP2 39 E4
Butts Rd. SP1 36 D5
Byways Clo. SP1 39 F2
Cambridge Rd. SP1 37 E5
Campbell Rd. SP1 37 E6
Canadian Av. SP2 36 B6
Capulet Rd. SP1 36 C4
Carmelite Way. SP1 39 E3
Carrion Pond Drove. SP2 38 B4
Castle Keep. SP1 36 C4
Castle Rd. SP1 36 D2
Castle St. SP1 36 D6
Catherine St. SP1 39 E2
Cecil Av. SP2 38 D4
Cecil Ter. SP2 38 A1
Cedar Clo. SP2 35 D2
Centurion Clo. SP2 36 A5
Chancery Clo. SP2 36 B6
Charles St. SP2 36 B6
Charnwood Rd. SP2 36 B6
Chatham Clo. SP1 36 C4
Cherry Clo. SP2 36 B6
Cherry Orchard La. SP2 36 B6
Cheshire Clo. SP2 36 A4
Chestnut Clo. SP1 37 G5
Cheverell Av. SP1 37 F5
Chichester Clo. SP2 39 E4
Chipper La. SP1 38 D1
Chiselbury Gro. SP2 37 G3
Choristers Sq. SP1 38 D2
Christie Miller Rd. SP2 36 B6
Christopher Clo. SP2 38 C5
Church La. SP2 36 A6
Church La. SP5 39 G5
Church Rd. SP1 37 G6
Churchfields Rd. SP2 38 B1
Churchill Way East. SP1 37 E6
Churchill Way Nth. SP1 37 E6
Churchill Way Sth. SP1 39 E3

Churchill Way
West. SP2 36 D6
Clarendon Rd. SP1 39 F1
Clifton Rd. SP2 36 C6
Coldharbour La. SP2 36 C6
College St. SP1 37 E6
Constable Way. SP2 38 C2
Cooks Clo. SP2 35 D1
Coombe Rd. SP2 38 B5
Cornwall Rd. SP1 36 D5
Coronation Rd. SP2 36 A5
Coronation Sq. SP2 35 B4
Courtwood Clo. SP1 39 F2
Cow La. SP1 37 F6
Crane St. SP1 38 D2
Cranebridge Rd. SP2 38 D1
Crestmount Dri. SP2 36 A5
Crown Ct. SP2 36 A5
Culver St. SP1 39 E2

Dairy Meadow La. SP1 39 G3
Dalewood Rise. SP1 37 G6
De Vaux Pl. SP1 38 D3
Denison Rise. SP1 37 F4
Devizes Rd. SP2 36 A3
Devonshire Rd. SP1 37 E5
Dews Rd. SP2 38 C1
Donaldson Rd. SP1 37 E5
Dorset Rd. SP1 37 E5
Douglas Haig Rd. SP1 36 D5
Down View Rd. SP1 37 G6
Downsway. SP1 37 E3
Downton Rd. SP2 39 E4
Drake Clo. SP1 37 F3
Dryden Clo. SP2 39 E4
Duck La. SP1 37 G6
Dublin Way. SP1 39 F2
Dunley Way. SP1 37 F3
Durnford Rd. SP1 36 B1

Eagle Field. SP2 36 A4
East St. SP2 38 D1
Edgam Pl. SP2 35 B4
Edison Rd. SP2 38 B1
Elm Clo. SP1 37 G5
Elm Ct. SP1 39 E1
Elm Gro. SP1 39 F1
Elm Gro Pl. SP1 39 F1
Elm Gro Rd. SP1 39 E1
Empire Rd. SP2 36 A6
Endless St. SP1 39 E1
Essex Sq. SP2 38 B3
Estcourt Rd. SP1 37 E6
Eveque Ct. SP2 35 B4
Eversglade. SP2 36 C6
Exeter St. SP1 39 E3
Eyres Way. SP1 39 E2

Fair View Rd. SP1 39 F1
Fair View Rd. SP2 35 A2
Fairfield Rd. SP1 36 D4
Falcons Way. SP2 38 D5
Faraday Rd. SP2 38 B1
Farley Rd. SP1 39 F2
Farm La. SP2 38 B1
Festival Av. SP2 35 D4
Feversham Rd. SP1 37 E4
Finchley Rd. SP2 36 B6
Fish Row. SP1 39 E1
Fisherton St. SP2 36 C6
Fison Walk. SP1 37 G4
Folkestone Rd. SP2 38 C4
Folly Clo. SP2 38 C4
Folly La. SP2 36 A5
Folly View. SP2 35 D2
Foots Hill. SP2 35 C4
Ford La. SP4 37 H2
Fotherby Cres. SP1 37 F4
Fowlers Hill. SP1 39 F2
Fowlers Rd. SP1 39 E2
Francis Way. SP2 38 D5
Friary La. SP1 39 E3
Fugglestone. SP2 35 A3
Fyfield Clo. SP1 37 G3

Gainsborough Clo. SP2 35 D3
Gas La. SP2 36 C6
Gawthorne Dri. SP2 38 C3
George St. SP2 36 C6
George St Sth. SP2 38 D1
Gibbs Clo. SP1 37 F2
Gigant St. SP1 39 E2
Gilbert Way. SP1 37 F4
Glendale Cres. SP1 39 G1
Glenmore Rd. SP1 37 F5
Glyndebourne Clo. SP2 35 D3
Godley Rd. SP2 38 D4
Gorringe Rd. SP2 36 B6
Grace Clo. SP2 35 D1
Gramshaw Rd. SP2 36 A6
Grange Gdns. SP1 37 F6
Grasmere Clo. SP2 38 D4
Green La. SP4 37 G1
Green Lane Clo. SP4 37 G2
Greencroft St. SP1 39 E1
Greenwood Av. SP1 39 G1
Greyfriars Clo. SP1 39 E2
Guilder La. SP1 39 E1
Gypsy La. SP1 39 H2

Hadrians Clo. SP2 36 A6
Hallum Clo. SP1 37 G4
Hamilton Rd. SP1 36 D6
Hampton Ct. SP2 35 B4
Harcourt Ter. SP2 38 D1
Harnham Rd. SP2 38 C3
Harnwood Rd. SP2 38 C4
Harper Rd. SP2 36 B6
Hartington Rd. SP2 36 C6
Hartley Way. SP1 37 F3
Harvard Clo. SP2 38 D5
Hatches La. SP1 39 G3
Hathaway Clo. SP1 36 C4
Hawks Ridge. SP2 38 D4
*Hawthorn Clo,
Wilton Rd. SP2 36 C6
Hazel Clo. SP2 35 C3
Heath Rd. SP2 36 A4
Hedley Davis Ct. SP2 38 B1
Herbert Rd. SP2 36 A5
Heronswood. SP2 38 D5
High Rd. SP5 39 F5
High St. SP1 38 D2
Highbury Av. SP2 36 B6
Highbury Clo. SP2 36 B6
Highfield Rd. SP2 36 B6
Highlands Rd. SP2 38 D4
Hill Rd. SP1 37 G6
Hill Top Way. SP1 36 D3
Hill View Rd. SP1 39 E1
Hoadley Grn. SP1 37 G4
Hollows Clo. SP2 38 C4
Homington Rd. SP2 38 B6
Hudson Rd. SP1 36 C4
Hulse Rd. SP1 36 D5

India Av. SP2 36 B6
INDUSTRIAL & RETAIL:
Churchfields Ind Est.
SP2 38 B1
Dolphin Trading Est.
SP1 39 F2
Harnham Trading Est.
SP2 38 A3
Milford Trading Est.
SP1 39 F2
Old Sarum Business Pk.
SP4 37 E1
Salisbury Business Pk.
SP1 39 G3
Salisbury Retail Pk.
SP1 37 G3
The Bourne Centre.
SP1 39 G3
Ivy St. SP1 39 E2

James St. SP2 36 C6
Jewell Clo. SP1 37 G4
*Jubilee Ct,
North St. SP2 38 D1
Juniper Dri. SP1 36 D3

Kelsey Rd. SP1 39 E1
Kensington Rd. SP2 36 C6
Kent Rd. SP2 38 B3
Kimpton Av. SP1 37 G3
Kingfisher Clo. SP2 38 D5
Kings Rd. SP1 37 E6
Kingsland Rd. SP2 36 C6
*Kivel Ct,
Scamells Rd. SP1 36 D6

Ladysmith Clo. SP2 36 A5
Laverstock Pk. SP1 37 G6
Laverstock Pk W. SP1 37 G6
Laverstock Rd. SP1 39 F1
Lees Ct. SP2 36 C6
Lime Kiln Way. SP2 38 D5
Linden Clo. SP1 39 G1
Lindford Rd. SP1 37 G3
Link Way. SP1 37 F5
Linnetsdene. SP2 38 D5
Locks La. SP2 35 B4
London Rd. SP1 37 F6
Longhill Dri. SP1 39 E4
Longland. SP2 36 B6
Love La. SP1 39 E2
Lovett Grn. SP1 37 F4
Lower Rd. SP5 39 G6
Lower Rd. SP2 35 B4
Lower St. SP2 38 C3
Lumley Clo. SP2 35 D2

Macklin Av. SP2 36 B5
Mallard Clo. SP2 38 C3
Malthouse La. SP2 38 D1
Manning Clo. SP1 37 F2
Manor Farm Rd. SP1 39 F1
Manor Rd. SP1 39 F1
Maple Cres. SP2 35 A3
Maplecroft. SP2 38 D4
Marina Rd. SP1 39 F2
Marlborough Rd. SP1 37 E6
Marsh La. SP2 36 C6
Martins Clo. SP2 38 D5
Maryland Clo. SP2 35 C2
Mayfair Rd. SP1 39 G1
Meadow Rd. SP2 36 C6
Meadow Rd Sth. SP2 38 D1
Melvin Clo. SP1 39 G1
Merrifield Rd. SP4 37 F2
Methuen Dri. SP1 39 E2
Meyrick Av. SP1 38 D4
Middle St. SP2 38 B2
Middleton Rd. SP2 36 D6
Milford Hill. SP1 39 E2
Milford Hollow. SP1 39 F2
Milford Manor Gdns.
SP1 39 F2
Milford Mill Rd. SP1 39 G2
Milford Pk. SP1 39 G2
Milford St. SP1 39 E1
Mill La. SP1 36 B3
Mill Rd. SP2 38 C1
Mill Stream App. SP1 38 D1
Millbrook. SP1 39 F1
Millennnium Clo. SP2 39 E5
Millers Clo. SP1 36 B3
Milton Rd. SP2 39 E4
Minster St. SP1 38 D1
Mitchell Rd. SP2 38 B1
Moberly Rd. SP1 36 D5
Montague Rd. SP2 38 A3
Montgomery Gdns.
SP2 36 B6
Monxton Clo. SP1 37 G3
Munks Clo. SP2 38 B3
Myrrfield Rd. SP1 37 G3

Nadder La. SP2 35 B5
Nadder Ter. SP2 38 B1
Napier Cres. SP1 39 G1
Neal Clo. SP1 37 F2
Nelson Rd. SP1 36 D6
Netheravon Clo. SP1 37 E5
Netheravon Rd. SP1 37 E5
Netherhampton Rd,
Harnham. SP2 38 A3
Netherhampton Rd,
Quidhampton. SP2 35 A6
Neville Clo. SP1 37 F4
New Bridge Rd. SP1 39 E3
New Canal. SP1 38 D2
New Harnham Rd. SP2 38 D4
New St. SP1 38 D2
New Zealand Av. SP2 36 A6
Newton Rd. SP2 38 B1
*Nightingale Walk,
Christie Miller Rd. SP2 36 B6
Norfolk Rd. SP2 38 B3
North St. SP2 38 D1
North Walk. SP1 38 D2
Norton Dri. SP4 37 G1
Nursery Rd. SP2 36 B6

Oak Tree Field. SP2 39 E6
Oakway Rd. SP1 37 E4
Odstock Rd. SP2 39 E5
Old Blandford Rd. SP2 38 B5
Old Castle Rd. SP1 36 D2
Old George Mall. SP2 38 D2
Old Meadows Walk.
SP2 38 B3
Old Shaftesbury Drove.
SP2 38 A5
Old St. SP2 38 D4
Oldfield Rd. SP1 37 F3
Olivier Clo. SP2 35 D1
Orchard Pl. SP2 36 C6
Orchard Rd. SP2 36 A6
Owls Wood. SP2 38 D5
Paddock Way. SP1 37 H6
Palmer Rd. SP2 36 B6
Park Clo. SP1 36 D4
Park La. SP5 39 G6
Park Clo. SP1 36 D4
Park La. SP1 36 D5
Park Rd. SP1 37 G6
Park St. SP1 37 E6
Parsonage Clo. SP1 36 B3
Parsonage Grn. SP2 38 C3
Pauls Dene Cres. SP1 37 E3
Pauls Dene Rd. SP1 36 D3
Paynes Hill. SP1 39 E2
Pearce Way. SP1 37 F2
Pembroke Rd. SP2 35 D4
Penning Rd. SP2 35 C3
Pennyfarthing St. SP1 39 E1
Penruddock Clo. SP2 35 D3
Peters Finger Rd. SP1 39 H3
Philip Ct. SP1 36 A5
Phillips La. SP1 36 B1
Pilgrims Mead. SP1 37 F3
Pinewood Clo. SP2 35 D2
Pinewood Way. SP2 35 C2
Polden Rd. SP1 39 F2
Poplar Way. SP1 37 F3
Portland Av. SP2 38 C5
Potters Way. SP1 39 G1
Primrose Rd. SP2 36 A4
Pullman Dri. SP2 35 C4
Queen Alexandra Rd.
SP2 36 A6
Queen Manor Rd. SP1 39 G2
Queen Mary Rd. SP2 36 A4
Queen St. SP1 39 E1
Queens Rd. SP1 37 E6
Queensberry Rd. SP1 36 D5

Radcliffe Rd. SP2 38 D4
Radnor Rd. SP1 36 D4
Rambridge Cres. SP2 35 C2
Ramleaze Dri. SP2 35 D1
Rampart Rd. SP1 39 E1
Ravenscroft. SP2 38 D5
Rawlence Rd. SP2 35 D3
Rectory Rd. SP2 38 C1
Redford Clo. SP1 37 F5
Richards Way. SP2 38 B3
Richmond Rd. SP2 36 C6
Ridgeway Rd. SP1 37 E5
Riverbourne Rd. SP1 39 G1
Riverside Clo. SP1 37 G6
Riverside Rd. SP1 37 G6
Roberts Rd. SP2 36 A5
Rogers Clo. SP2 35 B4
Rollestone St. SP1 39 E1
Roman Rd. SP2 36 A6
Romer Rd. SP2 38 D4
Rosemary Clo. SP1 37 G6
Rosemary La. SP1 38 D2
Rougemont Clo. SP1 39 E1
Rowan Clo. SP2 35 C3
Rowbarrow Clo. SP 39 E4
Russell Rd. SP2 36 B5

St Albans Clo. SP1 37 G3
St Andrews. SP1 37 G6
St Andrews Rd. SP2 36 A6
St Ann Pl. SP1 39 E2
St Ann St. SP1 39 E2
St Bedes Clo. SP1 37 G3
St Brendans Clo. SP1 37 F3
St Christophers Clo. SP1 37 F3
St Clair Rd. SP1 39 E3
St Clements Way. SP1 37 F3
St Davids Clo. SP1 37 F3
St Edmunds Church St.
SP1 39 E1
St Francis Cres. SP1 37 E3
St Francis Rd. SP1 36 D4
St Georges Rd. SP2 38 A3
St Gregory Av. SP2 36 A6
St James Clo. SP1 37 G3
St John St. SP1 39 E1
St Johns Clo. SP1 39 G2
St Josephs Clo. SP1 37 F3
St Judes Clo. SP1 37 G3
St Lawrence Clo. SP2 36 B3
St Lukes Clo. SP1 37 G3
St Margarets Clo. SP1 39 F2
St Marks Av. SP1 37 E5
St Marks Rd. SP1 37 E6
St Martins Church St.
SP1 39 E2
St Marys Rd. SP2 38 C3
St Matthews Clo. SP1 37 G3
St Michaels Rd. SP2 36 A4
St Michaels Rd. SP2 35 D2
St Nicholas Rd. SP1 38 D3
St Osmonds Clo. SP1 36 D3
St Pauls Rd. SP1 38 C1
St Peters Rd. SP1 37 F3
St Teresas Clo. SP1 37 F3
St Thomas Way. SP1 37 F3
St Ursulas Clo. SP1 37 F3
Saintes Clo. SP1 37 F3
Salisbury Rd. SP2 35 A3
Salt La. SP1 39 E1
Sarum Clo. SP2 36 B5
Saxon Rd. SP2 38 C3
Scamells Rd. SP1 36 D6
Scots La. SP1 38 D1
Senior Dri. SP2 39 E4
Seth Ward Dri. SP1 37 F5
Shady Bower. SP1 39 F2
Shady Bower Clo. SP1 39 F2
*Shakespeare Pl,
Windsor St. SP2 38 C1
Shakespeare Rd. SP1 36 C4
Sharrat Av. SP1 37 F3
Sheen Clo. SP2 35 D1
Shelley Dri. SP1 36 C4
Shropshire Clo. SP2 35 D2
Sidney St. SP2 36 C6
Silver St. SP1 38 D1
Silverwood Dri. SP1 37 H5
Skew Bridge Rd. SP2 36 A6
Skew Rd. SP2 35 C4
Smeaton Rd. SP2 38 B1
Somerset Rd. SP1 37 E5
South St. SP2 38 D1
South Western Rd. SP2 38 C1
Southampton Rd. SP1 39 E2
*Spring Ct,
Windsor Rd. SP1 38 C1
Stanley Little Rd. SP2 35 C3
Station Ter. SP2 38 C1
Stephens Clo. SP2 38 B3
Stephenson Rd. SP2 38 B1
Stockwood Clo. SP1 37 F5
Stratford Ct. SP1 36 D5
Stratford Rd. SP1 36 B2
Suffolk Rd. SP2 38 B3
Summerlock App. SP2 38 D1
Sunnyhill Rd. SP1 37 E4
Sussex Rd. SP2 38 B4
Swallow Mead. SP2 38 D5
Swan Clo. SP2 38 D4
Swaynes Clo. SP1 37 E6
Swift Down. SP2 38 D4
Sycamore Dri. SP1 37 F3
Syringa Ct. SP2 38 A1

Talbot Clo. SP1 37 F4
Telford Rd. SP2 38 B2
The Avenue, Fugglestone
St Peter. SP2 35 A3
The Avenue,
Laverstock. SP1 37 G6
The Avenue,
Salisbury. SP1 39 F1
The Beeches. SP1 39 F2
The Brambles. SP1 37 F6
The Crusades. SP1 37 F3
The Crescent. SP1 39 E1
The Friary. SP1 39 E2
*The Green,
Church Rd. SP1 37 G6
*The Hardings,
Devizes Rd. SP2 36 C6
The Kingsway. SP2 35 A2
The Maples. SP2 36 C6
The Meadows. SP1 39 G2
The Oak Bournes. SP1 37 F3
The Orchard. SP1 37 F6
The Portway. SP1 36 C4
The Steadings. SP4 37 G2
The Valley. SP2 35 D1
Thistlebarrow Rd. SP1 36 D3
Thompson Clo. SP2 38 C5
Tollgate Rd. SP1 39 E2
Tournament Rd. SP2 36 A5
Tower Mews. SP1 37 E6
Town Path. SP2 38 C2
Trinity St. SP1 39 E2
Tryhorn Dri. SP1 37 F3
Turner Clo. SP2 38 B3
Tylers Clo. SP2 38 B3

Upper St. SP2 38 B3

*Vanessa Av,
The Avenue. SP1 37 G6

Ventry Clo. SP1 37 E5
Verona Rd. SP1 36 C3
Victoria Ct. SP1 36 D4
Victoria Dri East. SP2 39 E6
Victoria Rd. SP1 36 D5
Viking Way. SP2 39 E4

Wain-a-long Rd. SP1 37 F6
Warwick Clo. SP1 37 D5
Waterloo Rd. SP1 39 F2
Waters Rd. SP1 36 D4
Watersmeet Rd. SP2 38 D3
Watt Rd. SP2 38 B2
Wavel Rd. SP2 38 D4
Wellington Way. SP2 36 A5
Wessex Rd. SP1 39 F1
West End Rd. SP2 36 B6
West St. SP2 38 C1
West Walk. SP1 38 D2
Westbourne Clo. SP1 39 F1
Western Way. SP2 35 C3
Westfield Clo. SP1 37 G6
Westminster Rd. SP2 36 C6
Westwood Rd. SP2 35 C2
Whitbred Rd. SP2 35 D1
Whitebridge Rd. SP1 39 G1
Whitefriars Way. SP1 39 E2
*William Clo,
  Riverside Rd. SP1 37 G6
Willow Clo. SP1 37 G6
Wilman Way. SP2 38 C5
Wilton Rd,
  Quidhampton. SP2 35 B3
Wilton Rd. SP2 36 A6
Wiltshire Rd. SP2 38 B3
Winchester St. SP1 39 E1
Winding Way. SP2 35 D3
Windlesham Rd. SP1 37 E4
Windsor Clo. SP2 38 C1
Windsor St. SP2 38 C1
Wolferston Dri. SP1 37 G3
Woodbury Gdns. SP2 39 E4
Woodford Rd. SP2 36 A1
Woodland Way. SP1 37 G6
Woodside Rd. SP2 35 D3
Woodstock Rd. SP1 37 E6
Woodville Rd. SP1 37 F4
Wordsworth Rd. SP1 37 E6
Wrenscroft. SP2 38 D5
Wylye Clo. SP2 35 B4
Wyndham Rd. SP1 36 D6
Wyndham Ter. SP1 37 E6

York Rd. SP2 36 C6

SWINDON

Abbey View Rd. SN2 41 E3
Abington Way. SN2 42 B2
Abney Moor. SN3 47 G5
Acacia Gro. SN2 41 H4
Acorn Clo. SN3 47 E3
Aden Ct. SN2 41 F1
Addison Cres. SN2 42 C3
Adwalton Clo. SN5 44 B4
Affleck Clo. SN5 44 C3
Ainsworth Rd. SN3 46 D4
Akenfield Clo. SN2 41 F2
Akers Way. SN2 40 D4
Alanbrooke Cres. SN2 41 F5
Alba Clo. SN5 44 A1
Albert St. SN1 46 A4
Albion St. SN1 45 G3
Aldborough Clo. SN5 44 C1
Aldbourne Clo. SN2 41 H1
Alder Clo. SN2 40 D2
Alexandra Rd. SN1 45 H1
Alfred St. SN1 46 A1
Allington Rd. SN2 41 G1
Allison Ct. SN2 41 F4
Alnwick. SN5 44 C4
Alpine Clo. SN5 44 B1
Alton Clo. SN2 41 H1
Alvescot Rd. SN3 46 B3
Alveston Clo. SN5 44 D2
Amber Ct. SN1 46 B1
Amberley Clo. SN2 41 H3
Ambrose Rd. SN1 46 A5
Amersham Rd. SN3 47 E4
Amesbury Clo. SN3 41 H1
Ancona Clo. SN5 44 B1
Anderson Clo. SN3 47 F4
Andover St. SN1 45 F3
Angelica Clo. SN2 40 D3
Angler Rd. SN5 44 B1

Anglesey Clo. SN5 44 C2
Angus Clo. SN5 44 B1
Anise Clo. SN2 40 C3
Ansty Walk. SN2 41 G1
Applewood Ct. SN5 44 D3
Archers Clo. SN2 42 C1
Argyle St. SN2 42 A5
Arkwright Rd. SN2 42 A1
Arley Clo. SN2 41 F1
Arlington Clo. SN3 47 E1
Arliss Clo. SN2 41 G1
Armstrong St. SN1 46 A1
Arnfield Moor. SN3 47 G5
Arun Rd. SN2 41 F3
Arundel Clo. SN3 46 C4
Ascham Rd. SN5 44 B2
Ash Gdns. SN5 40 B5
Ash Gdns. SN3 43 G3
Ash Gro. SN2 41 H4
Ashburnham Clo. SN5 44 A4
Ashbury Av. SN3 47 E1
Ashford Rd. SN1 45 G3
Ashie Clo. SN5 44 C3
Ashington Way. SN5 44 C3
Ashkirk Clo. SN3 46 B2
Ashley Clo. SN3 46 C2
Ashmore Clo. SN3 47 F2
Ashwell Clo. SN3 46 C3
Ashworth Dri. SN5 45 E2
Askerton Clo. SN5 40 A6
Askew Clo. SN5 44 A3
Atbara Clo. SN2 41 F3
Athena Av. SN2 42 B5
Attlee Cres. SN2 42 C3

*Atworth Clo,
  Chippenham Way.
  SN2 41 G1
Auden Clo. SN2 41 E1
Audley Clo. SN5 44 A4
Austen Cres. SN3 47 F3
Avebury Rd. SN2 41 G2
Avening St. SN2 42 A6
Avens Clo. SN2 40 D2
Avenue Rd. SN1 46 A4
Avocet Clo. SN3 42 D2
Avonmead. SN2 41 E3
Axbridge Clo. SN3 46 D3
Aylesbury St. SN1 45 H1
Aymer Pl. SN3 47 E3
Ayrshire Clo. SN5 44 B1
Azelin Ct. SN3 43 E4

Babington Pk. SN5 44 A3
Bainbridge Clo. SN5 44 A3
Baird Clo. SN5 40 B6
Bakers Clo. SN3 43 E4
Bale Clo. SN5 44 A3
Balmoral Clo. SN3 46 D5
Bampton Gro. SN3 46 B2
Banbury Clo. SN3 46 C4
Bancroft Clo. SN5 44 A2
Bankfoot Clo. SN5 44 C1
Bankside. SN1 45 F4
Banwell Av. SN3 46 D3
Barbury Clo. SN2 41 E3
Barn Moor Clo. SN3 47 G4
Barnard Clo. SN3 47 E1
Barnfield Clo. SN2 45 E1
Barnfield Rd. SN2 45 E1
Barnstable Clo. SN3 46 D3
Barnstead Clo. SN5 44 B4
Barnum Ct. SN2 45 F1
Baron Clo. SN3 43 E3
Barrington Clo. SN3 47 G5
Barrowby Gate. SN3 42 C5
Barry Glen Clo. SN2 45 E1
Barton Rd. SN2 41 E3
Basil Clo. SN2 40 D3
Basingstoke Clo. SN5 44 B4
Baskerville Rd. SN3 47 G5
Bath Rd. SN1 45 H4
Bathampton St. SN1 45 G2
Bathurst Rd. SN1 46 A1
Baxter Clo. SN2 41 F1
Baydon Clo. SN2 41 E3
Bayleaf Av. SN2 40 D2
Beales Clo. SN1 45 H1
Beatrice St. SN2 41 H6
Beauchamp Clo. SN2 41 E3
Beaufort Grn. SN3 47 E3
Beaulieu Clo. SN3 44 D4
Beaumaris Rd. SN5 44 C3
Beaumont Rd. SN3 46 C2
Beckhampton St. SN1 46 A2
Beddington Ct. SN5 44 D2
Bedford Rd. SN3 46 C2
Bedwyn Clo. SN2 42 A4

Beech Av. SN2 41 F4
Beech Dri. SN5 40 B4
Beechcroft Rd. SN2 42 B3
Beehive Clo. SN5 40 A6
Belgrave St. SN1 46 A3
Bell Gdns. SN3 43 G3
Belle Vue Rd. SN1 46 A3
Bellver. SN5 44 C3
Belmont Clo. SN3 42 D3
Belmont Cres. SN1 45 G5
Belsay. SN5 44 C3
Belvedere Rd. SN3 46 D4
Bembridge Clo. SN3 47 E3
Bentley Clo. SN3 46 D2
Benwell Clo. SN5 44 C2
Berenger Clo. SN1 46 B4
Beresford Clo. SN3 47 F4
Bergman Clo. SN2 41 G1
Berkeley Lawns. SN1 46 C5
Berkshire Dri. SN5 44 B1
Berrington Rd. SN3 46 D4
Berry Copse. SN5 40 A5
Bess Rd. SN5 44 A4
Bessemer Clo. SN2 41 F5
Bessemer Rd East. SN2 41 F5
Bessemer Rd West.
  SN2 41 F5
Betony Clo. SN2 41 E2
Bevan Clo. SN2 42 C4
Beverley. SN5 44 C4
Beverstone Gro. SN3 46 C4
Bevil. SN5 44 B4
Bevisland. SN3 47 E4
Bibury Rd. SN3 46 B3
Bicton Rd. SN3 46 D3
Bideford Clo. SN5 44 A3
Bindon Clo. SN5 45 F4
Birch St. SN1 45 F4
Birchwood Rd. SN3 43 E5
Birdbrook Rd. SN2 42 C2
Birdcombe Rd. SN5 44 C2
Bishopdale Clo. SN5 46 D3
Bisley Clo. SN3 46 D3
Bittern Rd. SN3 47 G2
Blackmore Clo. SN3 47 G1
Blackstone Av. SN3 47 F3
Blackthorn La. SN2 41 G3
Blake Cres. SN3 43 E4
Blakeney Av. SN3 47 E1
Blakesley Clo. SN3 46 D4
Blandford Ct. SN3 47 E2
Bletchley Clo. SN3 47 F4
Blockley Rise. SN3 42 D2
Bloomsbury Clo. SN5 44 B3
Blunsdon Rd. SN2 41 E1
Bodiam Dri. SN5 44 D3
Bodiam Dri North. SN5 44 D3
Bodiam Dri South. SN5 44 D4
Bodmin Clo. SN3 46 D2
Boldrewood. SN3 47 F4
Boleyn Clo. SN5 44 A2
Bolingbroke Rd. SN2 41 E4
Bonner Clo. SN5 44 A2
Borage Rd. SN2 40 D2
Boscombe Rd. SN2 41 E3
Bosham Clo. SN5 44 C3
Bosworth Rd. SN5 44 B2
Bothwell Rd. SN3 46 C1
Botley Copse. SN5 40 B4
Boundary Clo. SN2 42 C1
Bourne Rd. SN2 41 E4
Bourton Av. SN3 43 E5
Bouverie Av. SN3 46 B4
Bowles Rd. SN2 41 F2
Bowleymead. SN3 47 F2
Bowling Green La. SN1 46 A5
Bowman Clo. SN3 43 E4
Bowood Rd. SN1 45 G4
Boydell Clo. SN5 40 B6
Bradenham Rd. SN5 44 A3
Bradford Rd. SN1 46 A4
Bradley Rd. SN2 42 B3
Bradwell Moor. SN3 47 G5
Braemar Clo. SN3 46 D5
Bramble Clo. SN2 42 B5
Bramble Rd. SN2 42 C5
Bramdean Clo. SN2 41 F1
Bramwell Clo. SN2 42 C1
Brandon Clo. SN5 44 B3
Branksome Rd. SN2 41 E3
Bratton Clo. SN3 41 G2
Braybrooke Rd. SN5 40 A6
Brecon Clo. SN3 46 C5
Brem Hill Clo. SN2 41 H2
Brendon Walk. SN3 47 E2
Briar Fields. SN1 46 B1
Bridge End Rd. SN3 42 C6

Bridge St. SN1 45 G2
Bridgeman Clo. SN3 43 E4
Bridgemead Clo. SN5 44 D1
Bridgewater Clo. SN2 45 F1
Bridport Rd. SN3 46 D3
Briery Clo. SN3 42 D3
Bright St. SN2 42 B6
Brind Clo. SN3 47 G2
Brindley Clo. SN2 41 E6
Brington Rd. SN3 43 E6
Bristol St. SN1 45 G2
Britannia Pl. SN1 46 A4
Brixham Av. SN3 46 C3
Broad St. SN1 46 A3
Broadmead Walk. SN3 47 E1
Broadway. SN2 41 G2
Bromley Clo. SN3 46 C2
Bronte Clo. SN3 47 F4
Brook Lime Clo. SN2 40 D2
Brookdene. SN2 41 E2
Brooklands Av. SN2 41 F5
Brooks Clo. SN2 42 B2
Brooksby Way. SN3 44 D3
Broome Manor La. SN3 46 C5
Browning Clo. SN3 43 E3
Bruce St. SN2 45 F1
Bruddel Gro. SN3 46 B5
Brunswick St. SN1 45 H3
Bryanston Way. SN3 47 E2
Bryant Rd. SN2 40 C2
Bryony Way. SN2 40 D2
Buckhurst Cres. SN3 46 D2
Buckingham Rd. SN3 46 D5
Buckland Clo. SN3 46 D2
Bucklebury Clo. SN3 42 D5
Buckthorn Dri. SN2 40 D3
Buie Clo. SN5 40 C4
Buller St. SN2 42 B6
Bullfinch Clo. SN3 47 G2
Bunce Rd. SN3 42 D5
Burbage Rd. SN2 42 H1
Burden Clo. SN3 43 E5
Burford Av. SN3 46 B3
Burgess Clo. SN3 42 D5
Burghley Clo. SN3 46 D2
Burnet Clo. SN2 40 D2
Burnham Clo. SN3 46 D2
Burns Way. SN2 42 C3
Buttermere. SN3 47 G4
Butterworth St. SN1 45 F2
Byfield Way. SN3 43 E6
Byrd Clo. SN5 44 A3
Byron Ct. SN3 43 G2
Byron St. SN1 46 A3

Cabot Dri. SN5 44 A2
Cadley Clo. SN3 42 A4
Caen Vw. SN5 45 E3
Caernarvon Walk. SN3 46 C5
Cagney Dri. SN2 41 F1
Cairndow Way. SN2 42 B2
Calder Clo. SN2 41 F2
Callaghan Clo. SN3 42 D4
Callenders. SN5 44 D2
Calvert Rd. SN3 46 B2
Cambria Bri Rd. SN1 45 G2
Cambria Pl. SN1 45 G3
Cambridge Clo. SN3 46 C4
Camden Clo. SN5 44 A3
Cameron Clo. SN3 42 D5
Campden Rd. SN3 46 B3
Campion Gate. SN5 44 A2
Camton Rd. SN5 44 A1
Canal Walk. SN1 45 G2
Canford Clo. SN3 47 E2
Cannon St. SN1 46 A3
Canterbury Clo. SN3 46 A5
Capesthorne Dri. SN2 41 E1
Capitol Clo. SN3 43 F6
Caprice Clo. SN5 44 A1
Cardigan Clo. SN3 46 D4
Cardwell Clo. SN3 47 E1
Carey Clo. SN5 44 B3
Carfax St. SN1 45 H1
Carlisle Av. SN3 46 B4
Carlton Gate. SN3 46 D6
Carman Clo. SN3 47 F4
Carronbridge Rd. SN5 44 C2
Carshalton Rd. SN3 47 E4
Carslake Clo. SN3 43 E3
Carstairs Av. SN3 46 D4
Carter Clo. SN3 41 H1
Cartwright Dri. SN5 40 B6

Casson Rd. SN3 42 D4
Castilian Mews. SN5 44 B3
Castle Dore. SN5 44 B3
Castlefield Clo. SN5 44 C2
Castleton Rd. SN5 44 A1
Castleview Rd. SN3 43 F5
Catherine St. SN1 45 G2
Catherine Wayte Clo.
  SN2 41 F3
Caulfield Rd. SN2 40 D3
Caversham Clo. SN3 46 C3
Cavie Clo. SN5 40 A6
Caxton Clo. SN3 46 C3
*Caxton Ct,
  Caxton Clo. SN3 46 C3
Cayenne Pk. SN2 40 C3
Cecil Rd. SN3 46 D2
Cedars Clo. SN2 41 F4
Centurion Way. SN3 43 F6
Chadworth Gate. SN3 46 C6
Chalford Av. SN3 47 E1
Chamberlain Rd. SN3 42 D4
Chancellor Clo. SN5 44 A2
Chandler Clo. SN1 46 B3
Chandos Clo. SN5 44 B2
Chantry Rd. SN2 41 E4
Chapel Rd. SN3 43 G2
Chapel St. SN2 42 B6
Charfield Clo. SN3 46 D4
Charlbury Clo. SN2 41 E3
Charles McPherson
  Gdns. SN3 47 F3
Charlotte Mews. SN1 46 B4
Charlton Clo. SN2 42 A2
Charminster Clo. SN3 47 E2
Charolais Dri. SN5 44 B1
Chartley Grn. SN5 44 A3
Chase Wood. SN5 40 A5
Chatsworth Rd. SN2 41 F2
Cheddar Rd. SN2 41 E3
Chelmsford Rd. SN5 44 C1
Cheltenham St. SN1 45 G1
Chelworth Rd. SN2 41 E3
Cheney Manor Rd. SN2 41 F4
Chepstow Clo. SN5 44 C4
Cheraton Clo. SN3 41 E3
Cherhill Ct. SN2 41 E3
Cherry Tree Gro. SN2 41 H4
Chervil Clo. SN2 40 D2
Chesford Clo. SN3 46 D5
Chester St. SN1 45 G2
Chesterfield Clo. SN5 44 C2
Chestnut Av. SN2 42 A4
Chevalier Clo. SN5 44 A1
Cheviot Clo. SN5 44 B2
Chickerell Rd. SN3 46 D2
Chicory Clo. SN2 40 C3
Chilton Gdns. SN2 41 E4
Chilworth Clo. SN2 41 E1
Chippenham Clo. SN2 41 G1
Chippenham Way. SN2 41 G1
Chives Way. SN2 40 D3
Chobham Clo. SN3 42 D2
Christie Clo. SN3 47 F4
Chudleigh. SN5 44 B4
Church Grnd. SN3 43 H2
Church Pl. SN1 45 F2
Church St. SN3 43 E4
Church Walk. SN2 42 C4
Church Walk Nth. SN2 41 F3
Church Walk Sth. SN2 41 F4
Church Way. SN2 42 D5
Churchfield. SN2 41 E2
Churchward Av. SN2 41 F5
Cirencester Way. SN2 42 B6
Clanfield Rd. SN3 47 E3
Clare Walk. SN5 44 C3
Clarence St. SN1 45 H2
Clarendon La. SN1 45 F3
Clarke Dri. SN5 40 B6
Clary Rd. SN2 40 D2
Clayhill Copse. SN5 40 A5
Clays Clo. SN2 42 B3
Cleasby Clo. SN5 44 D2
Cleeve Lawns. SN1 46 C5
Clevedon Clo. SN3 46 D1
Cleves Clo. SN5 44 B2
Clifton St. SN1 45 G3
Clinton Clo. SN5 44 A3
Cloche Way. SN2 42 C4
Cloudberry Rd. SN2 41 E1
Clouts Wood. SN5 40 B4
Clover Lands. SN2 40 D2
Clover Pk. SN5 40 D3
Clydesdale Clo. SN5 44 B1

Cobden Rd. SN2   41 F6
Colbert Pk. SN2   41 F1
Colbourne St. SN1   46 B1
Colchester Clo. SN5   44 D4
Cole Clo. SN3   47 F2
Colebrook Rd. SN3   43 E6
Coleridge Rd. SN2   41 E1
College St. SN1   45 H2
Collett Av. SN2   41 F5
Collingsmead. SN3   47 F3
Collins La. SN5   40 A2
Colman Pk. SN2   41 F1
Coln Cres. SN2   41 F2
Colston Clo. SN3   46 D3
Comfrey Clo. SN2   40 D3
Commercial Rd. SN1   45 G2
Commonweal Rd. SN1   45 G4
Compton Clo. SN3   47 E4
Conan Doyle Walk. SN3   47 G4
Conisborough. SN5   44 C3
Conrad Clo. SN3   47 F4
Constable Rd. SN2   42 C4
Constantine Clo. SN3   43 F6
Conway Rd. SN3   47 F4
Conyers Clo. SN5   44 A3
Coombe Rd. SN2   41 E3
Cooper Fld. SN2   41 F1
Coppice Clo. SN2   40 D3
Copse Av. SN1   42 C6
Corby Av. SN3   46 B5
Corfe Clo. SN2   41 F3
Corfe Rd. SN5   44 C3
Coriander Way. SN2   40 D2
Corinium Way. SN3   43 F6
Cornflower Rd. SN2   40 D2
Cornmarsh Way. SN3   47 G1
Cornwall Rd. SN2   41 G5
Corporation St. SN1   46 A1
Corral Clo. SN5   40 B6
Corsham Rd. SN2   41 H2
Corton Cres. SN5   44 C2
Cottars Clo. SN3   43 E3
Cottington Clo. SN5   44 B4
County Rd. SN1   46 B1
Courtenay Rd. SN2   46 D2
Courtsknap Ct. SN1   45 F3
Covingham Dri. SN3   43 F6
Cowdrey Clo. SN5   44 C4
Cowleaze Walk. SN2   42 C3
Crabtree Copse. SN5   40 B5
Crampton Rd. SN3   46 D1
Cranborne Chase. SN2   40 C2
Cranmore Av. SN3   46 D4
Crawford Clo. SN5   44 B4
Crawley Av. SN3   43 E5
Cricklade Rd. SN2   42 A1
Cricklade St. SN1   46 B3
Crieff Clo. SN3   47 E2
Crispin Clo. SN3   43 E3
Croftmead. SN1   45 H5
Croft Rd. SN1   46 A6
Crombey St. SN1   45 G2
Crompton Rd. SN2   42 A1
Cromwell. SN5   44 B4
Cross St. SN1   46 A3
Crossways Av. SN2   41 H3
Crosswood Rd. SN3   46 D4
Crudwell Way. SN2   41 H1
Cuckoos Mead. SN3   47 G1
Cullerne Rd. SN3   43 F5
Cumberland Rd. SN3   46 B2
Cunetio Rd. SN3   43 F6
Cunningham Rd. SN2   41 G4
Curtis St. SN1   45 G3
Cypress Gro. SN2   41 G4

Dacre Rd. SN3   46 D2
Daisy Clo. SN2   40 D3
Dalefoot Clo. SN5   40 A5
Dallas Av. SN3   47 E1
Dalton Clo. SN3   46 D1
Dalwood Clo. SN3   47 E4
Dammas La. SN1   46 B4
Danestone Clo. SN5   44 A1
Darcey Clo. SN5   44 A2
Darius Way. SN3   41 F1
Darnley Clo. SN3   46 C2
Dart Av. SN2   41 G3
Darwin Clo. SN3   47 E1
Dave Watkins Ct. SN2   42 C4
Davenham Clo. SN3   46 D4
Davenwood. SN2   42 C2
Dawlish Rd. SN3   47 E2
Day House La. SN3   47 E5
Days Clo. SN3   42 D5
Deacon St. SN1   45 G3
Dean St. SN2   45 F2

Deben Cres. SN2   41 F2
Deburgh St. SN2   45 F2
Deerhurst Way. SN5   44 D3
Delamere Dri. SN3   42 D3
Denbeck Wood. SN5   44 C1
Denbigh Clo. SN3   46 C4
Denholme Rd. SN3   46 D4
Denton Ct. SN3   43 E4
Derby Clo. SN2   41 E5
Derwent Dri. SN2   42 C2
Desborough. SN5   44 B5
Deva Clo. SN3   43 F6
*Devereux Clo,
   Grindal Clo. SN5   44 A3
Devizes Rd. SN1   46 A4
Devon Rd. SN2   41 G5
Dewberry Clo. SN2   41 E2
Dewell Mews. SN1   46 B4
Dexter Clo. SN5   44 B2
Dickens Clo. SN3   47 F4
Dickenson Rd. SN2   40 C2
Dinmore Rd. SN2   41 F1
Dixon St. SN1   45 G3
Dobbin Clo. SN3   47 G1
Dockle Way. SN2   42 C3
Don Clo. SN2   41 F2
Donnington Gro. SN3   46 C4
Dorcan Way. SN3   47 E1
Dorchester Rd. SN1   46 C4
Dores Ct. SN2   42 B3
Dores Rd. SN2   42 B3
Douglas Rd. SN3   46 C2
Dover St. SN1   46 A3
Dovetrees. SN3   47 G1
Dowling St. SN1   45 H3
Downland Rd. SN2   40 D3
Downs View Rd. SN3   46 C6
Downton Rd. SN2   41 G2
Doyle Clo. SN3   40 C2
Drakes Mdw. SN3   46 C1
Drakes Way. SN3   46 C2
Draycott Clo. SN3   46 D2
Drew St. SN2   45 E1
Drove Rd. SN1   46 B3
Dryden St. SN1   45 G3
Duchess Way. SN2   42 B2
Dudley Rd. SN3   46 B2
Dudmore Rd. SN3   46 B2
Dukes Clo. SN2   42 B2
Dulverton Av. SN3   46 D3
Dunbarton Ter. SN1   46 A3
Dunbeath Rd. SN2   42 B5
Dunraven Clo. SN3   46 C4
Dunsford Clo. SN1   45 F3
Dunster Clo. SN3   46 C5
Dunwich Dri. SN5   44 D3
Durham St. SN1   46 A3
Durnford Rd. SN2   42 A2
Durrington Walk. SN2   41 H2

Eagle Clo. SN3   47 G1
Ealing Way. SN25   41 E1
Earl Clo. SN5   44 A1
East St. SN1   45 G2
Eastcott Hill. SN1   45 H3
Eastcott Rd. SN1   45 H3
Eastern Av. SN3   46 B2
Eastleaze Rd. SN5   44 C2
Eastmere. SN3   47 G4
Eastville Rd. SN2   41 H3
Eaton Clo. SN3   46 D4
Eaton Wood. SN5   40 A5
Eccleston Clo. SN3   47 E4
Ecklington. SN3   47 E3
Edale Moor. SN3   47 G5
Edgehill. SN3   44 B4
Edgeware Rd. SN1   45 H2
Edgeworth Clo. SN5   44 C1
Edinburgh St. SN2   42 A5
Edington Clo. SN3   44 C3
Edison Rd. SN3   47 F3
Edmund St. SN1   46 A3
Egerton Clo. SN3   47 E1
Elborough Rd. SN2   40 D3
Eldene Dri. SN3   47 E3
Elder Clo. SN2   40 D3
Elgin Dri. SN2   42 B5
Eliot Clo. SN3   47 G4
Elm Gro. SN5   40 B6
Elm Rd. SN2   41 F4
Elmina Rd. SN1   46 A1
Elmore. SN3   47 F2
Elmswood Clo. SN2   42 B2
Elsham Way. SN2   41 F2
Elsie Hazel Ct. SN5   44 B4
Elstree Way. SN2   41 F1
Ely Clo. SN5   44 D3

Emerson Clo. SN2   41 G1
Emlyn Sq. SN1   45 G2
Emmanuel Clo. SN2   41 F2
Enford Av. SN2   41 H1
Eric Long Clo. SN3   47 G2
Erlestoke Way. SN2   41 H1
Ermin St. SN3   42 C2
Espringham Pl. SN2   42 B2
Essex Walk. SN2   46 C2
Euclid St. SN1   46 A2
Euro Way. SN5   44 A5
Evelyn St. SN3   46 B5
Evergreens Clo. SN3   43 E5
Everleigh Rd. SN2   41 H2
Eworth Clo. SN5   44 A3
Exbury Clo. SN2   41 F1
Exe Clo. SN2   41 G2
Exeter St. SN1   45 G2
Exmouth St. SN1   45 G3

Fairfax Clo. SN3   46 C1
Fairford Cres. SN2   41 H3
Fairholme Way. SN2   42 C3
Fairlawn. SN3   47 F5
Fairview. SN1   45 G3
Falconscroft. SN3   47 F1
Falmouth Gro. SN1   46 C3
Faloner Mews. SN   41 G1
Fanstones Rd. SN3   47 E4
Faraday Rd. SN3   47 E3
Fareham Clo. SN3   47 E3
Faringdon Rd. SN1   45 G2
Farleigh Cres. SN3   46 C5
Farman Clo. SN3   47 F4
Farmer Cres. SN2   41 H1
Farnborough Rd. SN3   46 D5
Farnsby St. SN1   45 G2
Farrfield. SN2   42 C3
Farriers Clo. SN1   42 B6
Feather Wood. SN5   44 D3
Fenland Clo. SN5   44 A1
Fennel Clo. SN2   40 D2
Ferndale Rd. SN2   41 F6
Fernham Rd. SN3   41 E4
Ferrers Dri. SN5   44 A3
Field Rise. SN1   45 G5
Fieldfare. SN3   47 F1
Finchdale. SN3   43 F6
Fir Tree Clo. SN2   41 F4
Firecrest Vw. SN3   47 G2
Firth Clo. SN2   41 F3
Fitzmaurice Clo. SN3   47 F1
Fitzroy Rd. SN1   46 A5
Fleet St. SN1   45 G2
Fleetwood Ct. SN5   44 B4
Fleming Way. SN1   45 H2
Flint Hill. SN5   44 C4
Florence St. SN2   41 H6
Folkestone Rd. SN1   46 C3
Fonthill Walk. SN3   45 F3
Ford St. SN1   45 F3
Forester Clo. SN3   47 G3
Forsey Clo. SN3   47 G1
Forum Clo. SN3   43 F6
Fosse Clo. SN2   45 E2
Fovant Clo. SN5   40 B5
Fowey. SN5   44 B4
Fox Hill Clo. SN2   41 F3
Foxbridge. SN3   47 G1
Foxglove Rd. SN2   40 D2
Foxley Clo. SN2   42 B3
Foxwood. SN5   44 D3
Frampton Clo. SN5   44 C2
Francomes. SN2   41 E2
Frankland Rd. SN5   44 A5
Frankton Gdns. SN3   43 E5
Fraser Clo. SN3   47 E1
Freshbrook Way. SN5   44 B3
Friesian Clo. SN3   44 B1
Friesland Clo. SN3   44 B1
Frilford Dri. SN3   42 D5
Frith Copse. SN5   40 B4
Frobisher Dri. SN3   46 C2
Frome Rd. SN2   41 F3
Fry Clo. SN5   45 F3
Fullers Clo. SN3   42 C2
Furlong Clo. SN2   41 E2
Furze Clo. SN5   40 B5
Fyfield Av. SN2   41 F1
Fyne Clo. SN5   40 C5

Gable Clo. SN2   41 G1
Gainsborough Way.
   SN5   44 B4
Gairlock Clo. SN5   40 C4
Galloway Clo. SN5   44 B1
Galloway Rd. SN5   40 C2

Galsworthy Clo. SN3   47 G3
Gambia St. SN1   46 B2
Gantlett Dene. SN3   47 G2
Ganton Clo. SN2   42 C5
Ganton Way. SN2   42 C5
Garfield Clo. SN3   47 F4
Garrard Way. SN3   42 D6
Garside Grn. SN2   42 B2
Garson Rd. SN2   41 G1
Gartons Rd. SN5   44 A1
Gaynor Clo. SN2   41 F1
Gays Pl. SN2   42 C2
Gayton Way. SN3   43 E6
George St. SN1   45 F2
Gerard Walk. SN5   44 B2
Gibbs Clo. SN3   47 G1
Gifford Rd. SN3   43 E3
Gilberts Hill. SN1   45 H3
Gilling Way. SN3   47 G2
Gipsy La. SN2   42 B6
Gladstone St. SN1   46 A1
Glenmore Rd. SN2   40 C2
Glenwood Clo. SN1   46 A6
Glevum Rd. SN3   43 F6
Globe St. SN1   45 H3
Gloucester St. SN1   45 H1
Goddard Av. SN1   45 G4
Godolphin Clo. SN5   44 A4
Godwin Rd. SN3   43 E3
Goldcrest Walk. SN3   47 G1
Goldsborough Clo. SN5   44 C2
Gooch St. SN1   46 A1
Gordon Gdns. SN1   45 H2
Gordon Rd. SN1   46 A2
Goulding Clo. SN3   42 D4
Gower Clo. SN5   44 A3
Gower Clo. SN2   42 C4
Grafton Rd. SN2   42 A2
Graham St. SN1   46 A1
Grailey Clo. SN3   47 F4
Granary Clo. SN5   40 A6
Grandison Clo. SN3   44 A2
Grange Dri. SN3   42 D5
Grange Park Way. SN5   44 A4
Grantham Clo. SN5   44 B5
Grantley Clo. SN3   46 D4
Granville St. SN1   45 H2
Grasmere. SN3   47 G4
Graythwaite Clo. SN2   41 F1
Great Western Way.
   SN5   44 A5
Green Hill Rd. SN2   41 F4
Green Meadow Av. SN2   41 F3
Green Rd. SN2   42 B3
Green Valley Av. SN2   41 F2
Greenbridge Rd. SN3   46 D1
Greenfields. SN3   43 G2
Greenlands Rd. SN2   42 C4
Greenway Clo. SN3   47 E1
Greenwich Clo. SN2   41 F2
Gresham Clo. SN3   46 C2
Greywethers Av. SN3   46 B4
Griffiths Clo. SN3   43 E5
Grindal Dri. SN5   44 A3
Grosmont Dri. SN5   44 B3
Grosvenor Rd. SN1   45 F4
Groundwell Rd. SN1   46 A2
Grovelands Av. SN1   46 A5
Grovellly Clo. SN5   40 B5
Groves St. SN2   45 F2
Grundys. SN3   47 F4
Guildford Av. SN3   46 C5
Guppy St. SN1   45 F2

Hackett Clo. SN2   42 B2
Hackleton Rise. SN3   43 E6
Haddon Clo. SN5   44 A3
Hadleigh Clo. SN5   44 D2
Hadleigh Rise. SN3   42 D2
Hadrians Clo. SN3   43 F6
Haig Clo. SN2   42 B3
Hallam Moor. SN3   47 G5
Hamble Rd. SN2   41 F3
Hamilton Clo. SN3   46 C1
Hampshire Clo. SN5   44 B1
Hampton Dri. SN5   44 A2
Hamworthy Rd. SN3   47 F2
Hanbury Rd. SN3   46 D4
Handel St. SN2   41 H6
Hannington Clo. SN2   41 G1
Hanson Clo. SN5   44 B1
Harbour Clo. SN2   41 F3
Harcourt Rd. SN2   41 F6
Hardie St. SN2   42 D5
Hardwick Clo. SN2   41 F2
Hare Clo. SN3   42 C1
Harebell Clo. SN2   41 E2

Hargreaves Rd. SN2   42 B1
Harlech Clo. SN5   44 C4
Harlestone Rd. SN3   43 E6
Harptree Clo. SN5   40 A6
Harrington Walk. SN3   46 D1
Harris Rd. SN2   41 F5
Harrow Clo. SN3   42 D5
Hartland Clo. SN3   46 D3
Hartsthorn Clo. SN2   40 D3
Harvester Clo. SN5   40 A6
Harvey Gro. SN2   41 F5
Haslemere Clo. SN3   47 E4
Hatfield Clo. SN2   41 E1
Hathaway Rd. SN2   42 B2
Hatherall Clo. SN3   43 F5
Hatherley Rd. SN3   47 E1
Hathersage Moor. SN3   47 G5
Hatton Gro. SN3   46 C2
Havelock St. SN1   45 H2
Haven Clo. SN3   47 E3
Hawker Rd. SN3   47 F4
Hawkfinch Clo. SN3   47 G2
Hawkins St. SN2   45 F1
Hawkswood. SN3   43 F6
Hawksworth Way. SN2   45 G1
Hawthorn Av. SN2   41 H4
Hay La. SN4   44 A6
Haydon Ct. SN2   41 E2
Haydon Court Dri. SN2   41 E2
Haydon End La. SN2   41 E1
Haydon St. SN1   45 H1
Haydon View Rd. SN2   41 F2
Haydonleigh Dri. SN2   41 E2
Haynes Clo. SN3   47 E4
Hayward Clo. SN2   41 G1
Hazebury Cres. SN3   47 F1
Hazel Gro. SN2   41 H3
Headlands Gro. SN2   42 B4
Heath Way. SN3   43 E6
Heathcote Clo. SN5   40 B6
Heaton Clo. SN2   41 F1
Heddington Clo. SN2   41 H2
Hedgerow Clo. SN3   47 E3
Hedges Clo. SN3   43 E4
Helmsdale. SN3   41 E3
Helston Rd. SN3   46 D3
Henley Rd. SN3   46 D4
Henman Clo. SN2   41 F2
Henry St. SN1   45 G2
Hepworth Rd. SN3   47 F4
Hereford Lawns. SN3   46 C5
Hermitage La. SN2   42 B3
Heronbridge Clo. SN5   44 C2
Heronscroft. SN3   47 F1
Hertford Clo. SN3   46 C2
Hesketh Cres. SN3   46 A5
Hewitt Clo. SN3   47 F4
Hexham Clo. SN5   44 B3
Heytsbury Gdns. SN5   44 A4
Heywood Clo. SN2   41 G2
High St. SN2   41 E2
High St. SN1   46 B4
Highclere Av. SN2   46 C4
Highland Clo. SN5   44 B1
Highmoor Copse. SN5   40 A5
Highnam Clo. SN3   42 D5
Highwood Clo. SN2   40 D3
Highworth Rd. SN3   42 D3
Hill View Rd. SN3   43 F6
Hillary Clo. SN2   41 H3
Hillcrest Clo. SN1   45 G2
Hillingdon Rd. SN3   47 E4
Hillmead Dri. SN5   40 B6
Hillside Av. SN1   45 G4
Hillyard Clo. SN5   44 A3
Hilmarton Av. SN2   41 H1
Hinton St. SN2   42 B6
Hobley Dri. SN3   42 D4
Hodds Hill. SN5   44 B3
Holbein Field. SN5   44 B3
Holbein Mews. SN5   44 B3
Holbein Pl. SN5   44 B3
Holbein Walk. SN5   44 B3
Holbrook Way. SN1   45 G2
Holden Cres. SN2   41 G1
Holliday Clo. SN2   41 F1
Holinshed Pl. SN5   44 B3
Hollins Moor. SN3   47 G5
Holly Clo. SN2   41 F4
Holmleigh. SN2   41 E3
Honeylight Vw. SN2   41 F1
Honeysuckle Clo. SN2   40 D2
Honiton Rd. SN3   47 E2
Hook St. SN5   44 A4
Hoopers Pl. SN1   46 B4
Hopton Clo. SN5   44 C4
Horace St. SN2   45 F2

Horcott Rd. SN5 40 B4
Horder Mws. SN1 46 B4
Hornsey Gdns. SN3 42 D2
Horsham Cres. SN3 46 D3
Horseshoe Clo. SN5 40 A5
Horton Rd. SN2 42 C1
Howard Clo. SN3 46 C2
Huddleston Clo. SN2 42 B6
Hudson Way. SN2 41 F2
Hughes St. SN2 45 E1
Hugo Way. SN2 41 G1
Hungerford Clo. SN5 44 A1
Hunsdon Clo. SN3 46 D2
Hunt St. SN1 46 A3
Hunters Gro. SN2 41 G5
Huntley Clo. SN3 46 C1
Hunts Rise. SN3 43 E1
Hurst Cres. SN2 41 H4
Hyde Rd. SN2 42 B1
Hylder Clo. SN2 40 D3
Hysopp Clo. SN2 40 C3
Hythe Rd. SN1 45 H3

Icomb Clo. SN5 44 C4
Idovers Dri. SN5 44 C3
Iffley Rd. SN2 41 F6
Imber Walk. SN2 41 G1
INDUSTRIAL & RETAIL:
Axis Business Centre. SN5 44 D1
Blagrove Employment Area. SN5 44 A5
Britannia Trade Pk. SN3 42 C4
Cheney Manor Ind Est. SN2 41 E5
Churchward Pk. SN5 45 E3
Delta Business Pk. SN5 44 D2
Dorcan Ind Est. SN3 47 G3
Elgin Ind Est. SN2 42 B5
Europa Pk Employment Area. SN3 42 D4
Greenbridge Ind Est. SN3 42 D6
Groundwell Ind Est. SN2 42 B1
Hawksworth Ind Est. SN2 45 F1
Headlands Ind Est. SN2 42 B4
Hillmead Employment Area. SN5 40 B6
Honda Car Plant. SN3 43 E2
Isis Trading Est. SN1 42 C6
Kembrey Business Pk. SN2 42 B5
Kendrick Ind Est. SN2 41 E6
Mannington Employment Area. SN5 45 E3
Marshgate Ind Est. SN1 42 C6
Okus Ind Est. SN1 45 G4
Rivermead Ind Est. SN5 40 C6
Techno Trading Est. SN2 42 C5
Thornhill Ind Est. SN3 43 G3
Transfer Bridge Ind Est. SN2 42 B6
Westmead Ind Est. SN5 44 D1
Windmill Hill Business Pk. SN5 44 A4
Inglesham Rd. SN2 41 H2
Ipswich St. SN2 41 H6
Irston Way. SN5 44 B4
Isis Clo. SN2 41 G3
Islandsmead. SN3 47 F3
Islington St. SN1 45 H2
Ixworth Clo. SN5 44 B1

*Jack Thorne Clo, Linden Way. SN5 40 B4
Jacobs Walk. SN3 47 G3
James Watt Clo. SN2 45 F1
Jasmine Clo. SN2 40 D3
Jefferies Av. SN2 42 B4
Jennings St. SN2 45 F2
Jersey Pk. SN5 44 B1
Jewel Clo. SN5 44 A3
John Herring Cres. SN3 42 D5
John St. SN1 45 H2
Jole Clo. SN2 42 C2
Jolliffe St. SN1 45 F2
Joseph St. SN1 45 G3
Jubilee Rd. SN2 40 D4
Juliana Clo. SN5 44 B1
Juniper Clo. SN3 43 E6

Keats Cres. SN2 42 C3
Keble Clo. SN3 47 E1
Kelham Clo. SN3 46 C4
Kelly Gdns. SN2 41 F1
Kelmscot Rd. SN2 41 H3
Kelvin Rd. SN3 46 D1
Kemble Dri. SN2 45 F1
Kembrey St. SN2 42 A5
Kendal. SN5 44 C4
Kenilworth Lawns. SN3 46 C5
Kennedy Dri. SN3 47 F4
Kennet Av. SN2 41 G3
Kent Rd. SN1 45 G3
Kenton Clo. SN3 47 E2
Kenwin Clo. SN3 43 E4
Kerry Clo. SN5 44 B2
Kershaw Rd. SN3 47 F4
Kestrel Dri. SN3 47 G2
Keswick Rd. SN3 47 E4
Keycroft Copse. SN5 40 A5
Keyneston Rd. SN3 47 F2
Keynsham Walk. SN3 47 E4
Kilben Clo. SN5 44 A1
Kiln La. SN2 41 F5
Kilsby Way. SN3 43 E6
Kilsyth Clo. SN5 44 B3
Kimberley Rd. SN3 46 D4
Kimbolton Clo. SN5 44 B4
Kimmeridge Clo. SN3 47 E2
King Charles Rd. SN5 44 B4
King Henry Dri. SN5 44 A3
King John St. SN1 46 A3
King St. SN1 45 H2
King William St. SN1 46 A3
Kingfisher Dri. SN3 47 F1
Kingscote Clo. SN5 40 A6
Kingsdown Rd. SN2 42 C2
Kingshill Ct. SN1 45 G3
Kingshill Rd. SN1 45 F3
Kingsley Way. SN2 42 B2
Kingsthorpe Gro. SN3 43 F6
Kingston Rd. SN3 46 D4
Kingsway Clo. SN3 46 D3
Kingswood Av. SN3 46 D3
Kipling Gdns. SN2 42 C3
Kirby Clo. SN3 46 C4
Kirkstall Clo. SN5 44 C3
Kirktonhill Rd. SN5 44 D2
Kitchener St. SN2 41 H6
Knapp Clo. SN2 41 F4
Knowsley Rd. SN3 46 D4

Laburnum Rd. SN2 41 H4
Lacock Rd. SN2 42 A2
Lady La. SN2 41 E1
Lagos St. SN1 46 A1
Lakeside. SN3 46 B4
Lambert Clo. SN5 44 B4
Lambourne Av. SN3 46 B5
Lamora Clo. SN5 40 A6
Lanac Rd. SN3 42 D6
Lancaster Mews. SN3 43 F1
Lancaster Pl. SN3 43 F1
Langdale Dri. SN5 44 B4
Langford Gro. SN3 46 B2
Langport Clo. SN5 44 B3
Langstone Way. SN5 44 C2
Lanhydrock Clo. SN5 44 B3
Lansbury Dri. SN2 42 C3
Lansdown Rd. SN1 45 H3
Lapwing Clo. SN3 47 G2
Larchmore Clo. SN2 41 G3
Larksfield. SN3 47 F1
Latton Clo. SN2 41 G1
Lawrence Clo. SN3 47 F3
Lawton Clo. SN3 46 D4
Leamington Gro. SN3 46 C5
Leicester St. SN1 46 A2
Leigh Rd. SN2 41 H2
Leighton Av. SN3 46 D4
Lennox Dri. SN3 46 C2
Leslie Clo. SN5 44 B3
Lethbridge Rd. SN1 46 A4
Letterage Rd. SN5 40 B4
Leven. SN5 44 B5
Leverton Gate. SN3 46 C6
Lewisham Clo. SN2 41 E4
Lichen Clo. SN2 40 D3
Liddington St. SN2 42 A4
Liden Dri. SN3 47 F4
Limes Av. SN2 41 G4
Lincoln St. SN1 46 A2
Linden Av. SN2 41 H4
Linden Way. SN5 40 B4
Lineacre Clo. SN5 44 A4
Link Av. SN5 44 C2
Linley Clo. SN1 46 A5
Linnetsdene. SN3 43 F6
Linslade St. SN2 45 F2
Liskeard Way. SN5 44 B4
Lisle Clo. SN5 44 A3
Little Av. SN2 41 F5
Little London. SN1 46 A3
Littlecote Clo. SN5 44 D3
Locksgreen Cres. SN2 41 E3
Logan Clo. SN3 46 B2
Lomond Clo. SN5 40 C5
London St. SN1 45 G2
Longstock Ct. SN5 44 C2
Longthorpe Clo. SN5 44 D3
Lorne St. SN1 45 G2
Loughborough Clo. SN5 44 A3
Louviers Way. SN1 46 A5
Loveage Clo. SN2 40 D3
Lovell Clo. SN3 47 F1
Loveridge Clo. SN2 42 B1
Lowes Clo. SN5 40 C4
Lucerne Clo. SN5 44 A1
Luddesdown Rd. SN5 44 C4
Ludlow Clo. SN3 46 C4
Lulworth Rd. SN2 41 E3
Lumley Clo. SN5 44 A3
Lyddon Way. SN2 41 F3
Lydford Clo. SN5 40 B6
Lyme Way. SN2 41 F2
Lyndhurst Cres. SN3 46 D2
Lyneham Clo. SN2 41 H1
Lynton Rd. SN2 41 E5
Lynwood Gro. SN2 40 D3
Lytchett Way. SN3 47 F2

Mackenzie Clo. SN3 47 G4
Magpie La. SN3 47 G1
Maidstone Rd. SN1 45 G3
Maitland Rd. SN3 46 D1
Majestic Clo. SN5 44 A1
Maldwyn Clo. SN5 44 A1
Mallard Clo. SN3 47 G2
Mallow Clo. SN2 40 D2
Malvern Rd. SN2 41 H5
Manchester Rd. SN1 45 H1
Mannington La. SN5 44 D3
Mannington Pk. SN2 45 E1
Manor Cres. SN2 41 E4
Manor Gdns. SN2 41 F5
Manor Mdws. SN3 43 G3
Manor Pk. SN3 43 G3
Manor St. SN1 45 F3
Manton St. SN2 45 F1
Maple Gro. SN2 41 H4
March Clo. SN2 41 F1
Mardale Clo. SN5 40 A6
Marigold Clo. SN2 40 D2
Marjoram Clo. SN2 40 D2
Markenfield. SN5 44 D3
Market St. SN1 45 G2
Markham Clo. SN3 46 C1
Marlborough La. SN3 46 B5
Marlborough Rd. SN3 46 B4
Marlborough St. SN1 45 F3
Marlowe Av. SN3 46 D1
Marney Rd. SN5 44 B2
Marsh Farm La. SN1 46 B1
Marshall Rd. SN5 40 B6
Marshfield Way. SN3 42 D5
Marshgate. SN1 42 C6
Marsland Rd. SN2 42 B4
Marston Av. SN2 42 A2
Martinfield. SN3 47 F1
Masefield Av. SN2 42 B4
Mason Rd. SN25 41 G1
Matley Moor. SN3 47 G5
Maxey Clo. SN5 40 B6
Maxwell St. SN1 45 G2
May Clo. SN2 41 H5
Mayfield Clo. SN3 47 E1
Mead Way. SN5 44 C1
Meadow Rd. SN2 45 E1
Meadowcroft. SN2 42 C2
Meadowsweet Clo. SN2 41 E1
Meares Dri. SN5 40 B6
Medgbury Rd. SN1 46 A2
Medina Way. SN2 42 C2
Medway Rd. SN2 41 F3
Melbourne Clo. SN3 46 D5
Melfort Clo. SN5 40 C5
Melford Walk. SN3 47 E1
Melksham Clo. SN2 41 G1
Mellow Ground. SN2 41 E2
Melrose Clo. SN5 44 C1
Melville Clo. SN3 46 C2
Melvyn Webb Pl. SN2 42 B6
Mendip Clo. SN2 41 H3
Menham Clo. SN2 42 A4
Merlin Way. SN3 43 F6
Merrivale Gro. SN1 46 B3
Merton Av. SN2 42 B3
Merton St. SN1 45 H2
Middleleaze Dri. SN5 44 A1
Middleton Clo. SN3 46 C2
Midhurst Av. SN3 47 E2
Midwinter Clo. SN5 40 B5
Midwinter Gdns. SN3 42 D4
Mildenhall Way. SN2 41 G1
Mildmay Clo. SN5 44 A3
Milford St. SN1 45 H2
Mill La. SN1 45 F5
Millbuck Clo. SN2 42 C5
Miller Clo. SN5 44 A1
Milston Av. SN2 41 H2
Milton Rd. SN1 45 G2
Minety Rd. SN2 41 G1
Mint Clo. SN2 40 D3
Monet Clo. SN2 41 F1
Monkton Clo. SN3 47 E4
Monmouth Clo. SN3 46 C4
Montagu St. SN2 45 E1
Monteagle Clo. SN5 44 A3
Montgomery Av. SN2 41 G5
Montrose Clo. SN2 41 E4
Moorhen Clo. SN3 47 G2
Moray Rd. SN2 42 B5
Moredon Pk. SN2 40 D3
Moredon Rd. SN2 41 E3
Moresby Clo. SN5 44 C2
Morie Clo. SN5 40 C5
Morley St. SN1 45 H2
Morris St. SN2 45 E2
Morrison St. SN2 45 E1
Morse St. SN1 45 G3
Mortimer Clo. SN5 44 C1
Mulberry Gro. SN2 41 F4
Mulcaster Av. SN5 44 A3
Mundy Av. SN3 47 E3
Munro Clo. SN3 46 B2
Murdoch Rd. SN3 47 G2
Myrtle Gdns. SN2 41 H4

Nantwich. SN5 44 B5
Napier Clo. SN2 45 F1
Naunton Rd. SN3 46 D2
Nelson St. SN1 45 F3
Ness Clo. SN5 40 C4
Netherton Clo. SN3 47 E4
Nevis Clo. SN5 40 C4
New Bridge Clo. SN1 45 H1
New Bridge Sq. SN1 45 H2
New Meadow Copse. SN5 40 B5
Newark Clo. SN5 44 B4
Newburn Cres. SN1 45 F3
Newbury Dri. SN5 44 B4
Newcastle St. SN1 46 A2
Newcome Dri. SN2 45 F1
Newhall St. SN1 45 H3
Newland Rd. SN2 41 F3
Newport St. SN1 46 A4
*Newstead Clo, Bicton Rd. SN2 41 F1
Newton Way. SN2 41 H3
Nightingale Rd. SN3 43 H3
Nightwood Copse. SN5 40 B5
Nindum Rd. SN3 43 E5
Norcliffe Rd. SN3 46 D4
Norfolk Clo. SN3 46 D2
Norman Rd. SN2 41 H6
North St. SN1 46 A3
North Star Av. SN2 45 G1
Northampton St. SN1 46 B2
Northbrook Rd. SN2 41 G5
Northern Rd. SN2 41 G6
Northfield Way. SN3 47 E1
Northleaze Clo. SN2 41 F4
Norton Gro. SN3 46 B2
Norwood Clo. SN3 47 F4
Noyes Clo. SN2 40 C2
Nuffield Clo. SN5 44 C1
Nuthatch Clo. SN3 47 G2
Nutmeg Clo. SN2 40 D3
Nyland Rd. SN3 47 E1
Nythe Rd. SN3 43 E5

Oak Garden. SN3 42 D3
Oak Tree Av. SN2 42 A4
Oakford Walk. SN3 46 D2
Oakham Clo. SN5 44 C3
Oakie Clo. SN2 41 G1
Oaksey Rd. SN2 41 H2
Oakwood Rd. SN5 44 C1
Oasthouse Clo. SN5 40 A6
Oberon Way. SN2 41 F2
Ocotol Way. SN1 46 B1
Odstock Rd. SN2 41 H1
Okebourne Pk. SN3 47 F5
Okeford Clo. SN3 47 E1
Okus Gro. SN2 42 B3
Okus Rd. SN1 45 F4
Old Mill La. SN3 46 B4
Old Shaw La. SN5 44 B1
Olive Gro. SN2 41 G4
Oliver Clo. SN5 44 A2
Omdurman St. SN2 41 H6
Orchard Gro. SN2 42 B3
Orchid Clo. SN2 41 H3
Oriel St. SN1 45 H2
Orkney Clo. SN5 44 B2
Orlando Clo. SN5 44 A3
Orrin Clo. SN5 40 C5
Orwell Clo. SN2 41 F2
Osborne St. SN2 41 G6
Osprey Clo. SN3 47 G2
Osterley Rd. SN2 41 E1
Overbrooke. SN3 47 E4
Overton Gdns. SN3 43 E5
Owl Clo. SN3 47 G2
Oxford Rd. SN3 42 D5
Oxford St. SN1 45 G2

Packington Clo. SN5 44 B1
Paddington Dri. SN5 45 E2
Paddock Clo. SN2 41 E2
Pakenham Rd. SN3 47 E4
Parham Walk. SN5 44 A3
Park La. SN1 45 F2
Park Side. SN3 42 D4
Park Springs. SN5 44 D3
Park St. SN3 43 E5
Parklands Rd. SN3 46 B3
Parr Clo. SN5 44 A2
Parsley Clo. SN2 40 D2
Parsonage Rd. SN3 42 D3
Partridge Clo. SN3 47 H2
Passmore Clo. SN3 47 G1
Pasture Clo. SN2 45 E1
Patney Walk. SN2 41 G1
Paulet Clo. SN5 44 A3
Peaks Down. SN5 40 B4
Pearce Clo. SN2 42 C1
Pearl Rd. SN5 44 A1
Peatmoor Way. SN5 40 B5
Pembroke Gdns. SN2 41 E4
Pembroke St. SN1 45 G3
Pen Clo. SN2 41 G3
Pencarrow. SN2 41 E1
Pendennis Rd. SN5 44 B4
Penfold Gdns. SN1 45 H4
Penhill Dri. SN2 41 H1
Penny La. SN3 46 C1
Pennycress Clo. SN2 41 E2
Pentridge Clo. SN3 47 F1
Penzance Dri. SN5 45 E3
Pepperbox Hill. SN5 40 B5
Percheron Clo. SN5 44 B1
Percy St. SN2 45 F1
Peregrine Clo. SN3 43 F6
Periwinkle Clo. SN2 40 C3
Petersfield Rd. SN3 47 E4
Pevensey Way. SN5 44 C3
Pewsham Rd. SN2 42 A2
Pheasant Clo. SN3 47 G2
Pickwick Clo. SN2 42 B2
Picton Rd. SN5 44 B1
Pigeon House La. SN3 42 D4
Pilgrim Clo. SN5 44 B1
Pilton Clo. SN5 40 A6
Pinehurst Rd. SN2 41 G5
Pinetree Rise. SN2 41 G4
Pinnegar Way. SN3 47 G2
Pinnocks Pl. SN2 42 C3
Pioneer Clo. SN5 44 A1
Pipers Way. SN3 46 A6
Pipitdene. SN3 47 G1
Plattes Clo. SN5 40 C6
Pleydell Rd. SN1 46 A5
Plymouth St. SN1 46 A2
Poltondale. SN3 47 G1
Pond St. SN2 41 E2
Ponting St. SN1 46 A1
Poole Rd. SN2 41 E3
Pope Clo. SN2 41 E1
Poplar Av. SN2 41 H4
Popplechurch Dri. SN3 47 G1

Portal Rd. SN2 — 41 G5
Portland Av. SN1 — 45 G4
Portmore Clo. SN5 — 40 C5
Portsmouth St. SN1 — 46 B2
Potterdown Rd. SN2 — 41 H1
Poulton St. SN2 — 41 H6
Pound La. SN2 — 41 G4
Poynings Way. SN5 — 44 A3
Primrose Clo. SN2 — 40 D2
Princes St. SN1 — 46 A2
Priory Rd. SN3 — 46 D4
Pritchard Clo. SN2 — 42 C2
Prospect Hill. SN1 — 46 A3
Prospect Pl. SN1 — 46 A3
Purbeck Clo. SN3 — 47 E1
Purley Av. SN1 — 47 E5
Purley Rd. SN4 — 47 H6
Purslane Clo. SN2 — 40 C3
Purton Rd. SN2 — 40 D3

Quarry Brook Clo. SN3 — 43 G2
Quarry Mews. SN1 — 45 H4
Quarry Rd. SN1 — 45 H4
Queen Elizabeth Dri. SN2 — 40 C2
Queen St. SN1 — 45 G2
Queenborough. SN5 — 44 C4
Queens Dri. SN3 — 46 B2
Queensfield. SN2 — 42 B1
Quentin Rd. SN3 — 46 B4

Radcot Clo. SN5 — 40 B6
Radley Clo. SN3 — 47 E1
Radnor St. SN1 — 45 G3
Radstock Av. SN3 — 47 E2
Radway Rd. SN3 — 42 D4
Raglan Clo. SN3 — 46 C5
Rainer Clo. SN3 — 43 E4
Raleigh Av. SN3 — 46 C2
Ramleaze Dri. SN5 — 44 B1
Ramsbury Av. SN2 — 41 G1
Ramsden Rd. SN5 — 44 A5
Ramsthorne Clo. SN2 — 40 D3
Randall Cres. SN5 — 44 B1
Randolph Clo. SN5 — 46 C2
Rannoch Clo. SN5 — 40 C5
Ransome Clo. SN5 — 40 B6
Ratcombe Rd. SN5 — 40 B4
Ravenglass Rd. SN5 — 44 C2
Ravenscroft. SN3 — 47 F1
Rawlings Clo. SN3 — 43 G3
Rawston Clo. SN5 — 47 F2
Ray Clo. SN2 — 41 F2
Raybrook Cres. SN2 — 45 E2
Rayfield Gro. SN2 — 41 G6
Read St. SN1 — 45 G3
Reading St. SN1 — 45 G2
Redcap Gdns. SN5 — 44 B1
Redcliffe St. SN2 — 45 F2
Redlynch Clo. SN2 — 41 H1
Redruth Clo. SN3 — 47 E3
Regent St. SN1 — 45 H2
Regents Pl. SN1 — 42 C6
Retingham Way. SN3 — 42 D2
Revell Clo. SN2 — 42 B2
Rhuddlan. SN5 — 44 C4
Richmond Rd. SN2 — 41 F6
Ridge Grn. SN5 — 44 C1
Ridge Nether Moor. SN3 — 47 G5
Ridgeway Clo. SN2 — 41 E4
Ridgeway Rd. SN2 — 42 B1
Ringwood Clo. SN3 — 47 E2
Rinsdale Clo. SN5 — 40 C5
Ripley Rd. SN1 — 46 A4
Ripon Way. SN3 — 46 D4
Ripplefield. SN5 — 44 B4
Risingham Mead. SN5 — 44 C3
Rivenhall Rd. SN5 — 44 C2
Riverdale Clo. SN1 — 46 A6
Rivermead Dri. SN5 — 44 C1
Robins Grn. SN5 — 47 F1
Robinson Clo. SN3 — 47 F2
Roche Clo. SN3 — 47 F4
Rochester Clo. SN5 — 44 B4
Rochford Clo. SN5 — 44 A3
Rockdown St. SN2 — 41 H2
Rodbourne Grn. SN2 — 41 F5
Rodbourne Rd. SN2 — 41 F6
Rodwell Clo. SN3 — 46 D3
Rogers Clo. SN3 — 46 D1
Roman Cres. SN1 — 45 G5
Romney Way. SN5 — 44 B2
Romsey St. SN2 — 45 F1
Rose Dale Rd. SN3 — 46 D4
Rose St. SN2 — 45 E1
Rosebery St. SN2 — 46 A1

Rosemary Clo. SN2 — 40 D2
Ross Gdns. SN3 — 42 D2
Rother Clo. SN2 — 41 E2
Roughmoor Farm. SN5 — 40 A5
Roughmoor Way. SN5 — 44 B1
Roundway Down. SN5 — 44 C5
Rowan Rd. SN2 — 41 F4
Rowland Hill Clo. SN3 — 47 G4
Rowton Heath Way. SN5 — 44 B3
Royston Rd. SN3 — 46 D4
Ruckley Gdns. SN3 — 43 E5
Rushall Clo. SN2 — 46 D4
Rushton Rd. SN3 — 46 D4
Ruskin Av. SN2 — 42 C3
Russell Walk. SN3 — 46 C2
Russley Clo. SN5 — 40 A5
Ryan Clo. SN5 — 40 C4
Rycote Clo. SN5 — 44 B2
Rydal Clo. SN2 — 41 F2
Rye Clo. SN5 — 44 B1

Sackville Clo. SN3 — 46 C1
Saddleback Rd. SN5 — 44 B2
Sadler Walk. SN3 — 46 C3
Saffron Clo. SN2 — 40 D3
Sage Clo. SN2 — 40 D2
St Albans Clo. SN2 — 45 E1
St Ambrose Clo. SN3 — 47 G2
St Andrews Grn. SN3 — 47 G1
St Austell Way. SN2 — 45 F2
St Helens Vw. SN1 — 45 F4
St James Clo. SN2 — 42 B2
St Katherines Grn. SN3 — 47 G1
St Margarets Grn. SN3 — 43 E4
St Margarets Rd. SN3 — 46 A4
St Marys Gro. SN2 — 41 G6
St Pauls Dri. SN3 — 47 F1
St Pauls St. SN2 — 41 H6
St Philips Rd. SN2 — 42 B3
Salcombe Gro. SN3 — 46 C5
Salisbury St. SN1 — 46 A1
Saltram Clo. SN3 — 46 D4
Sandacre Rd. SN5 — 40 A6
*Sandford Ct,
  Springfield Rd. SN1 — 46 A4
Sandgate. SN3 — 43 E5
Sandown Av. SN3 — 46 B4
Sandpiper Bri. SN3 — 47 G1
Sandringham Rd. SN3 — 46 C4
Sandwood Clo. SN5 — 40 C5
Sandy La. SN1 — 45 G4
Sanford St. SN1 — 45 H2
Sarsen Clo. SN1 — 45 F4
Savernake St. SN1 — 45 H3
Sawyer Clo. SN25 — 41 G1
Scarborough Rd. SN2 — 41 F6
School Clo. SN3 — 42 D3
School Row. SN2 — 41 E3
Scotby Av. SN3 — 46 B5
Scotney Cres SN2 — 41 F1
Seaton Clo. SN2 — 41 F2
Sedgebrook. SN3 — 47 F5
Selby Cres. SN5 — 44 B3
Severn Av. SN2 — 41 F2
Seymour Rd. SN3 — 46 C2
Shaftesbury Av. SN3 — 47 E5
Shakespeare Path. SN2 — 42 C3
Shalbourne Clo. SN2 — 41 G2
Shanklin Rd. SN2 — 42 D4
Shaplands. SN3 — 42 D4
Shapwick Clo. SN3 — 47 F1
Sharp Clo. SN5 — 44 C1
Shaw Rd. SN5 — 44 C1
Shearwood Rd. SN5 — 40 B5
Sheen Clo. SN5 — 44 A4
Shelfinch. SN5 — 44 D4
Shelley St. SN1 — 45 G4
Shenton Clo. SN3 — 43 E4
Sheppard St. SN1 — 45 G2
Shepperton Way. SN2 — 41 F1
Sherbourne Pl. SN3 — 47 E1
Sherford Rd. SN3 — 41 E3
Sherston Av. SN2 — 41 H2
Sherwold Clo. SN3 — 43 E3
Sherwood Rd. SN3 — 47 E4
Shetland Clo. SN5 — 44 B1
Shipley Dri. SN2 — 41 E1
Shipton Gro. SN3 — 46 B3
Shire Clo. SN5 — 44 B1
Shire Ct. SN1 — 45 F3
Shirley Clo. SN3 — 46 C1
Shrewsbury Rd. SN3 — 46 C2
Shrewton Walk. SN2 — 41 H1
Shrivenham Rd. SN1 — 46 B1
Shropshire Clo. SN5 — 44 B1
Sidney Clo. SN5 — 44 A3

Sigerson Rd. SN25 — 40 C1
Signal Way. SN3 — 46 B4
Silbury Mews. SN25 — 40 D3
Silchester Way. SN5 — 44 C2
Silto Ct. SN2 — 41 F5
Silverton Rd. SN3 — 47 E2
Simnel Clo. SN5 — 44 A3
Slade Dri. SN3 — 42 D6
Slaters Orchard. SN3 — 43 E3
Sleaford Clo. SN5 — 44 A2
Smitan Brook. SN3 — 47 F2
Snowdrop Clo. SN2 — 40 D2
Snowshill Clo. SN2 — 41 F2
Somerdale Clo. SN5 — 44 C2
Somerford Clo. SN3 — 42 A3
Somerset Rd. SN2 — 41 F5
Somerville Rd. SN3 — 46 C2
Sound Copse. SN5 — 40 B4
South St. SN1 — 46 A3
South View Av. SN3 — 46 B2
Southampton St. SN1 — 46 B2
Southbrook St. SN2 — 41 G6
Southernwood Dri. SN2 — 40 C2
Southwick Av. SN2 — 41 G6
Sparcells Dri. SN5 — 40 C4
Speedwell Clo. SN2 — 41 E1
Spencer Clo. SN5 — 44 A1
Spencer Clo. SN3 — 46 D1
Speresholt. SN5 — 44 D4
Spring Gdns. SN1 — 46 A2
Spring Hill Clo. SN5 — 44 C3
Springfield Rd. SN1 — 46 A4
Spur Way. SN2 — 42 C3
Squires Copse. SN5 — 40 B5
Stafford St. SN1 — 45 G3
Stamford Clo. SN5 — 44 C3
Stanbridge Pk. SN5 — 44 B1
Stancombe Pk. SN5 — 44 B1
Standings Clo. SN5 — 40 A6
Stanier St. SN1 — 45 H3
Stanley St. SN1 — 46 A3
Stanmore St. SN1 — 45 G3
Stansfield Clo. SN5 — 44 D4
Stanway Clo. SN3 — 46 D3
Stapleford Clo. SN2 — 41 G1
Staring Clo. SN5 — 40 A6
Station App. SN1 — 46 A4
Station Rd. SN1 — 45 H1
Stenness Clo. SN5 — 40 C4
Stephens Rd. SN3 — 42 D6
Stevenson Rd. SN2 — 40 C2
Stewart Clo. SN2 — 41 G1
Stirling Rd. SN3 — 43 F1
*Stockbridge Copse,
  Ratcombe Rd. SN5 — 40 B4
Stockton Rd. SN2 — 41 H2
Stokesay Dri. SN5 — 44 C3
Stone La. SN5 — 40 A5
Stonecrop Way. SN2 — 41 E1
Stonefield Clo. SN5 — 44 C1
Stonehill Grn. SN5 — 40 D2
Stonehurst Rd. SN3 — 42 D6
Stoneybeck Clo. SN5 — 40 D2
Stour Rd. SN5 — 44 B3
Stratford Rd. SN5 — 44 D3
Stratton Orchard. SN3 — 42 D4
Stratton Rd. SN1 — 42 C6
Stratton St Margaret
  By-Pass. SN2 — 42 D4
Stuart Clo. SN3 — 46 D2
Stubsmead. SN3 — 47 F3
Studland Clo. SN3 — 47 E4
Sudeley Way. SN5 — 44 B3
Suffolk St. SN2 — 41 H6
Summers St. SN2 — 45 F1
Sunningdale Rd. SN2 — 41 H3
Sunnyside Av. SN1 — 45 F3
Surrey Rd. SN2 — 41 F5
Sutton Rd. SN3 — 47 F4
Swallowdale. SN3 — 47 F1
Swallowfield Av. SN3 — 46 C3
Swanage Walk. SN2 — 41 E3
Swanbrook. SN3 — 43 F6
Swindon Rd. SN3 — 42 D6
Swindon Rd. SN1 — 46 A3
Swinley Dri. SN5 — 40 A5
Sycamore Gro. SN2 — 41 H4
Symonds. SN5 — 44 B5
Syon Clo. SN2 — 41 F1
Sywell Rd. SN3 — 43 F6

Tavistock Rd. SN3 — 47 E2
Tawny Owl Clo. SN3 — 43 E6
Taylor Cres. SN3 — 42 D2
Tealsbrook. SN3 — 47 G1
Tedder Clo. SN2 — 41 G5
Tees Clo. SN3 — 47 E2
Teesdale Clo. SN5 — 44 B2
Telford Way. SN5 — 44 D3
Temple St. SN1 — 45 H2
Tenby Clo. SN3 — 46 C4
Tennyson St. SN1 — 45 G2
Tensing Gdns. SN2 — 41 H3
Terncliff. SN3 — 47 G1
Tewkesbury Way. SN5 — 44 A1
Thackeray Clo. SN3 — 47 F4
Thames Av. SN2 — 41 E2
The Acorns. SN3 — 46 D5
The Birches. SN3 — 46 D5
The Bramptons. SN5 — 44 C1
The Brow. SN2 — 41 E2
The Bungalows. SN2 — 41 G4
The Buntings. SN3 — 47 F1
The Chesters. SN5 — 44 D2
The Circle. SN2 — 41 H4
The Close. SN3 — 43 E4
The Crescent. SN5 — 40 A4
The Drive. SN3 — 47 E1
The Ferns. SN2 — 41 H6
*The Fields,
  Cameron Clo. SN3 — 42 D5
The Fox. SN5 — 40 A3
The Forum. SN5 — 44 C3
The Harriers. SN3 — 47 F1
The Heights. SN1 — 45 F4
The Holbein. SN5 — 44 B3
The Knoll. SN1 — 46 A5
The Mall. SN1 — 45 G4
The Marsh. SN4 — 47 H5
The Orchards. SN3 — 46 C6
The Owletts. SN3 — 47 G1
The Paddocks. SN3 — 42 D5
The Parade. SN1 — 45 H2
The Planks. SN3 — 46 B4
The Quarries. SN1 — 45 H4
The Square. SN1 — 46 B4
The Street. SN2 — 41 E3
The Weavers. SN3 — 46 B4
The Willows. SN5 — 40 A4
Theobald St. SN1 — 45 G2
Thetford Way. SN2 — 40 C2
Thirlmere. SN3 — 47 G4
Thomas St. SN3 — 45 F1
*Thorley Ct,
  Emerson Clo. SN3 — 41 G1
Thornbridge Av. SN3 — 46 D4
Thorne Rd. SN3 — 47 F4
Thornford Dri. SN5 — 44 C2
Thornhill Rd. SN3 — 43 G4
Thresher Dri. SN2 — 41 H1
Thrushel Clo. SN3 — 41 E3
Thurlestone Rd. SN3 — 46 B3
Thurney Dri. SN5 — 44 A3
Thyme Clo. SN2 — 40 C3
Tilleys La. SN3 — 42 D5
Tilshead Walk. SN2 — 41 H1
Timandra Clo. SN2 — 41 F1
Tintagel Clo. SN5 — 44 C4
Tisbury Clo. SN2 — 41 H1
Tismeads Cres. SN1 — 45 A5
Titchfield Clo. SN5 — 44 A3
Tithe Barn Cres. SN1 — 45 F4
Tiverton Rd. SN2 — 41 H5
Tockenham Way. SN2 — 41 H1
Tollard Clo. SN3 — 47 F2
Toppers Clo. SN2 — 41 G3
Torridge Clo. SN2 — 41 E3
Totterdown Clo. SN3 — 47 G1
Tovey Rd. SN2 — 41 G5
Towcester Rd. SN3 — 43 E6
Tower Rd. SN5 — 40 B5
Tracy Clo. SN3 — 47 F1
Trajan Rd. SN3 — 43 F6
Tree Courts Rd. SN2 — 41 G4
Tregantle Walk. SN3 — 47 E2
Tregoze Way. SN5 — 44 A2
Trent Rd. SN2 — 41 F3
Trentham Clo. SN3 — 46 D4
Trinity Clo. SN3 — 46 D4
Trueman Clo. SN3 — 47 F3
Truro Path. SN5 — 44 C3
Tryon Clo. SN3 — 47 G5
Tudor Cres. SN3 — 43 E5
Tulip Tree Clo. SN2 — 41 H4
Turl St. SN1 — 45 H2
Turner St. SN1 — 45 F3
Turnham Grn. SN5 — 44 B4
Tweed Clo. SN2 — 41 E2

Twyford Clo. SN3 — 46 D1
Tyburn Clo. SN5 — 44 B2
Tydeman St. SN2 — 42 A5
Tye Gdns. SN5 — 44 A3
Tyndale Path. SN5 — 44 A2
Tyneham Rd. SN3 — 47 E2
Ullswater Clo. SN3 — 47 G4
Union St. SN1 — 46 A3
Upfield. SN3 — 47 G4
Upham Rd. SN3 — 46 B3
Upton Clo. SN25 — 41 F2
Uxbridge Rd. SN3 — 44 A4
Valleyside. SN1 — 45 F4
Vanbrugh Gate. SN3 — 46 D6
Ventnor Clo. SN2 — 41 E3
Verney Clo. SN3 — 47 G2
Verulam Clo. SN3 — 43 F6
Verwood Clo. SN3 — 46 D3
Vespasian Clo. SN3 — 43 F6
Vicarage Rd. SN2 — 41 E2
Victoria Rd. SN1 — 46 A3
Vilett St. SN1 — 45 G2
Villiers Clo. SN5 — 44 A2
Viscount Way. SN3 — 43 F1
Volpe Clo. SN5 — 44 A3
Volta Rd. SN1 — 46 A2
Waggoner Clo. SN25 — 41 G1
Wagtail Clo. SN3 — 43 E6
Wainwright Clo. SN3 — 47 F3
Wakefield Clo. SN5 — 44 B3
Walcot Rd. SN3 — 46 B3
Wallingford Clo. SN5 — 44 C4
Wallsworth Rd. SN3 — 46 D3
Walsingham Rd. SN3 — 46 C2
Walter Clo. SN5 — 44 B2
Walton Clo. SN3 — 46 B3
Walwayne Field. SN3 — 42 D2
Wanborough Rd,
  Covingham. SN3 — 47 G1
Wanborough Rd,
  Lower Stratton. SN3 — 43 F5
Warbeck Gate. SN5 — 44 A3
Wardley Clo. SN3 — 46 D4
Wardour Clo. SN5 — 46 C5
Wareham Clo. SN5 — 44 B3
Warminster Av. SN2 — 41 H1
Warneford Clo. SN5 — 44 D4
Warner Clo. SN3 — 43 E3
Watercrook Mews. SN5 — 44 D3
Watling Clo. SN2 — 45 E2
Wavell Rd. SN2 — 41 G4
Waverley Rd. SN3 — 43 E6
Wayne Clo. SN3 — 41 F1
Wayside Clo. SN5 — 45 E1
Webbs Wood. SN5 — 40 B4
Wedgewood Clo. SN5 — 45 F1
Weedon Rd. SN3 — 43 E6
Welcombe Av. SN3 — 46 D3
Welford Clo. SN3 — 43 E6
Wellington St. SN1 — 45 H1
Wells St. SN1 — 46 A2
Welton Rd. SN5 — 44 D2
Wembley St. SN2 — 41 F6
Wensleydale Clo. SN5 — 44 B2
Wentworth Park. SN5 — 44 B3
Wesley St. SN1 — 46 A3
West End Rd. SN3 — 42 D5
Westmead Dri. SN5 — 44 D1
Westbrook Rd. SN2 — 41 G5
Westbury Rd. SN2 — 41 H2
Westcott Pl. SN1 — 45 F3
Westcott St. SN1 — 45 F3
Western St. SN1 — 46 A3
Westfield Way. SN2 — 40 D3
Westlea Dri. SN5 — 44 C2
Westlecot Rd. SN1 — 45 G5
Westminster Rd. SN5 — 44 C3
Westmorland Rd. SN1 — 46 B2
Westview Walk. SN3 — 47 E1
Westwood Rd. SN3 — 41 H1
Wey Clo. SN5 — 41 G2
Weyhill Clo. SN3 — 46 D3
Wharf Rd. SN4 — 43 B6
Wheatlands. SN3 — 41 E3
Wheatstone Rd. SN3 — 47 G3
Wheeler Av. SN2 — 42 B4
Whilestone Way. SN3 — 43 E5
Whitbourne Av. SN3 — 47 G3
Whitbread Clo. SN5 — 44 B1
Whitby Gro. SN2 — 41 F6
White Castle. SN5 — 44 C4
White Edge Moor. SN3 — 47 G5
Whitefield Cres. SN5 — 40 A5
Whitehead St. SN1 — 45 F4

Whitehill Way. SN5	44 A4	Court St Clo. SP3	51 C1	Broadcloth La. BA14 50 F1

Whitehill Way. SN5 44 A4
Whitehouse Rd. SN2 41 H6
Whitelands Rd. SN3 44 A4
Whiteman St. SN2 41 H6
Whitgift Clo. SN5 44 A2
Whitmore Clo. SN5 44 A2
Whitney St. SN1 45 H3
Whittington Rd. SN5 44 C2
Whitworth Rd. SN2 41 F4
Wichelstok Clo. SN1 45 H5
Wick La. SN3 47 G6
Wickdown Av. SN2 44 A3
Wicks Clo. SN2 41 E2
Wigmore Av. SN3 46 C4
Wilcot Av. SN2 42 A2
Wilcox Clo. SN2 41 H4
Wildern Sq. SN3 42 D3
Wilkins Clo. SN2 42 C2
William St. SN1 45 G3
Willowherb Clo. SN2 41 E1
Willows Av. SN2 42 A3
Wills Av. SN1 42 C6
Wilmot Clo. SN5 44 A2
Wilton Walk. SN2 41 H1
Wiltshire Av. SN2 41 G6
Wimpole Clo. SN3 46 D4
Winchcombe Clo. SN5 44 A2
Winchester Clo. SN3 43 E5
Windbrook Mdw. SN3 42 D3
Windermere. SN3 47 G4
Windflower Rd. SN2 41 E1
Windrush Rd. SN2 41 F3
Windsor Rd. SN3 46 C5
Wingfield. SN3 42 D2
Wingfield Av. SN2 41 H1
Winifred St. SN3 46 B4
Winsley Clo. SN2 41 H2
Winstanley Clo. SN5 44 B4
Winterslow Rd. SN2 41 G2
Winwick Rd. SN5 44 B4
Wiseman Clo. SN3 47 G2
Witham Way. SN2 42 C2
Wolsely Av. SN3 46 D4
Wood Hall Dri. SN2 40 D3
Wood St. SN1 46 A4
Woodbine Ter. SN3 47 F5
Woodbury Clo. SN5 40 A6
Woodchester. SN5 44 C2
Woodford Clo. SN2 41 H1
Woodside Av. SN3 46 C3
Woodsman Rd. SN25 41 G1
*Woodspring Ct,
  Grovelands Av. SN1 46 A5
Woodstock Rd. SN3 43 E6
Woollaton Clo. SN5 44 B3
Wootton Bassett Rd.
  SN1 45 E3
Wordsworth Dri. SN2 42 C3
Worlidge Dri. SN5 44 C1
Worsley Rd. SN5 44 A4
Wrenswood. SN3 47 F1
Wylye Clo. SN3 41 E3
Wyndham Rd. SN2 45 F1
Wynndale Clo. SN3 42 D3
Wynwards Rd. SN2 41 G1
Wyvern Clo. SN1 46 A5

Yardley Clo. SN2 41 E4
Yarmouth Clo. SN5 44 B3
Yarnton Clo. SN5 40 B6
Yarrow Clo. SN2 40 D3
*Yellowhammer Clo,
  Wagtail Clo. SN3 43 F6
Yeoman Clo. SN5 44 A1
Yeovil Clo. SN3 43 G3
Yew Tree Gdns. SN3 43 G3
Yiewsley Cres. SN3 43 E5
York Rd. SN1 46 B2

TISBURY

Ansty Rd. SP3 51 B3
Becket St. SP3 51 B2
Brook Clo. SP3 51 B3
Castle Mount. SP3 51 B3
Chantry Vw. SP3 51 B2
Chicks Grove Rd. SP3 51 D1
Chilmark Rd. SP3 51 D1
Church St. SP3 51 B3
Church St Clo. SP3 51 B2
Churchill Clo. SP3 51 B2
Churchill Est. SP3 51 B2
Coton Down. SP3 51 B2
Court St. SP3 51 C1

Court St Clo. SP3 51 C1
Cuffs La. SP3 51 B1
Doctors Pl. SP3 51 B1
Duck St. SP3 51 B2
Dunworth Rise. SP3 51 B2
High St. SP3 51 B3
High View Clo. SP3 51 B3
Hill Clo. SP3 51 C1
Hindon La. SP3 51 B1
Kipling Clo. SP3 51 B2
Lady Down Vw. SP3 51 C1
Monmouth Rd. SP3 51 A3
Mount Pleasant. SP3 51 A3
Nadder Clo. SP3 51 B2
Oddford Vale. SP3 51 B3
Overhouse Dri. SP3 51 A3
Park Rd. SP3 51 B2
Queens Rd. SP3 51 C1
St Johns Clo. SP3 51 B3
Snows Hill. SP3 51 C1
Springfield Pk. SP3 51 A3
Station Rd. SP3 51 B2
Taramah Gdns. SP3 51 B2
Targetts Mead. SP3 51 C1
Temperence Row. SP3 51 B2
The Avenue. SP3 51 B2
The Causeway. SP3 51 B2
The Cross. SP3 51 B1
The Mallards. SP3 51 B3
The Old Farmyard. SP3 51 C2
The Paddock. SP3 51 C2
Tisbury Row. SP3 51 C1
Tuckingmill Rd. SP3 51 A3
Union Rd. SP3 51 B3
Vicarage Rd. SP3 51 B2
Weaveland Rd. SP3 51 B1

TROWBRIDGE

Acacia Cres. BA14 48 B6
Adcroft Dri. BA14 48 D4
Adcroft St. BA14 48 D4
Aintree Ave. BA14 50 E4
Alastair Ct. BA14 50 D2
Albany Clo. BA14 49 F4
Albert Rd. BA14 49 F3
Albion St. BA14 48 B6
Aldeburgh Pl. BA14 50 A3
Alder Clo. BA14 50 C3
Alderton Way. BA14 50 E4
Allen Rd. BA14 50 C2
Alma St. BA14 49 E6
Almond Gro. BA14 50 C3
Alum Clo. BA14 50 F1
Amour Acre. BA14 49 F6
Angcaster Clo. BA14 48 B5
Apsley Clo. BA14 49 H4
Arnolds Hill. BA14 50 A1
Arras Clo. BA14 50 D2
Ashleigh Gro. BA14 50 D2
Ashmead. BA14 50 D2
Ashmead Ct. BA14 50 E2
Ashton Rise. BA14 49 H3
Ashton Road. BA14 49 H3
Ashton St. BA14 49 E5
Avenue Rd. BA14 50 C1
Avon Vale Rd. BA14 49 E3
Avon Way. BA14 49 E2
Axe and
  Cleaver La. BA14 50 D4
Azalea Dri. BA14 50 A2
Back St. BA14 48 D5
Balmoral Rd. BA14 50 C4
Barn Glebe. BA14 49 F5
Barnack Clo. BA14 48 B5
Barnes Clo. BA14 50 B2
Baydon Clo. BA14 50 D3
Beatrice Way. BA14 49 F6
Beech Gro. BA14 50 C3
Bellefield Cres. BA14 49 E5
Berkeley Rd. BA14 48 B6
Bewley Rd. BA14 50 B2
Biss Meadow. BA14 48 B6
Blair Rd. BA14 50 B2
Bond St. BA14 50 C1
Bond St Blds. BA14 50 C1
Boundary Walk. BA14 50 D4
Bradford Rd. BA14 48 C5
Bradley Rd. BA14 50 D2
Bramley La. BA14 50 E1
Brewery Wk. BA14 49 E5
Bridge Av. BA14 48 B6
British Row. BA14 48 D5
Broad Mead. BA14 48 A4
Broad St. BA14 48 D5

Broadcloth La. BA14 50 F1
Broadcloth La East.
  BA14 49 F6
Brook Rd. BA14 48 A6
Broughton Rd. BA14 50 D4
Brown St. BA14 50 E1
Buckleaze Clo. BA14 50 E3
Burderop Clo. BA14 50 E3
Burnett Rd. BA14 50 E2
Bythesea Rd. BA14 48 D6
Cadby Clo. BA14 49 G6
Campion Dri. BA14 50 E3
Canal Rd. BA14 48 D4
Carders Cnr. BA14 50 E2
Carisbrooke Cres. BA14 49 F1
Carlton Row. BA14 50 D2
Castell Clo. BA14 49 H5
Castle St. BA14 48 D5
Castley Rd. BA14 49 G4
Cavendish Dri. BA14 50 A2
Cedar Gro. BA14 50 C3
Chaffinch Dri. BA14 50 B6
Chalfont Clo. BA14 48 A5
Charles St. BA14 48 D4
Charlotte Ct. BA14 49 E5
Charlotte St. BA14 48 D5
Charlotte Sq. BA14 49 E4
Charnwood Rd. BA14 48 A5
Chepston Pl. BA14 48 A5
Cherry Gdns,
  Hilperton. BA14 49 H3
Cherry Gdns,
  Lower Studley. BA14 50 E2
Cherry Gdns Clo. BA14 50 E2
Chestnut Gro. BA14 50 C3
Cheverell Clo. BA14 50 E3
Cheviot Rd. BA14 50 F1
Chilmark Rd. BA14 48 A5
Chirton Pl. BA14 50 E3
Christin Ct. BA14 48 A6
Church Fields. BA14 50 B3
Church La. BA14 50 B3
Church St,
  Hilperton. BA14 49 G3
Church St,
  Trowbridge. BA14 48 D5
Church Walk. BA14 49 E5
Clarence Rd. BA14 49 G6
Clarendon Av. BA14 49 F6
Clarendon Rd. BA14 49 F6
Clarks Pl. BA14 49 F4
Cleveland Gdns. BA14 49 F4
Clipsham Rise. BA14 48 B5
Cloford Clo. BA14 48 B5
Clothier Leaze. BA14 50 E1
Clydesdale Clo. BA14 50 D4
Cock Hill. BA14 48 B4
Cockhill House Ct.
  BA14 48 B5
College Rd. BA14 50 B3
Collingbourne Clo. BA14 50 E3
Comfrey Clo. BA14 50 F3
Compton Clo. BA14 48 D5
Conigre. BA14 48 D5
Coniston Rd. BA14 49 E4
Copper Beeches. BA14 49 G3
Corbin Rd. BA14 49 G4
Cornbrash Rise. BA14 49 G5
Coronation St. BA14 50 E1
County Way. BA14 49 E6
Court St. BA14 48 D6
Cranmore Clo. BA14 48 B5
Crawley Cres. BA14 48 B6
Cross St. BA14 49 E5
Cusance Way. BA14 49 G5
Delamere Rd. BA14 49 E4
Devizes Rd. BA14 49 H3
Dovecote Clo. BA14 48 B6
Downhayes Rd. BA14 49 E4
Downside Pk. BA14 49 E3
Downside Vw. BA14 49 E3
Drynham Drove. BA14 50 E4
Drynham La. BA14 50 E4
Drynham Pk. BA14 50 E2
Drynham Rd. BA14 50 E2
Duke St. BA14 49 E5
Dunford Clo. BA14 50 E2
Dursley Rd. BA14 50 D1
Dymott Sq. BA14 49 G2
Eastbourne Gdns. BA14 49 E5
Eastbourne Rd. BA14 49 E5
Eastview Rd. BA14 50 B2
Elcombe Clo. BA14 50 D3
Elliot Pl. BA14 48 B5
Elmdale Rd. BA14 50 B2
Epsom Rd. BA14 50 F4
Everleigh Clo. BA14 50 E3

Fairwood Clo. BA14 49 G4
Farleigh Av. BA14 48 B6
Farm Clo. BA14 48 B5
Faverole Way. BA14 49 G4
Field Way. BA14 50 A3
Firs Hill. BA14 50 B4
Fleece Cotts. BA14 50 F2
Fore St. BA14 48 D5
Foxglove Dri. BA14 49 E2
Frampton Ct. BA14 50 B3
Francis St. BA14 48 C4
Frome Rd. BA14 50 B3
Fulford Rd. BA14 49 E4
Fulney Clo. BA14 49 F3
Furlong Gdns. BA14 49 F5
Gainsborough Rise.
  BA14 50 B3
George St. BA14 48 D5
Gibbs Leaze. BA14 49 G4
Gladstone Rd. BA14 50 C1
Glebe Rd. BA14 50 B2
Gloucester Rd. BA14 50 C1
Goodwood Clo. BA14 50 F4
Grasmere. BA14 49 F4
Green La. BA14 49 F6
Green Ter. BA14 48 D4
Greenhill Gdns. BA14 49 G2
Greenway Gdns. BA14 49 E3
Hackett Pl. BA14 49 H4
Haden Rd. BA14 50 E1
Halfway Clo. BA14 49 G4
Halfway La. BA14 49 F5
Hammond Way. BA14 49 E1
Hanover Clo. BA14 49 F1
Harford St. BA14 48 D6
Hargreaves Rd. BA14 50 F1
Harmony Pl. BA14 50 D1
Havelock Rd. BA14 50 D1
Hawthorn Gro. BA14 50 C3
Hayes Clo. BA14 49 E2
Hazel Gro. BA14 50 C3
Heather Shaw. BA14 50 E4
Heddington Clo. BA14 50 D3
Helmdon Clo. BA14 48 A5
Helmdon Rd. BA14 48 A5
Henderson Clo. BA14 50 C1
Hewitt Clo. BA14 50 F2
Hill St, Hilperton. BA14 49 G1
Hill St,
  Trowbridge. BA14 48 D5
Hilperton Clo. BA14 49 G4
Hilperton Rd. BA14 49 E5
Holbrook La. BA14 50 D3
Holyrood Clo. BA14 50 C4
Home Clo. BA14 50 E1
Honeymans Clo. BA14 49 G6
Honeysuckle Clo. BA14 49 F6
Horse Rd. BA14 49 F2
Hungerford Av. BA14 50 B1
Hyde Rd. BA14 48 D4
INDUSTRIAL & RETAIL:
  Canal Bridge
    Ind Est. BA14 48 D5
  The Spitfire Retail Pk.
    BA14 50 D4
  White Horse Business
    Centre. BA14 50 E4
Ingleham Clo. BA14 50 E4
Innox Footpath. BA14 48 C5
Innox Mill Clo. BA14 48 C5
Innxox Rd. BA14 49 E4
Islington. BA14 49 E4
James St. BA14 48 D4
Jasmine Way. BA14 49 F6
Jenkins St. BA14 49 E4
Keates Clo. BA14 49 E4
Kennet Way. BA14 49 E4
Kensington Clo. BA14 49 E4
Kensington Fields
  BA14 50 A2
Kenton Dri. BA14 49 G4
Kenwood Clo. BA1 449 F6
Ketton Clo. BA14 48 B4
Kew Dri. BA14 50 B1
Kings Gdns. BA14 49 E1
Kingsdown Rd. BA14 49 H4
Kingsley Pl. BA14 48 A5
Kingswood Chase.
  BA14 50 A2
Knightstone Ct. BA14 49 E6
Laburnum Gro. BA14 50 C3
Lacock Dri. BA14 49 H4
Ladydown. BA14 48 D3
Lamb Ale Grn. BA14 50 E3
Lambrok Clo. BA14 50 A3
Lambrok Rd. BA14 50 A3
Langford Rd. BA14 48 D4

Langley Rd. BA14 50 D4
Lansdown Clo. BA14 50 C2
Larch Gro. BA14 50 C3
Lark Down. BA14 49 F5
Laurel Gro. BA14 50 D3
Lavender Clo. BA14 50 F1
Leafield Pl. BA14 48 A5
Leap Gate. BA14 49 H5
Leigh Clo. BA14 50 E3
Liddington Way. BA14 50 D4
Lilac Gro. BA14 50 B3
Linden Pl. BA14 48 C5
Lockeridge Clo. BA14 50 E3
Lodge Ct. BA14 49 F6
Longfield Rd. BA14 50 E1
Lower Alma St. BA14 49 F6
Lower Bond St Blds.
  BA14 50 C1
Lower Court. BA14 49 E4
Lowmead. BA14 49 E4
Lydiard Way. BA14 50 E3
Lynham Way. BA14 49 G6
Lynwood Dri. BA14 48 B5
Magnolia Rise. BA14 50 F1
Mallow Clo. BA14 50 E3
*Manley Clo,
  Shails La. BA14 48 D5
Manor Clo. BA14 50 B2
Manor Rd. BA14 50 B2
Manton Clo. BA14 50 E3
Manver St. BA14 48 D5
Maple Gro. BA14 50 D2
Marden Walk. BA14 50 E3
Marine Dri. BA14 49 F1
Market St. BA14 48 D5
Marsh Rd. BA14 49 F1
Marshmead. BA14 49 G1
Marston Rd. BA14 50 C4
Meadway. BA14 48 A6
Melton Rd. BA14 48 A6
Meridian Walk. BA14 48 B6
Middle La. BA14 49 F4
Mill La. BA14 48 D5
Mill St. BA14 48 D6
Millhand Villas. BA14 50 F2
Millington Dri. BA14 50 B1
Montague Ct. BA14 49 G5
Mortimer St. BA14 50 D1
Moyle Pk. BA14 49 H5
Murray Rd. BA14 49 E4
Navigator Clo. BA14 49 E1
Newhurst Pk. BA14 49 H4
Newleaze. BA14 49 G2
Newtown. BA14 50 D1
Nightingale Rd. BA14 50 B6
Nursery Clo. BA14 49 G3
Oak Tree Clo. BA14 48 B5
Orchard Ct. BA14 50 E1
Orchard Rd. BA14 50 E1
Oriel Clo. BA14 49 G2
Orpington Way. BA14 49 H5
Osborne Rd. BA14 49 F3
Painters Mead. BA14 49 E4
Palmer Rd. BA14 49 E4
Park Rd. BA14 50 D1
Park St. BA14 50 D1
Parklands. BA14 49 H5
Parsonage Rd. BA14 49 H5
Pavely Gdns. BA14 49 G5
Paxcroft Way. BA14 49 F6
Pembroke Clo. BA14 50 E2
Pepperacre La. BA14 49 F4
Pitman Av. BA14 50 C2
Pitman Ct. BA14 50 C2
Polebarn Rd. BA14 49 E5
Pound Farm Clo. BA14 49 F2
Princess Gdns. BA14 49 F1
*Proby Pl,
  Corbin Rd. BA14 49 G4
Prospect Pl. BA14 49 G4
Quarterway La. BA14 49 F5
Queens Club Gdns.
  BA14 48 B6
Queens Gdns. BA14 48 D4
Queens Rd. BA14 50 D1
Quilling Clo. BA14 50 F1
Ragleth Gro. BA14 49 F4
Raleigh Ct. BA14 49 E5
Rambler Clo. BA14 48 B5
Ramsbury Walk. BA14 50 E3
Ravenscroft Gdns.
  BA14 49 F5
Red Hat La. BA14 48 D5
Redgrave Clo. BA14 50 E2
Regents Clo. BA14 50 A3
Richmond Clo. BA14 50 B1
River Way. BA14 48 C5

Rock Rd. BA14 50 C2
Rodwell Pk. BA14 49 F4
Rosedale Gdns. BA14 48 A5
Rossett Gdns. BA14 48 B6
Roundstone St. BA14 49 E5
Rutland Cres. BA14 50 D2
Ryeland Way. BA14 50 F2
St Augustines Rd. BA14 48 C6
St Johns Cres. BA14 50 A3
St Margarets Clo. BA14 50 B3
St Marys Clo. BA14 49 F1
St Marys Gdns. BA14 49 F2
St Michaels Clo. BA14 49 G3
St Stephens Pl. BA14 49 E6
St Thomas Pass. BA14 49 E5
St Thomas Rd. BA14 49 E5
Sanders Rd. BA14 48 D4
Sandown Centre. BA14 50 F4
Sandringham Rd. BA14 50 C3
Saxon Dri. BA14 49 E1
School La. BA14 48 D1
School La Clo. BA14 48 D1
Seymour Ct. BA14 48 D5
Seymour Rd. BA14 48 D4
Shaftesbury Ct. BA14 50 B2
Shails La. BA14 48 D5
Shearman St. BA14 50 E2
Sheepcote Barton. BA14 50 F1
Sherborne Rd. BA14 48 A5
Sheridon Gdns. BA14 50 A2
Shore Pl. BA14 48 A5
Shrewton Clo. BA14 50 E3
Silver Birch Gro. BA14 50 C3
Silver Mdws. BA14 50 B3
Silver St. BA14 49 E5
Silver St La. BA14 50 B3
Slowgrove Clo. BA14 49 F6
Smallbrook Gdns. BA14 49 E1
Smithy Well Clo. BA14 49 G5
Sorrell Clo. BA14 50 E3
South View Rd. BA14 50 E3
Southway. BA14 50 E1
Southwood Rd. BA14 49 G6
Speedwell Clo. BA14 50 E3
Spinners Croft. BA14 50 E1
Spring Mdws. BA14 50 B3
Springfield Clo. BA14 49 F4
Springfield Pk. BA14 49 F4
Stallard St. BA14 48 D6
Stancomb Av. BA14 49 E5
Stanton Clo. BA14 50 E3
Station Way. BA14 48 D5
Stokehill. BA14 49 H5
Stonelea. BA14 49 H3
Stuart Clo. BA14 49 E1
Studley Rise. BA14 50 E2
Summerdown Walk. BA14 50 D4
Summerleaze. BA14 50 B2
Surrey Pl. BA14 50 D1
Swallow Dri. BA14 48 B6
Swan Dri. BA14 49 F1
Sycamore Gro. BA14 50 C3
Talbot Rd. BA14 50 B2
Taylors Vw. BA14 49 E5
The Beeches. BA14 49 G4
The Croft. BA14 50 D2
The Down. BA14 49 E4
The Halve. BA14 49 E5
The Knapp. BA14 49 G3
The Mount. BA14 49 E4
The Nestings. BA14 50 B4
The Poplars. BA14 50 B3
The Slipway. BA14 49 F1
Thestfield Dri. BA14 49 E2
Timbrell St. BA14 49 E5
Tower Clo. BA14 50 B1
Town Bridge. BA14 48 D5
Towpath Rd. BA14 49 E1
Trowbridge Rd. BA14 49 G3
Trowle. BA14 48 A2
Tudor Dri. BA14 49 E1
Tyning Clo. BA14 50 A1
Union St. BA14 49 E5
Upper Broad St. BA14 48 D5
Victoria Gdns. BA14 49 F3
Victoria Rd. BA14 49 F3
Walmesley Chase. BA14 49 G5
Walnut Gro. BA14 50 C3
Warbler Clo. BA14 48 B6
Warburton Clo. BA14 50 B2
Waterford Beck. BA14 50 A2
Waterworks Rd. BA14 50 C1
Weavers Dri. BA14 50 E1
Webbers Ct. BA14 50 A3
Wesley Rd. BA14 50 D1
West Ashton Rd. BA14 49 E6
West St. BA14 50 C1
Westbourne Gdns. BA14 48 C6
Westbourne Rd. BA14 50 C1
Westcroft St. BA14 48 D4
Westfield Clo. BA14 50 B2
Westfield Rd. BA14 50 A2
Westmead Cres. BA14 50 C4
Westwood Rd. BA14 48 A5
Whaddon La. BA14 49 H2
White Hart Yard. BA14 49 E5
White Horse Clo. BA14 50 E2
White Row Hill. BA14 50 B4
White Row Pk. BA14 50 B3
Wicker Hill. BA14 48 D5
Widbrook Meadow. BA14 48 A6
Wilcot Clo. BA14 50 D3
Willow Gro. BA14 50 C3
Wilton Dri. BA14 50 E2
Wiltshire Dri. BA14 50 D3
Windermere Rd. BA14 49 E4
Windsor Dri. BA14 50 C4
Wingfield Rd. BA14 50 B1
Winterslow Rd. BA14 50 C4
Withy Clo. BA14 49 E2
Woburn Clo. BA14 48 B5
Woodborough Clo. BA14 50 E3
Woodmill Ter. BA14 49 H3
Woodhouse Gdns. BA14 49 H4
Woolpack Mdws. BA14 50 F2
Worsted Clo. BA14 50 F1
Wren Ct. BA14 48 C6
Wyke Rd. BA14 49 E2
Yarn Ter. BA14 50 F2
Yeoman Way. BA14 50 D2
Yerbury St. BA14 49 E5
York Buildings. BA14 49 E4

WARMINSTER

Alcock Crest. BA12 52 B4
Arn Vw. BA12 52 C1
Ash Walk. BA12 52 C3
Ashley Coombe. BA12 52 C6
Ashley Pl. BA12 52 C6
Avon Rd. BA12 52 D5
Azalea Dri. BA12 52 B3
Barley Clo. BA12 53 F5
Bath Rd. BA12 52 B1
Battlesbury Rd. BA12 53 G4
Beacon View. BA12 52 A4
Beavens Ct. BA12 53 E3
Beckfield Clo. BA12 53 E4
Beech Av. BA12 52 C4
Beech Gro. BA12 52 D2
Bell Clo. BA12 52 C5
Bell Hill. BA12 52 C5
Bishopstrow Ct. BA12 53 H5
Bishopstrow Rd. BA12 53 G5
Blackdown Clo. BA12 52 D2
Blenheim Clo. BA12 52 C3
Boot Hill. BA12 52 C5
Bore Hill. BA12 52 C6
Boreham Clo. BA12 53 E4
Boreham Field. BA12 53 G4
Boreham Rd. BA12 53 E4
Bourbon Clo. BA12 52 D5
Bourne Clo. BA12 52 D5
Bradfield Clo. BA12 53 F5
Bradley Clo. BA12 52 B6
Bradley Rd. BA12 52 B6
Bramley Clo. BA12 52 C3
Bread St. BA12 52 C5
Broadway. BA12 52 B5
Broadwood Clo. BA12 52 C2
Brook Clo. BA12 52 B4
Brook St. BA12 52 B5
Broxburn Rd. BA12 52 A4
Buttons Yard. BA12 53 E4
Camelia Dri. BA12 52 B3
Cannimore Clo. BA12 52 B5
Cannimore Rd. BA12 52 A6
Canons Clo. BA12 52 E5
Chain La. BA12 53 E4
Chalfield Clo. BA12 52 C1
Chancery La. BA12 53 E4
Chantry Mews. BA12 52 A3
Chapel St. BA12 52 C5
*Chathat Ct, Yard Ct. BA12 53 E3
Chelwood Ct. BA12 53 E4
Chiltern Clo. BA12 52 D2
Christchurch Ter. BA12 52 C4
Church St. BA12 52 C3
Cley Vw. BA12 52 B4
Cobbett Pl. BA12 52 C4
Cobbett Rise. BA12 53 H6
Coldharbour La. BA12 52 B2
Coleridge Clo. BA12 52 A4
Conference Clo. BA12 52 B3
Copheap La. BA12 53 E2
Copheap Rise. BA12 53 E2
Coppice Clo. BA12 52 C4
Corner Grd. BA12 53 G5
Cotswold Clo. BA12 52 D2
Cotton House Gdns. BA12 53 E3
Cuckoos Nest La. BA12 52 B4
Damask Way. BA12 52 D5
Daniell Crest. BA12 52 C4
Deverill Rd. BA12 52 C6
Dorothy Walk. BA12 52 C2
Downs Vw. BA12 53 F4
East End Av. BA12 52 D4
East St. BA12 53 E4
Ebble Cres. BA12 52 C5
Elm Hill. BA12 53 E2
Emwell St. BA12 52 C3
Epping Clo. BA12 52 D2
Factory La. BA12 52 C4
Fairfield Rd. BA12 53 E3
Fanshaw Way. BA12 52 D5
Ferris Mead. BA12 52 D4
Firbank Cres. BA12 53 F2
Flers Ct. BA12 52 C3
Folly La. BA12 52 A5
Fore St. BA12 52 C5
Foxley Clo. BA12 52 C2
Freesia Clo. BA12 52 B3
Furlong. BA12 53 E4
Furnax La. BA12 52 C2
George St. BA12 52 D3
George St Pl. BA12 52 D3
Gipsy La. BA12 53 E4
Glebe Field. BA12 52 D4
Goodwin Clo. BA12 53 G2
Grange La. BA12 53 G5
Grenadier Clo. BA12 52 C3
Grovelands Way. BA12 52 B3
Hampton La. BA12 52 C5
Haygrove Clo. BA12 52 A4
Heathlands. BA12 52 B5
Henfords Marsh. BA12 53 E6
Heron Slade. BA12 53 F5
High St. BA12 52 D3
Highbury Pk. BA12 53 E4
Hillbourne Clo. BA12 52 D3
Hillwood Clo. BA12 52 C5
Hillwood La. BA12 52 C5
Hollybush Rd. BA12 52 C2
Houghton Clo. BA12 53 F4
Houldsworth Av. BA12 53 G2
Imber Rd. BA12 53 E3
Imber Way. BA12 53 F3
Imberwood Clo. BA12 53 E3

INDUSTRIAL & RETAIL:

Crusader Park Business Pk. BA12 52 B2
Woodcock Ind Est. BA12 53 F3
Kennet Clo. BA12 52 C5
King Ct. BA12 52 B5
King La. BA12 52 B5
King St. BA12 52 B5
Kings Rise. BA12 52 B5
Langholme Av. BA12 52 A4
Langholme Clo. BA12 52 A4
Little Orchard. BA12 52 C4
Lower Marsh Rd. BA12 52 D5
Ludlow Clo. BA12 52 C6
Luxfield Rd. BA12 52 B3
Lyme Av. BA12 52 C4
Maddocks Hill. BA12 52 B5
Malvern Clo. BA12 52 D2
Manor Gdns. BA12 52 C3
Market Pl. BA12 52 D3
Marsh St. BA12 52 C5
Martin Crest. BA12 52 B5
Masefield Rd. BA12 52 A4
Melrose Av. BA12 52 B4
Melrose Clo. BA12 52 B4
Mendip Clo. BA12 52 D2
Middleton Clo. BA12 52 B4
Minster Vw. BA12 52 B3
Morley Fields. BA12 53 E3
Mount La. BA12 52 C5
Myrtle Av. BA12 52 C4
Newopaul Way. BA12 52 C1
Newport. BA12 52 D3
Norridge Vw. BA12 52 B3
North La. BA12 52 A3
North Row. BA12 52 D3
Orchard Clo. BA12 53 E2
Pampas Ct. BA12 52 A4
Pepper Pl. BA12 53 F3
Perriwinkle Clo. BA12 52 A4
Pit Mead La. BA12 53 H6
Plants Grn. BA12 53 E4
Portway. BA12 52 D3
Portway La. BA12 52 C2
Poulsden Clo. BA12 52 D5
Pound Row. BA12 52 B4
Pound St. BA12 52 B4
Prestbury Dri. BA12 53 E5
Primrose Wk. BA12 52 B3
Princecroft La. BA12 52 B4
Princess Gdns. BA12 53 G4
Quantock Clo. BA12 52 D2
Queensway. BA12 53 G4
Rectory Clo. BA12 52 C2
Regal Ct. BA12 52 D4
Robin Clo. BA12 53 E4
Rock La. BA12 53 F4
Ruskin Dri. BA12 52 A4
Russett Ct. BA12 52 C3
Sack Hill. BA12 53 H1
St Andrews Rd. BA12 52 A5
St Georges Clo. BA12 53 G5
St Johns Rd. BA12 53 E5
Sambourne Chase. BA12 52 C3
Sambourne Gdns. BA12 52 C4
Sambourne Rd. BA12 52 C4
Sassoon Clo. BA12 52 A4
Savernake Clo. BA12 52 D2
Saxons Acre. BA12 52 A4
Shelley Way. BA12 52 A4
Sherwood Clo. BA12 52 C2
Silver St. BA12 52 C3
Smallbrook La. BA12 53 F5
Smallbrook Rd. BA12 53 E4
South St. BA12 52 B5
Southleigh Vw. BA12 53 B5
Station Rd. BA12 52 D3
Stephens Way. BA12 52 C2
Stuart Grn. BA12 52 D4
Swallow Clo. BA12 52 B5
Swift Mead. BA12 52 B5
Teichman Clo. BA12 53 E4
Tennyson Clo. BA12 52 A4
Thames Clo. BA12 52 D5
The Avenue. BA12 52 D3
The Beeches. BA12 52 C4
The Close. BA12 52 D3
The Dene. BA12 53 G4
The Downlands. BA12 53 E3
The Grove. BA12 52 D3
The Homelands. BA12 52 B5
The Maltings. BA12 52 C4
The Mead. BA12 52 D2
The Mews. BA12 52 D3
The Oaks. BA12 52 D2
The Paddock. BA12 53 E4
The Pippins. BA12 52 C3
The Ridgeway. BA12 52 D4
The Teasels. BA12 52 C4
The Uplands. BA12 53 E3
The Woodlands. BA12 52 D1
Thornhill Rd. BA12 52 A5
Upper Marsh Rd. BA12 52 D4
Upton Clo. BA12 52 B4
Vicarage St. BA12 52 C3
Victoria Mews. BA12 52 B4
Victoria Rd. BA12 52 A4
Virginia Dri. BA12 52 B3
Watery La. BA12 53 H6
Were Clo. BA12 52 B3
West Leigh. BA12 52 B4
West Parade. BA12 52 C4
West St. BA12 52 B4
West St Pl. BA12 52 B4
Westbury Rd. BA12 52 D1
Weymouth St. BA12 52 D4
Whitfield Clo. BA12 53 E3
Willow Cres. BA12 53 E5
Wilson Sq. BA12 53 F3
Woodcock Gdns. BA12 53 F4
Woodcock La. BA12 53 E3
Woodcock Rd. BA12 53 E3
Woodland Rd. BA12 52 B4
Woodman Mead. BA12 52 C3
Wren Clo. BA12 52 B5
Wylye Clo. BA12 52 C5
Wylye Rd. BA12 52 C5
Yard Ct. BA12 53 E3

WESTBURY

Abbotts Ct. BA13 54 B3
Alfred St. BA13 54 C3
All Saints Cres. BA13 54 C3
Anne Clo. BA13 54 A3
Arundell Clo. BA13 54 D2
Ash Gro. BA13 54 A3
Audley Gate. BA13 54 B4
Avebury Clo. BA13 54 B2
Beech Gro. BA13 54 A3
Bell Orchard. BA13 54 C2
Bitham Mill. BA13 54 C3
Bitham Pk. BA13 54 D2
Blackhorse La. BA13 54 A6
Boulton Clo. BA13 54 A5
Bramble Dri. BA13 54 B2
Bratton Rd. BA13 54 C3
Bremeridge Rd. BA13 54 D3
Breton Rd. BA13 54 B4
Briar Clo. BA13 54 B2
Bridge Ct. BA13 54 B3
Brook La. BA13 54 A2
Brunel Clo. BA13 54 C2
Campion Clo. BA13 54 C1
Castle Vw. BA13 54 D3
Cedar Gro. BA13 54 A3
Chalford Gdns. BA13 54 B5
Chantry La. BA13 54 C3
Chestnut Gro. BA13 54 B4
Cheyney Walk. BA13 54 D3
Chichester Pk. BA13 54 C2
Church La. BA13 54 A5
Church St. BA13 54 C3
Cleveland Way. BA13 54 A4
Coach Rd. BA13 54 D1
Dales Rd. BA13 54 A5
Danvers Way. BA13 54 D3
Dene Clo. BA13 54 B6
Devon Dri. BA13 54 C1
Dog Kennel La. BA13 54 B5
Dorney Clo. BA13 54 B6
Dorset Dri. BA13 54 C2
Downsview Rd. BA13 54 C2
Eden Vale Rd. BA13 54 B4
Edward St. BA13 54 C3
Elm Gro. BA13 54 A3
Fairdown Av. BA13 54 D3
Farleigh Gro. BA13 54 B2
Fell Rd. BA13 54 A4
Field Clo. BA13 54 C2
Fore St. BA13 54 C2
Fountain Ct. BA13 54 C3
Frogmore Rd. BA13 54 B1
Gibbs Clo. BA13 54 D3
Gloucester Walk. BA13 54 C1
Gooselands. BA13 54 B5
Grassy Slope. BA13 54 D6
Great Roc Rd. BA13 54 A3
Green La. BA13 54 B5
Gryphon Clo. BA13 54 A3
Ham Rd. BA13 54 A1
Hampshire Gdns. BA13 54 C2
Hampton Mews. BA13 54 B4
Hawkeridge Pk. BA13 54 A1
Hawkeridge Rd. BA13 54 B1
Hawthorn Gro. BA13 54 B4
Haynes Rd. BA13 54 C3
Hayward Pl. BA13 54 B2
Hazel Gro. BA13 54 B4
Heather Clo. BA13 54 B2
High St. BA13 54 C3
Hillside Pk. BA13 54 D3
Hospital Rd. BA13 54 C4
Hunters Chase. BA13 54 B4
Indigo Gdns. BA13 54 B4

INDUSTRIAL & RETAIL:

Brook Lane Ind Est. BA13 54 A2
Woodland Ind Est. BA13 54 B4
Ingram Clo. BA13 54 B2
Jubilee Clo. BA13 54 C3
Kendrick Clo. BA13 54 C4
Kingfisher Dri. BA13 54 C2
Lanhams Clo. BA13 54 C4
Laverton Ct. BA13 54 C3
Laverton Grn. BA13 54 B6
Laverton Rd. BA13 54 B5
Leigh Clo. BA13 54 A6
Leigh Rd. BA13 54 B5
Leighton Grn. BA13 54 C5
Leighton La. BA13 54 C5
Leighton Park N. BA13 54 B6

Leighton Park Rd. BA13 54 B6
Leighton Park W. BA13 54 B6
Ley Rd. BA13 54 A5
Lilac Gro. BA13 54 A4
Lopes Way. BA13 54 B2
Ludlow Clo. BA13 54 B2
Mallard Clo. BA13 54 C2
Maristow St. BA13 54 C2
Market Pl. BA13 54 C3
Matthew Ley Clo. BA13 54 B4
Matravers Clo. BA13 54 B3
Meadow Clo. BA13 54 B3
Meadow La. BA13 54 B3
Merlin Clo. BA13 54 B2
Morgan Walk. BA13 54 A4
Newtown. BA13 54 D3
Nightingale Dri. BA13 54 D2
Old Dilton Rd. BA13 54 B6
Oldfield Park. BA13 54 B3
Oldfield Rd. BA13 54 A3
Orchard Rd. BA13 54 C4
Park View Dri. BA13 54 B5
Paveley Clo. BA13 54 A3
Penleigh Park. BA13 54 A3
Penleigh Rd. BA13 54 B4
Penwood Clo. BA13 54 A3
Phipps Clo. BA13 54 B2
Phoenix Rise. BA13 54 A3
Pintail Way. BA13 54 D2
Prospect Sq. BA13 54 C4
Queens Rd. BA13 54 A3
Queens Sq. BA13 54 A3
Redland La. BA13 54 B4
Rocher Clo. BA13 54 B3
Rosefield Way. BA13 54 B2
Rothe Rise. BA13 54 B6
Salisbury Clo. BA13 54 A5
Sand Hole La. BA13 54 A6
Sarum Gdns. BA13 54 C2
Saxon Clo. BA13 54 C3
School La. BA13 54 A5
Shetland Clo. BA13 54 A4
Shire Way. BA13 54 A5
Shoreland Clo. BA13 54 B3
Silbury Clo. BA13 54 B2
Slag La. BA13 54 A2
Snappersnipes. BA13 54 C4
Somerset Dri. BA13 54 C2
Sparrick La. BA13 54 A5
Springfield Rd. BA13 54 B4
Station App. BA13 54 A2
Station Rd. BA13 54 A1
Storridge Rd. BA13 54 A1
Studland Pk. BA13 54 D4
Summer Rd. BA13 54 B2
Summerdown Ct. BA13 54 C3
Sun La. BA13 54 A6
Sycamore Gro. BA13 54 B3
Teal Clo. BA13 54 C2
The Avenue. BA13 54 B3
The Butts. BA13 54 C4
The Crescent. BA13 54 C3
The Knoll. BA13 54 D2
The Mead. BA13 54 C2
The Stables. BA13 54 C4
The Tynings. BA13 54 B5
Thornbury Rd. BA13 54 B2
Tickle Belly La. BA13 54 B6
Timor Rd. BA13 54 A4
Trowbridge Rd. BA13 54 D2
Uplands Rise. BA13 54 D4
Vista Clo. BA13 54 C4
Warminster Rd. BA13 54 B6
Wellhead Drove. BA13 54 C5
Wellhead La. BA13 54 C5
Wessex Walk. BA13 54 B3
West End. BA13 54 C3
Westbury Leigh. BA13 54 A6

White Horse Way. BA13 54 C3
Whiteland Rise. BA13 54 D4
Willoughby Clo. BA13 54 B5
Willow Gro. BA13 54 A3
Wiltshire Way. BA13 54 C2
Windsor Dri. BA13 54 D3
Wyvern Walk. BA13 54 A3

WILTON

Adelphi Ct. SP2 55 D3
Albany Ter. SP2 55 D3
Bell La. SP2 55 C4
Bishopstone Rd. SP2 55 B6
Bulbridge Rd. SP2 55 B5
Burcombe La. SP2 55 A4
Castle La. SP2 55 D3
Chantry Rd. SP2 55 C5
Churchill Ct. SP2 55 D3
Crow La. SP2 55 C3
Downside. SP2 55 B4
Elizabeth Rd. SP2 55 B1
Fairfield Cotts. SP2 55 D2
Greyhound La. SP2 55 D3
Grovely Vw. SP2 55 B5
Hare Warren Clo. SP2 55 C5
INDUSTRIAL & RETAIL:
Kingsway Trading Est. SP2 55 D2
King St. SP2 55 D3
Kings Ct. SP2 55 D3
Kingsbury Sq. SP2 55 D3
Lampard Ter. SP2 55 C4
Lower Folly. SP2 55 B5
Market Pl. SP2 55 D3
Minster St. SP2 55 D3
Nadder Ter. SP2 55 C4
North St. SP2 55 D3
Northleigh Ter. SP2 55 C5
Oak Ash Grn. SP2 55 B1
Olivier Rd. SP2 55 C3
Pembroke Ct. SP2 55 D3
Pennys La. SP2 55 B2
Philip Rd. SP2 55 B2
Primrose Hill. SP2 55 D3
Priory Clo. SP2 55 D2
Queen St. SP2 55 D2
Randalls Croft Rd. SP2 55 B5
Rawlence Rd. SP2 55 B4
Riverside. SP2 55 D3
Russell St. SP2 55 D3
Russell Ter. SP2 55 C3
Saddlers Mead. SP2 55 B5
St Andrews Clo. SP2 55 C5
St Ediths Clo. SP2 55 C5
St Johns Ct. SP2 55 C3
St Johns Sq. SP2 55 C3
St Marys Clo. SP2 55 B5
St Michaels Clo. SP2 55 B5
St Nicholas Clo. SP2 55 B5
St Peters Clo. SP2 55 B5
Seagrim Rd. SP2 55 A3
Shaftesbury Rd. SP2 55 B3
Shortlands. SP2 55 C3
Silver St. SP2 55 C4
South St. SP2 55 B5
Swayne Rd. SP2 55 D2
The Hollows. SP2 55 B6
The Kingsway. SP2 55 D2
Upper Folly. SP2 55 B3
Victoria Clo. SP2 55 C5
Victoria Rd. SP2 55 B3
Warminster Rd. SP2 55 C1
Washern Clo. SP2 55 B5
Water Ditchampton. SP2 55 C2

WOOTTON BASSETT

Alderney Clo. SN4 56 D4
Arran Clo. SN4 56 D4
Aspen Clo. SN4 56 B3
Badger Clo. SN4 56 C4
Baileys Mead. SN4 56 D4
Bardsey Clo. SN4 56 C4
Bath Rd. SN4 56 A5
Beamans La. SN4 56 A4
Bennett Hill Clo. SN4 56 C4
Betjeman Av. SN4 56 C3
Bincknoll La. SN4 56 A4
Blackthorn Clo. SN4 56 B2
Blenheim Clo. SN4 56 C3
Boroughfields. SN4 56 B4
Bradene Clo. SN4 56 C4
Branscombe Dri. SN4 56 C4
Briars Clo. SN4 56 B2
Brynards Hill. SN4 56 B5
Byron Av. SN4 56 B3
Chaucer Clo. SN4 56 C3
Church Hill Clo. SN4 56 D3
Church St. SN4 56 A4
Clarendon Dri. SN4 56 B4
Coleridge Clo. SN4 56 C3
Coxstalls. SN4 56 B4
Dianmer Clo. SN4 56 C1
Downs View. SN4 56 C3
Dryden Pl. SN4 56 C3
Dunnington Rd. SN4 56 B6
Eastwood Av. SN4 56 B4
Elm Clo. SN4 56 B2
Elm Park. SN4 56 B5
Englefield. SN4 56 B4
Eveleigh Rd. SN4 56 C4
Fairfield. SN4 56 B3
Farne Way. SN4 56 D4
Fox Brook. SN4 56 C4
Gainsborough Av. SN4 56 C3
Garraways. SN4 56 B4
Glebe Rd. SN4 56 A5
Glenville Clo. SN4 56 B6
Goughs Way. SN4 56 C4
Hazelend. SN4 56 C5
High Fold. SN4 56 C5
High Mead. SN4 56 C4
High St. SN4 56 A5
Home Ground. SN4 56 D4
Homefield. SN4 56 C4
Honeyhill. SN4 56 B5
Horsell Clo. SN4 56 C4
Huntsland. SN4 56 C4
INDUSTRIAL & RETAIL:
Cannons Ind Est. SN4 56 B5
Interface Business Centre. SN4 56 D4
Templars Way Ind Est. SN4 56 B6
Keats Clo. SN4 56 C3
Kingsley Av. SN4 56 B3
Laburnam Dri. SN4 56 B3
Lime Kiln. SN4 56 B3
Linden Clo. SN4 56 B2
Lindisfarne. SN4 56 D3
Longfellow Cres. SN4 56 C3
Longleaze. SN4 56 B3
Lucerne Clo. SN4 56 B2
Malmesbury Rd. SN4 56 A1
Maple Dri. SN4 56 B2

Marlborough Ct. SN4 56 C3
Marlborough Rd. SN4 56 B6
Marlowe Way. SN4 56 C3
Masefield. SN4 56 C3
Meadow Clo. SN4 56 B3
Middle Ground. SN4 56 D4
Miltons Way. SN4 56 A4
Morstone Rd. SN4 56 B5
New Rd. SN4 56 A5
Nore Marsh Rd. SN4 56 B5
Noredown Way. SN4 56 C4
Northbank Rise. SN4 56 C4
Old Court. SN4 56 B4
Old Malmesbury Rd. SN4 56 C2
Orchard Mead. SN4 56 D4
Otter Way. SN4 56 C4
Parhams Ct. SN4 56 C4
Parsons Way. SN4 56 B4
Pipers Clo. SN4 56 B5
Princess Gdns. SN4 56 B4
Queens Rd. SN4 56 D3
Ravens Walk. SN4 56 D3
Richards Clo. SN4 56 A5
Robins Clo. SN4 56 D3
Roebuck Clo. SN4 56 C4
Rope Yard. SN4 56 A4
Rowan Dri. SN4 56 C5
Ruskin Dri. SN4 56 C3
Rylands Way. SN4 56 B4
Saffron Clo. SN4 56 B2
Salt Spring Dri. SN4 56 C3
Shakespeare Rd. SN4 56 C3
Shelley Av. SN4 56 C3
Shepherds Breach. SN4 56 B4
Sherfields. SN4 56 C5
Sheridan Dri. SN4 56 C3
Showfield. SN4 56 A5
Skewbridge Clo. SN4 56 A5
Sorrell Clo. SN4 56 B2
Southbank Glen. SN4 56 C4
Springfield Cres. SN4 56 A3
Squires Hill Clo. SN4 56 D4
Squirrel Cres. SN4 56 B4
Station Rd. SN4 56 B4
Stoneover La. SN4 56 D4
Swallows Mead. SN4 56 D4
Swinburne Pl. SN4 56 C3
Swindon Rd. SN4 56 B3
Tanners Clo. SN4 56 B4
Templars Firs. SN4 56 B6
Templars Way. SN4 56 B6
Tennyson Rd. SN4 56 B4
The Burlongs. SN4 56 B4
The Lawns. SN4 56 A4
The Maltings. SN4 56 A5
The Meadows. SN4 56 C1
The Mulberrys. SN4 56 B4
The Oaks. SN4 56 C4
The Rosary. SN4 56 B6
The Steadings. SN4 56 B4
Tinkers Field. SN4 56 B4
Vale View. SN4 56 A5
Victory Row. SN4 56 A4
Vowley View. SN4 56 C5
Washbourne Rd. SN4 56 B6
Westbury Park. SN4 56 A5
Whitehill La. SN4 56 A5
Whitethorn Clo. SN4 56 B2
Withy Clo. SN4 56 B2
Wood St. SN4 56 A4
Woodshaw Mead. SN4 56 D4
Wordsworth Clo. SN4 56 C3

WROUGHTON

Anthony Rd. SN4 51 B5

Artis Av. SN4 51 D4
Ashencopse Rd. SN4 51 B5
Baileys Way. SN4 51 B5
Bakers Rd. SN4 51 D6
Barcelona Cres. SN4 51 C5
Barrett Way. SN4 51 C6
Beaufort Rd. SN4 51 C4
Berkeley Rd. SN4 51 D5
Bladen Clo. SN4 51 B5
Blenheim Rd. SN4 51 B5
Boness Rd. SN4 51 C4
Brimble Hill. SN4 51 D6
Burderop Clo. SN4 51 B4
Charterhouse Rd. SN4 51 B5
Church Hill. SN4 51 B6
Coombe Clo. SN4 51 D6
Coronation Rd. SN4 51 C5
Coventry Clo. SN4 51 B5
Cowleaze Cres. SN4 51 B5
Devizes Rd. SN4 51 C6
Dunbar Rd. SN4 51 C4
Edgar Row Clo. SN4 51 B5
Elcombe Av. SN4 51 B5
Ellingdon Rd. SN4 51 B4
Falkirk Way. SN4 51 C4
Greens La. SN4 51 C4
Hackpen Clo. SN4 51 C4
Halifax Clo. SN4 51 B4
Hall Clo. SN4 51 C6
Hicks Clo. SN4 51 C4
High St. SN4 51 B5
INDUSTRIAL & RETAIL:
Wroughton Business Park. SN4 51 D4
Inverary Rd. SN4 51 C4
Kellsboro Av. SN4 51 B4
Kennet Rd. SN4 51 B5
Kerrs Way. SN4 51 C4
Lancaster Rd. SN4 51 D4
Lister Rd. SN4 51 D4
Manor Clo. SN4 51 D4
Marine Clo. SN4 51 D4
Markham Pl. SN4 51 B5
Markham Rd. SN4 51 B6
Marlborough Rd. SN4 51 D6
Maskeleyne Way. SN4 51 B5
Maunsell Way. SN4 51 B4
Mill Clo. SN4 51 C5
Moat Wk. SN4 51 C6
Moormead Rd. SN4 51 D5
Overtown Hill. SN4 51 C5
Perrys La. SN4 51 C5
Petter Clo. SN4 51 B4
Plummer Clo. SN4 51 B5
Priors Hill. SN4 51 C6
Purley Clo. SN4 51 C5
Roberts Clo. SN4 51 C6
St Andrews Clo. SN4 51 C4
St Andrews Ct. SN4 51 C4
St Johns Rd. SN4 51 C5
Savill Cres. SN4 51 B4
Snapps Clo. SN4 51 C5
Stirling Clo. SN4 51 B4
Summerhouse Rd. SN4 51 B4
Swindon Rd. SN4 51 D5
The Mountings. SN4 51 C6
The Pitchens. SN4 51 C6
Victoria Cross Rd. SN4 51 D4
Wanshot Clo. SN4 51 D6
Weirside Av. SN4 51 C5
Whalley Cres. SN4 51 B5
Wharf Rd. SN4 51 A4
Willow Wk. SN4 51 C6
Zoar Clo. SN4 51 B6

ESTATE PUBLICATIONS

RED BOOKS

ALDERSHOT, CAMBERLEY
ALFRETON, BELPER, RIPLEY
ASHFORD, TENTERDEN
AYLESBURY, TRING
BANGOR, CAERNARFON
BARNSTAPLE, ILFRACOMBE
BASILDON, BILLERICAY
BASINGSTOKE, ANDOVER
BATH, BRADFORD-ON-AVON
BEDFORD
BIRMINGHAM, WOLVERHAMPTON, COVENTRY
BODMIN, WADEBRIDGE
BOURNEMOUTH, POOLE, CHRISTCHURCH
BRACKNELL
BRENTWOOD
BRIGHTON, LEWES, NEWHAVEN, SEAFORD
BRISTOL
BROMLEY (London Bromley)
BURTON-UPON-TRENT, SWADLINCOTE
BURY ST. EDMUNDS
CAMBRIDGE
CARDIFF
CARLISLE
CHELMSFORD, BRAINTREE, MALDON, WITHAM
CHESTER
CHESTERFIELD
CHICHESTER, BOGNOR REGIS
COLCHESTER, CLACTON
CORBY, KETTERING
COVENTRY
CRAWLEY & MID SUSSEX
CREWE
DERBY, HEANOR, CASTLE DONINGTON
EASTBOURNE, BEXHILL, SEAFORD, NEWHAVEN
EDINBURGH, MUSSELBURGH, PENICUIK
EXETER, EXMOUTH
FALKIRK, GRANGEMOUTH
FAREHAM, GOSPORT
FLINTSHIRE TOWNS
FOLKESTONE, DOVER, DEAL & ROMNEY MARSH
GLASGOW, & PAISLEY
GLOUCESTER, CHELTENHAM
GRAVESEND, DARTFORD
GRAYS, THURROCK
GREAT YARMOUTH, LOWESTOFT
GRIMSBY, CLEETHORPES
GUILDFORD, WOKING
HARLOW, BISHOPS STORTFORD
HARROGATE, KNARESBOROUGH
HASTINGS, BEXHILL, RYE
HEREFORD
HERTFORD, HODDESDON, WARE
HIGH WYCOMBE
HUNTINGDON, ST. NEOTS
IPSWICH, FELIXSTOWE
ISLE OF MAN
ISLE OF WIGHT TOWNS
KENDAL
KIDDERMINSTER
KINGSTON-UPON-HULL
LANCASTER, MORECAMBE
LEICESTER, LOUGHBOROUGH
LINCOLN
LLANDUDNO, COLWYN BAY
LUTON, DUNSTABLE
MACCLESFIELD
MAIDSTONE
MANSFIELD, MANSFIELD WOODHOUSE
MEDWAY, GILLINGHAM
MILTON KEYNES
NEW FOREST TOWNS
NEWBURY, THATCHAM
NEWPORT, CHEPSTOW
NEWQUAY
NEWTOWN, WELSHPOOL
NORTHAMPTON
NORTHWICH, WINSFORD
NORWICH
NOTTINGHAM, EASTWOOD, HUCKNALL, ILKESTON
NUNEATON, BEDWORTH
OXFORD, ABINGDON
PENZANCE, ST. IVES
PETERBOROUGH
PLYMOUTH, IVYBRIDGE, SALTASH, TORPOINT
PORTSMOUTH, HAVANT, WATERLOOVILLE
READING
REDDITCH, BROMSGROVE

REIGATE, BANSTEAD, LEATHERHEAD, DORKING
RHYL, PRESTATYN
RUGBY
ST. ALBANS, WELWYN, HATFIELD
ST. AUSTELL
SALISBURY, AMESBURY, WILTON
SCUNTHORPE
SEVENOAKS
SHREWSBURY
SITTINGBOURNE, FAVERSHAM, ISLE OF SHEPPEY
SLOUGH, MAIDENHEAD, WINDSOR
SOUTHAMPTON, EASTLEIGH
SOUTHEND-ON-SEA
STAFFORD
STEVENAGE, HITCHIN, LETCHWORTH
STIRLING
STOKE-ON-TRENT
STROUD, NAILSWORTH
SWANSEA, NEATH, PORT TALBOT
SWINDON, CHIPPENHAM, MARLBOROUGH
TAUNTON, BRIDGWATER
TELFORD
THANET, CANTERBURY, HERNE BAY, WHITSTABLE
TORBAY (Torquay, Paignton, Newton Abbot)
TRURO, FALMOUTH
TUNBRIDGE WELLS, TONBRIDGE, CROWBOROUGH
WARWICK, ROYAL LEAMINGTON SPA &
   STRATFORD UPON AVON
WATFORD, HEMEL HEMPSTEAD
WELLINGBOROUGH
WESTON-SUPER-MARE, CLEVEDON
WEYMOUTH, DORCHESTER
WINCHESTER, NEW ARLESFORD
WORCESTER, DROITWICH
WORTHING, LITTLEHAMPTON, ARUNDEL
WREXHAM
YORK

COUNTY RED BOOKS (Town Centre Maps)

BEDFORDSHIRE
BERKSHIRE
BUCKINGHAMSHIRE
CAMBRIDGESHIRE
CHESHIRE
CORNWALL
DERBYSHIRE
DEVON
DORSET
ESSEX
GLOUCESTERSHIRE
HAMPSHIRE
HEREFORDSHIRE
HERTFORDSHIRE
KENT
LEICESTERSHIRE & RUTLAND
LINCOLNSHIRE
NORFOLK
NORTHAMPTONSHIRE
NOTTINGHAMSHIRE
OXFORDSHIRE
SHROPSHIRE
SOMERSET
STAFFORDSHIRE
SUFFOLK
SURREY
SUSSEX (EAST)
SUSSEX (WEST)
WILTSHIRE
WORCESTERSHIRE

OTHER MAPS

KENT TO CORNWALL (1:460,000)
CHINA (1:6,000,000)
INDIA (1:3,750,000)
INDONESIA (1:4,000,000)
NEPAL (1,800,000)
SOUTH EAST ASIA (1:6,000,000)
THAILAND (1:1,600,000)

STREET PLANS

CARDIFF
EDINBURGH TOURIST PLAN
ST. ALBANS
WOLVERHAMPTON

OFFICIAL TOURIST & LEISURE MAPS

SOUTH EAST ENGLAND (1:200,000)
KENT & EAST SUSSEX (1:150,000)
SUSSEX & SURREY (1:150,000)
SUSSEX (1:50,000)
SOUTHERN ENGLAND (1:200,000)
ISLE OF WIGHT (1:50,000)
WESSEX (1:200,000)
DORSET (1:50,000)
DEVON & CORNWALL (1:200,000)
CORNWALL (1:180,000)
DEVON (1:200,000)
DARTMOOR & SOUTH DEVON COAST (1:100,000)
EXMOOR & NORTH DEVON COAST (1:100,000)
GREATER LONDON M25 (1:80,000)
EAST ANGLIA (1:200,000)
CHILTERNS & THAMES VALLEY (1:200,000)
THE COTSWOLDS (1:110,000)
COTSWOLDS & SEVERN VALLEY (1:200,000)
WALES (1:250,000)
THE SHIRES OF MIDDLE ENGLAND (1:250,000)
THE MID SHIRES (Staffs, Shrops, etc.) (1:200,000)
PEAK DISTRICT (1:100,000)
SNOWDONIA (1:125,000)
YORKSHIRE (1:200,000)
YORKSHIRE DALES (1:125,000)
NORTH YORKSHIRE MOORS (1:125,000)
NORTH WEST ENGLAND (1:200,000)
ISLE OF MAN (1:60,000)
NORTH PENNINES & LAKES (1:200,000)
LAKE DISTRICT (1:75,000)
BORDERS OF ENGLAND & SCOTLAND (1:200,000)
BURNS COUNTRY (1:200,000)
HEART OF SCOTLAND (1:200,000)
GREATER GLASGOW (1:150,000)
EDINBURGH & THE LOTHIANS (1:150,000)
ISLE OF ARRAN (1:63,360)
FIFE (1:100,000)
LOCH LOMOND & TROSSACHS (1:150,000)
ARGYLL THE ISLES & LOCH LOMOND (1:275,000)
PERTHSHIRE, DUNDEE & ANGUS (1:150,000)
FORT WILLIAM, BEN NEVIS, GLEN COE (1:185,000)
IONA (1:10,000) & MULL (1:115,000)
GRAMPIAN HIGHLANDS (1:185,000)
LOCH NESS & INVERNESS (1:150,000)
SKYE & LOCHALSH (1:130,000)
ARGYLL & THE ISLES (1:200,000)
CAITHNESS & SUTHERLAND (1:185,000)
HIGHLANDS OF SCOTLAND (1:275,000)
WESTERN ISLES (1:125,000)
ORKNEY & SHETLAND (1:128,000)
ENGLAND & WALES (1:650,000)
SCOTLAND (1:500,000)
HISTORIC SCOTLAND (1:500,000)
SCOTLAND CLAN MAP (1:625,000)
BRITISH ISLES (1:1,100,000)
GREAT BRITAIN (1:1,100,000)

EUROPEAN LEISURE MAPS

EUROPE (1:3,100,000)
BENELUX (1:600,000)
FRANCE (1:1,000,000)
GERMANY (1:1,000,000
IRELAND (1:625,000)
ITALY (1:1,000,000)
SPAIN & PORTUGAL (1,1,000,000)
CROSS CHANNEL VISITORS' MAP (1:530,000)
WORLD (1:35,000,000)
WORLD FLAT

TOWNS IN NORTHERN FRANCE STREET ATLAS
BOULOGNE SHOPPERS MAP
CALAIS SHOPPERS MAP
DIEPPE SHOPPERS MAP

ESTATE PUBLICATIONS are also
Distributors in the UK for:

INTERNATIONAL TRAVEL MAPS, Canada
HALLWAG, Switzerland
ORDNANCE SURVEY

Catalogue and prices from:
ESTATE PUBLICATIONS
Bridewell House, Tenterden, Kent. TN30 6EP.
Tel: 01580 764225   Fax: 01580 763720
www.estate-publications.co.uk